LIVING THE WORD

*Scripture Reflections
and Commentaries
for Sundays and
Holy Days*

Dennis D. Sylva
and
Rev. James A. Wallace, CSsR

LIVING THE WORD

Scripture Reflections and Commentaries
for Sundays and Holy Days

Vol. 24   November 30, 2008–November 22, 2009

Published annually

Individual copy: $14.95
(2-9 copies: $10.95 per copy;
10-24 copies: $9.95 per copy;
25-99 copies: $8.95 per copy;
100 or more copies: $6.95 per copy)

Scripture readings are taken from the *Lectionary for Mass* Copyright © 1970, 1997, 1998, Confraternity of Christian Doctrine, Washington D.C. All rights reserved. Used by permission.

The English translation of some psalm responses from *Lectionary for Mass*, © 1969, 1981, 1997, International Committee on English in the Liturgy (ICEL). All rights reserved.

Excerpt from Pierre Teilhard de Chardin, *The Divine Milieu*, Copyright © 1960 by William Collins Sons & Co., Ltd., London, and Harper & Row, Publishers, Incorporated, New York. All rights reserved. Reprinted by permission of HarperCollins Publishers.

Editor: Michael E. Novak
Copy Editor: Marcia T. Lucey
Typesetter: Tejal Patel
Cover Design: Paula Wendland and Tejal Patel
Director of Publications: Mary Beth Kunde-Anderson

Published with ecclesiastical approval.

Copyright © 2008 by World Library Publications,
the music and liturgy division of J. S. *Paluch Company,* Inc.
3708 River Road, Suite 400, Franklin Park, IL 60131-2158
800 566-6150 • fax 888 957-3291
wlpcs@jspaluch.com • www.wlpmusic.com
All rights reserved.

Printed in the United States of America
WLP 006773 • (ISSN) 1079-4670 • (ISBN) 978-1-58459-397-3

Our renewed liturgy has generated a great deal of interest in sacred scripture. In turn, a richer appreciation of the readings for Mass has done much for participation in our liturgical celebrations. *Living the Word* is designed to help facilitate this twofold deepening of the Christian life. It is our hope that individuals, homilists, catechumens, candidates, discussion groups, religious education classes, and similar gatherings will all benefit from the commentaries and reflections found on these pages.

The readings for each Sunday, holy day, and major celebration from November 2008 through November 2009, Year B of the Lectionary cycle, are presented here, along with a brief passage intended to suggest a focus or approach to consider while reading them. Following the readings is a commentary that provides a context for understanding them, incorporating both biblical scholarship and the Church's age-old wisdom. A reflection section develops the initial focus and ties it together with the commentary. The discussion questions and suggestions for responses that follow offer help in moving from reflection to action, inviting those who use this volume to go about truly "Living the Word."

Whether reflecting on the scriptures in a group setting or individually, it is best to do so in the context of prayer. Consider creating an atmosphere that will foster prayerful reflection when you are using this book. In a quiet space, perhaps with lit candles and simple seasonal decoration (incense or soft music may also be appropriate), begin with a prayer and read aloud the Scriptures for that day, even if you are alone. Groups can encourage members to focus on one word or idea that speaks to them from each reading. Participants might want to share these ideas with one another before continuing.

After listening to the readings, ask yourself how they have changed you, enlightened you, moved you. Proceed to the commentary, reflection, and response. Use the discussion questions to shape your conversation or as a springboard for your own questions. How does the brief "Responding to the Word" reflection invite you to "live the word" in your relationship with God, with family and friends, at work, school, or church, or in the broader community?

Having started with prayer, perhaps once you have spent time in reflection or discussion it will be appropriate to lift up someone or something in a prayer that is related to the readings or your reflections. Pray spontaneously as you think about the texts' meaning for you, or invite people in the group to offer prayers informally.

Finally, what action will you take this week that grows out of your prayerful reflection on this week's scriptures? You may propose your own prayer for help to do something in response to the readings or simply stand and pray the Lord's Prayer. If you are in a group, offer one another a sign of peace before departing. If alone, extend yourself to another in a gesture of peace later in the day or week, in person, by phone, or by offering a simple prayer.

Repeating this pattern over time can help your prayerful reflection to deepen your appreciation for and commitment to God's word every day of your life.

Table of Contents

Prayers Before Reading Scripture

Lord Jesus,
we give you praise.
Speak to us as we read your word,
and send your Spirit into our hearts.
Guide us today and each day in your service,
for you are our way, our truth, our life.

Lord Jesus, we love you:
keep us in your love for ever and ever. *Amen*!

or

Blessed are you, Lord God,
king of all creation:
you have taught us by your word.
Open our hearts to your Spirit,
and lead us on the paths of Christ your Son.

All praise and glory be yours for ever. *Amen*!

or

Lord, open our hearts:
let your Spirit speak to us
as we read your word. *Amen*!

or

Lord Jesus,
to whom shall we go?
You have the words of eternal life.

Speak, Lord,
your servants are listening:
here we are, Lord,
ready to do your will. *Amen*!

Prayers After Reading Scripture

Blessed are you, Lord God,
maker of heaven and earth,
ruler of the universe:
you have sent your Holy Spirit
to teach your truth to your holy people.
We praise you for letting us read your word today.

Grant that we may continue to think and pray
over the words we have read,
and to share your thoughts with others
throughout this day.

Loving God, we praise you
and thank you in Jesus' name. *Amen*!

or

God of all graciousness, we thank you
for speaking to us today
through your holy word. *Amen*!

The readings for Advent and Christmas are about new beginnings initiated by God. These beginnings are filled with life and hope because God promises not to leave humanity alone, and continues to come in life-expanding and life-enriching ways. The Gospel on the First Sunday of Advent establishes the necessity of being prepared for Christ's second coming by caring for others. This reading from Mark's Gospel inspires a heroic concern for others by showing their great value. The second reading on the following Sunday, from the Second Letter of Peter, encourages us by showing how life is moving toward decisive final events and why virtue matters.

On each succeeding Sunday, the Lectionary looks at past decisive comings of God into the world and what they have meant. The Old Testament readings, especially those from the prophet Isaiah, and the Gospel passages illustrate God's entering into communion with all people. The Gospel reading for the Third Sunday of Advent presents John the Baptist, the herald of Jesus Christ. From John we learn of the type of witness to Jesus that prepares his coming into the lives of others. The Gospels next move to Luke's account of the annunciation to Mary, in which we see how great faith is possible in the face of life's seemingly insurmountable obstacles.

The Gospel for the Christmas Vigil is from Matthew, and it illustrates his perspective on a divine order that supports human compassion. For the Feast of the Holy Family we return to Luke's Gospel, where we find two characters who have grown old while remaining dedicated to God: Simeon and Anna. Their long-term dedication is a model for us who need to learn to be open to God's future expansive plans. On the Solemnity of Mary, the Mother of God, we hear a reading about Mary as an example of attentiveness to God, who is revealed in the scriptures and in her life. This posture of her heart moves her toward action and feeling for others. In the Gospel proclaimed on Epiphany the magi, who came to recognize Jesus as the newborn "king of the Jews," give us a guide to discerning the reign of God. Finally, the reading from the Gospel of Mark on the Feast of the Baptism of the Lord reflects on how Jesus brings the Spirit that liberates humanity.

November 30, 2008

FIRST SUNDAY OF ADVENT

Today's Focus: A Time to Live, a Time to Die,
a Time to Wake Up . . .

*Advent begins with a trumpet blast: Wake up! Watch out! The call to be watchful
and alert is a call to readiness, not to let our spirits get sluggish and slip off into a state
of un-consciousness. But it is hard at times to stay up, to keep watch. Is Jesus being
unreasonable here?*

**FIRST
READING**
*Isaiah 63:
16b–17, 19b;
64:2–7*

You, LORD, are our father,
  our redeemer you are named forever.
Why do you let us wander, O LORD, from your ways,
  and harden our hearts so that we fear you not?
Return for the sake of your servants,
  the tribes of your heritage.
Oh, that you would rend the heavens and come down,
  with the mountains quaking before you,
while you wrought awesome deeds we could not hope for,
  such as they had not heard of from of old.
No ear has ever heard, no eye ever seen, any God but you
  doing such deeds for those who wait for him.
Would that you might meet us doing right,
  that we were mindful of you in our ways!
Behold, you are angry, and we are sinful;
  all of us have become like unclean people,
  all our good deeds are like polluted rags;
we have all withered like leaves,
  and our guilt carries us away like the wind.
There is none who calls upon your name,
  who rouses himself to cling to you;
for you have hidden your face from us
  and have delivered us up to our guilt.
Yet, O LORD, you are our father;
  we are the clay and you the potter:
  we are all the work of your hands.

**PSALM
RESPONSE**
Psalm 80:4

Lord, make us turn to you; let us see your face and we shall be
saved.

<table>
<tr><td align="right">SECOND
READING
1 Corinthians 1:
3–9</td><td>Brothers and sisters: Grace to you and peace from God our Father and the Lord Jesus Christ.

I give thanks to my God always on your account for the grace of God bestowed on you in Christ Jesus, that in him you were enriched in every way, with all discourse and all knowledge, as the testimony to Christ was confirmed among you, so that you are not lacking in any spiritual gift as you wait for the revelation of our Lord Jesus Christ. He will keep you firm to the end, irreproachable on the day of our Lord Jesus Christ. God is faithful, and by him you were called to fellowship with his Son, Jesus Christ our Lord.</td></tr>
<tr><td align="right">GOSPEL
Mark 13:33–37</td><td>Jesus said to his disciples: "Be watchful! Be alert! You do not know when the time will come. It is like a man traveling abroad. He leaves home and places his servants in charge, each with his own work, and orders the gatekeeper to be on the watch. Watch, therefore; you do not know when the lord of the house is coming, whether in the evening, or at midnight, or at cockcrow, or in the morning. May he not come suddenly and find you sleeping. What I say to you, I say to all: 'Watch!'"</td></tr>
</table>

Understanding the Word

Today's Gospel passage stands at the conclusion of a recitation of the tribulations that will occur in the final times. Jesus exhorts his disciples to keep awake. This exhortation is grounded in the way that Jesus' followers are to think about themselves: They are servants who are to take care of the home while the master is away (13:34). In other words, Jesus, in going away, is entrusting to his disciples what is precious to him, as symbolized by home and the family that lives there. The challenging command to keep awake at all hours of the day and night when doing one's duty reflects the great value of those whom the servants are guarding and attending.

How we keep awake and what it means to guard and care for what is precious to Jesus is soon developed in another passage that repeats the imagery of watching at night, and so is linked to the Gospel passage for today. Following the Last Supper, Jesus leads his disciples into the Garden of Gethsemane. Leaving the rest of the disciples at one place in the garden, Jesus takes Peter, James, and John and proceeds further with them (Mark 14:32–33). This is an inner circle of disciples who are particularly close to Jesus. To these three he confides that his sorrow is so great that it may itself cause his death (14:34). It is in this context that Jesus asks these three disciples to "[r]emain here and keep watch" (14:34).

They are to be Jesus' support group, as shown by the fact that Jesus only goes a "little" way from them and then comes back to them in between his prayers. Because they keep falling asleep, however, Jesus admonishes them that prayer will give them the power to overcome their weakness (14:38). Prayer energizes the spirit to combat the fatigue of the flesh.

Thus, watching at all hours means providing support at all times to those entrusted to us. Prayer undergirds such rigorous support, as does the realization that the ones we are called to care for are loved by Jesus as family members. Disciples are those entrusted with Jesus' family.

Surely Jesus does not mean that we are to stay awake at all hours? Not only our bodies but our minds and our spirits need rest, both the rest of sleep and what we rightfully call re-creation. We need time to recharge our batteries, let our spirits play, give our souls room for leisure activities.

Jesus is saying that part of our life's work is always to be in a state of readiness to welcome him, the one who will come to judge the living and the dead. Our faith reminds us that we are a people who wait for the Lord to return, just like a parent is always waiting for a child to return home late at night.

One of the most difficult times to stay awake is after the Thanksgiving Day meal. All that stuffing—and not just what goes into the turkey! In his book *Consumed*, Benjamin Barber points out how our consumer culture encourages adults to remain as infantile as possible, while it trains children to consume at an ever younger age. Such consumption, he says, makes for a bloated people whose spirits are weighed down and sluggish.

We all have moments when we feel alert, when our senses are primed to take in what is happening, when our hearts and minds are open. That is what the Lord is asking us to achieve, if not 24/7, perhaps a little more frequently than we presently do. One of the traditional ways of achieving this state of alertness has been the spiritual discipline of fasting. Another is prayer.

CONSIDER/ DISCUSS:

- When did you last feel fully alert and alive? Truly awake and watchful?
- Do you find yourself like the people Isaiah writes about when he says that "we have all withered like leaves, / and our guilt carries us away like the wind" (Isaiah 64:5)?
- What can you do to take on the attitude of actively waiting for the Lord?

Responding to the Word

We can ask God to help us live these coming days alert and attentive to the hope that has been placed in our hearts. Let us pray that God "will keep [us] firm to the end, irreproachable on the day of our Lord Jesus Christ" (1 Corinthians 1:8).

December 7, 2008

SECOND SUNDAY OF ADVENT

Today's Focus: A Time to Take Inner Inventory

There had to be something magnetic about John the Baptist, a person who clothed himself in camel's hair, ate locusts and wild honey, and shouted out for repentance. He brought crowds of people out in the desert, lining up to be baptized as a sign that they had repented their sins. What does he have to say to us? Why should we change our lives?

FIRST READING
Isaiah 40:1–5, 9–11

Comfort, give comfort to my people,
   says your God.
Speak tenderly to Jerusalem, and proclaim to her
   that her service is at an end,
   her guilt is expiated;
indeed, she has received from the hand of the LORD
   double for all her sins.

A voice cries out:
In the desert prepare the way of the LORD!
   Make straight in the wasteland a highway for our God!
Every valley shall be filled in,
   every mountain and hill shall be made low;
the rugged land shall be made a plain,
   the rough country, a broad valley.
Then the glory of the LORD shall be revealed,
   and all people shall see it together;
   for the mouth of the LORD has spoken.

Go up onto a high mountain,
   Zion, herald of glad tidings;
cry out at the top of your voice,
   Jerusalem, herald of good news!
Fear not to cry out
   and say to the cities of Judah:
   Here is your God!
Here comes with power
   the Lord GOD,
   who rules by his strong arm;
here is his reward with him,
   his recompense before him.
Like a shepherd he feeds his flock;
   in his arms he gathers the lambs,
carrying them in his bosom,
   and leading the ewes with care.

PSALM RESPONSE
Psalm 85:8

Lord, let us see your kindness, and grant us your salvation.

Do not ignore this one fact, beloved, that with the Lord one day is like a thousand years and a thousand years like one day. The Lord does not delay his promise, as some regard "delay," but he is patient with you, not wishing that any should perish but that all should come to repentance. But the day of the Lord will come like a thief, and then the heavens will pass away with a mighty roar and the elements will be dissolved by fire, and the earth and everything done on it will be found out.

Since everything is to be dissolved in this way, what sort of persons ought you to be, conducting yourselves in holiness and devotion, waiting for and hastening the coming of the day of God, because of which the heavens will be dissolved in flames and the elements melted by fire. But according to his promise we await new heavens and a new earth in which righteousness dwells. Therefore, beloved, since you await these things, be eager to be found without spot or blemish before him, at peace.

The beginning of the gospel of Jesus Christ the Son of God.

As it is written in Isaiah the prophet:
Behold, I am sending my messenger ahead of you;
he will prepare your way.
A voice of one crying out in the desert:
"Prepare the way of the Lord,
make straight his paths."

John the Baptist appeared in the desert proclaiming a baptism of repentance for the forgiveness of sins. People of the whole Judean countryside and all the inhabitants of Jerusalem were going out to him and were being baptized by him in the Jordan River as they acknowledged their sins. John was clothed in camel's hair, with a leather belt around his waist. He fed on locusts and wild honey. And this is what he proclaimed: "One mightier than I is coming after me. I am not worthy to stoop and loosen the thongs of his sandals. I have baptized you with water; he will baptize you with the Holy Spirit."

Understanding the Word

The false teachers about whom the Second Letter of Peter warns were claiming that the fact that Christ's second coming had not occurred in the lifetime of the apostles showed that no such coming was to be expected. They said that nothing ever changes from one generation to the next; the world goes on without any decisive breaking in by God (2 Peter 3:4). On this basis these teachers were advocating a live-it-up-now lifestyle, one free from any sexual or sensual restraints (2:2–3, 13–14, 18–19). Their reasoning was that if there is to be no decisive day of reckoning, then why discipline oneself instead of grabbing all the gusto one can?

Second Peter responds that God takes a long-range view and does so in order to give people the time to mend their ways and be saved (3:8–9). Thus, the delay in the Second Coming is an opportunity and neither a cause for doubt about judgment nor an encouragement to immoral living. Moreover, our actions have a role in determining the day of this coming: A good life can hasten the coming, which is not only for judgment but also for the creation of "a new heavens and a new earth in which righteousness dwells" (3:13). Thus, Second Peter claims that the discipline of a life of self-control and virtue cooperates with God's plan of bringing about a new just world of personal integrity.

The language of destruction found in this passage is actually for the purpose of assuring readers that what they do is consequential, is seen by God, has an effect. Thus, at the Second Coming not only will the heavens pass away, but the astral bodies will as well (3:10, 12). When this occurs, "the earth and everything done on it will be found" (3:10). These are the best readings of 3:10 and 12, and they indicate that the flaming heavens and the astral bodies at the endtime are means of revealing the secret works of people on the earth. People's lives will be revealed, and so the rigor of virtue matters.

 ## Reflecting on the Word

Both this week and next our Gospel readings focus on the figure of John the Baptist. Today we will reflect on his message; next week, on his person. John's message was a simple one: One is coming who will baptize you with the Holy Spirit, so prepare the way of the Lord, make straight his paths.

That God came and that God will come can be an easier message to handle than that God is coming now. The past can be seen as offering us information and the future as . . . whatever it will be, but the present demands a response. Every Advent calls us to respond to this message. He comes and he comes today. Jesus continues to come now and to immerse us in the life of the Holy Spirit. He comes to us in the word of God and in the sacrament of the Eucharist.

So we are to make straight a path for him so that he can take up residence in our minds and hearts. This baptism with the Holy Spirit is an ongoing process, just as the first Pentecost began an ongoing process in the church. The Holy Spirit that blew out doors and sent out the first disciples with enflamed hearts and tongues continues to come in surprising ways. (Pick up the Acts of the Apostles and read it through if you need reminding.)

So as a new year begins in the Church, making straight a path involves some inner inventory.

- What is presently taking up room in our hearts?
- What is engaging our minds these days? What energizes our wills and flows over into action?
- Do any of these serve as obstacles to God entering in and taking possession of our hearts and minds and spirits?

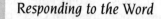

Responding to the Word

We can get used to living with obstacles that block access to our hearts, like we get used to construction projects that tie up access to our streets and roads. This week, pray that God will help us to recognize and remove those things that block God's entry into our lives at this moment.

December 8, 2008

THE IMMACULATE CONCEPTION OF THE BLESSED VIRGIN MARY

Today's Focus: Grace Overflowing

Today we celebrate God's gracious action in Mary from the first moment of her existence. The Church teaches that from the beginning she was free from all stain of sin because of God's grace. This privilege anticipated Christ's saving death and was part of God's plan of salvation for us.

FIRST READING
Genesis 3: 9–15, 20

After the man, Adam, had eaten of the tree, the LORD God called to the man and asked him, "Where are you?" He answered, "I heard you in the garden; but I was afraid, because I was naked, so I hid myself." Then he asked, "Who told you that you were naked? You have eaten, then, from the tree of which I had forbidden you to eat!" The man replied, "The woman whom you put here with me — she gave me fruit from the tree, and so I ate it." The LORD God then asked the woman, "Why did you do such a thing?" The woman answered, "The serpent tricked me into it, so I ate it."

Then the LORD God said to the serpent:
"Because you have done this, you shall be banned
    from all the animals
    and from all the wild creatures;
on your belly shall you crawl,
    and dirt shall you eat
    all the days of your life.
I will put enmity between you and the woman,
    and between your offspring and hers;
he will strike at your head,
    while you strike at his heel."

The man called his wife Eve, because she became the mother of all the living.

PSALM RESPONSE
Psalm 98:1a

Sing to the Lord a new song, for he has done marvelous deeds.

SECOND READING
Ephesians 1: 3–6, 11–12

Brothers and sisters: Blessed be the God and Father of our Lord Jesus Christ, who has blessed us in Christ with every spiritual blessing in the heavens, as he chose us in him, before the foundation of the world, to be holy and without blemish before him. In love he destined us for adoption to himself through Jesus Christ, in accord with the favor of his will, for the praise of the glory of his grace that he granted us in the beloved.

In him we were also chosen, destined in accord with the purpose of the One who accomplishes all things according to the intention of his will, so that we might exist for the praise of his glory, we who first hoped in Christ.

GOSPEL
Luke 1:26–38

The angel Gabriel was sent from God to a town of Galilee called Nazareth, to a virgin betrothed to a man named Joseph, of the house of David, and the virgin's name was Mary. And coming to her, he said, "Hail, full of grace! The Lord is with you." But she was greatly troubled at what was said and pondered what sort of greeting this might be. Then the angel said to her, "Do not be afraid, Mary, for you have found favor with God. Behold, you will conceive in your womb and bear a son, and you shall name him Jesus. He will be great and will be called Son of the Most High, and the Lord God will give him the throne of David his father, and he will rule over the house of Jacob forever, and of his kingdom there will be no end." But Mary said to the angel, "How can this be, since I have no relations with a man?" And the angel said to her in reply, "The Holy Spirit will come upon you, and the power of the Most High will overshadow you. Therefore the child to be born will be called holy, the Son of God. And behold, Elizabeth, your relative, has also conceived a son in her old age, and this is the sixth month for her who was called barren; for nothing will be impossible for God." Mary said, "Behold, I am the handmaid of the Lord. May it be done to me according to your word." Then the angel departed from her.

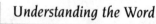

Understanding the Word

The Gospel for today's feast is Luke's account of the angel Gabriel's appearance to Mary, announcing what God was doing for her and for all of humanity. This reading illustrates God's power to bring new life and a new quality of life in human weakness, and Mary's willingness to accept this divine power in the face of its seeming impossibility.

The divine power is highlighted in a number of ways. First, the angel who is sent with this announcement is Gabriel. The name "Gabriel" means "the power of God." Angels are manifestations of the divine presence actualized in particular ways. This is why when Zechariah questions this same angel how he can know if what Gabriel says will occur, the angel begins his response by saying, "I am Gabriel" (1:19). In other words, Zechariah can know because the divine power is before him in the presence of Gabriel. This godly might is also shown in the child that Mary will bear, who "will be called Son of the Most High," a Davidic king whose kingdom is eternal (1:32–33). The divine strength is highlighted in relation to human weakness as well. Mary will conceive despite the fact that she has "no relations with a man" because "the power of the Most High will overshadow" her (1:34–35). Elizabeth, although old and previously barren, also conceives because, as Gabriel says, "nothing will be impossible for God" (1:37).

16

Mary believes this announcement of Gabriel, whose words recall the words of God to Abraham, promising the childless Abraham and Sarah a son: "Is anything too marvelous for the LORD to do?" (Genesis 18:14). On the feast of the Immaculate Conception Luke presents us an image of Mary who, because she is rooted in God's gifts of new life in the past, is open, even in situations of weakness, to such life and even more in the future.

Reflecting on the Word

Today we get two vivid pictures of the relationship we can have with God: the scene in the garden and the one at Nazareth. Both reveal God as a God of grace, who wishes to communicate and enter into intimate communion with us.

God created the man and woman in the divine image, set them in a garden, and entrusted it to their care. God asked one thing: that they be obedient by not eating the fruit of one tree in the middle of the garden. Of course, they did eat and God came calling soon after. Hear the sadness and disappointment in God's words: "You have eaten, then, from the tree of which I had forbidden you to eat!" (Genesis 3:11). Even so, God does not give up on humans.

In the scene at Nazareth once again human creatures are called into an intimate communion with God, only this time in a most startling way. One of us is to bear the Son of God. Mary considers, questions, and consents. All of creation must have been holding still in that moment before she said, "May it be done to me according to your word" (Luke 1:38). The intimate relationship with God that she entered into was the gift of a loving God. We call this intimate relationship grace. Mary was full of grace, totally open to God. Mary's relationship signals the relationship God wishes to have with us.

The Letter to the Ephesians reminds us that we have been blessed in Christ with every spiritual blessing in the heavens because God chose us in Christ before the world began. We entered into this relationship at the time of our baptism, when we began to die to sin and live for God.

CONSIDER/ DISCUSS:
- How is God inviting you to enter into deeper intimacy?
- How can the words of Mary to the angel—"Behold, I am the handmaid of the Lord"—find resonance in your own life as you serve God?

Responding to the Word

Today we can make our own the greeting of the angel: "Hail, full of grace! The Lord is with you" (Luke 1:28). Let us pray to Mary that she teach us openness to the will of God. We can pray her words: "May it be done to me according to your word" (1:38).

December 14, 2008

THIRD SUNDAY OF ADVENT

Today's Focus: Who Are You?

Once again we meet John the Baptist in the desert. Today we hear how the Jewish leaders in Jerusalem sent people to find out just who this strange preacher was. John gives us an account of his identity, inviting us to think about our own.

FIRST READING
Isaiah 61:1–2a, 10–11

The spirit of the Lord GOD is upon me,
    because the LORD has anointed me;
he has sent me to bring glad tidings to the poor,
    to heal the brokenhearted,
to proclaim liberty to the captives
    and release to the prisoners,
to announce a year of favor from the LORD
    and a day of vindication by our God.

I rejoice heartily in the LORD,
    in my God is the joy of my soul;
for he has clothed me with a robe of salvation
    and wrapped me in a mantle of justice,
like a bridegroom adorned with a diadem,
    like a bride bedecked with her jewels.
As the earth brings forth its plants,
    and a garden makes its growth spring up,
so will the Lord GOD make justice and praise
    spring up before all the nations.

PSALM RESPONSE
Isaiah 61:10b

My soul rejoices in my God.

SECOND READING
1 Thessalonians 5: 16–24

Brothers and sisters: Rejoice always. Pray without ceasing. In all circumstances give thanks, for this is the will of God for you in Christ Jesus. Do not quench the Spirit. Do not despise prophetic utterances. Test everything; retain what is good. Refrain from every kind of evil.

May the God of peace make you perfectly holy and may you entirely, spirit, soul, and body, be preserved blameless for the coming of our Lord Jesus Christ. The one who calls you is faithful, and he will also accomplish it.

GOSPEL
*John 1:6–8,
19–28*

A man named John was sent from God. He came for testimony, to testify to the light, so that all might believe through him. He was not the light, but came to testify to the light.

And this is the testimony of John. When the Jews from Jerusalem sent priests and Levites to him to ask him, "Who are you?" he admitted and did not deny it, but admitted, "I am not the Christ."

So they asked him, "What are you then? Are you Elijah?" And he said, "I am not." "Are you the Prophet?" He answered, "No." So they said to him, "Who are you, so we can give an answer to those who sent us? What do you have to say for yourself?" He said:

"I am *the voice of one crying out in the desert,*
make straight the way of the Lord,
as Isaiah the prophet said."

Some Pharisees were also sent. They asked him, "Why then do you baptize if you are not the Christ or Elijah or the Prophet?" John answered them, "I baptize with water; but there is one among you whom you do not recognize, the one who is coming after me, whose sandal strap I am not worthy to untie." This happened in Bethany across the Jordan, where John was baptizing.

Understanding the Word

The Gospel today begins the Johannine portrayal of John the Baptist as a figure who points the way to true witness.

The portrait begins by looking through John rather than at John (John 1:6–8). As soon as the Baptist is mentioned we hear of him repeatedly in terms of his connection to God and Jesus. John is a relational figure who is defined (and who defines himself) by his relation to the divine. Thus, we first read that God sent him, even before we hear his name. Next, there are three notices that John testifies to the light. The conclusion of this introduction to John's character states what he is not (the light) but rather what he does (testifies to the light—1:6–8). Thus, the narrator describes John the Baptist as a figure whose personality points away from himself and toward Jesus.

This initial sketch is confirmed and developed when next we read the account that John gives of himself (1:19–23). Leaders from Jerusalem send representatives to find out his identity, showing that John has achieved enough visibility to appear on their radar. Five times the delegates ask him who he is. He responds to their first three queries in terms of who he is not, and each response becomes shorter and shorter (five words, three words, one word). This is a man who is not about to promote himself when he is presented with the opportunity to do so. He becomes expansive, however, when he speaks about who Jesus is. At this point, he also defines himself in relation to Jesus as simply a voice announcing Jesus' coming and as one who is unworthy to untie the strap of Jesus' sandal (1:23, 26–27).

Given these observations, we can say that the portrayal of John the Baptist in the Gospel of John conveys the message that witness involves defining oneself in relation to Jesus, consistent refusal to seek personal renown, and acclaiming Jesus as the one in whom eternal life and light reside.

Reflecting on the Word

One of the most poignant moments of Arthur Miller's *Death of a Salesman* occurs at the end of the play when the family and one friend of Willie Loman, the salesman of the title, are gathered at his gravesite. Willie has committed suicide. His son Biff says, "He never knew who he was." These sad words hang in the air. This man lived his whole life not knowing who he was.

Today we hear the words of John the Baptist, who knew who he was and who he was not: "I am not the Christ. I am not Elijah. I am not the Prophet. I am the voice of one crying out in the desert, 'Make straight the way of the Lord' " (see John 1:19–23). John had a unique role to play: He was the best friend of the bridegroom who was coming and in whom God and humanity would be joined.

These days of Advent call us to know who we are—children of God who in the fullness of time sent the Son into the world so that we might have life, so that we might know our God as Father, Son, and Holy Spirit and open ourselves to be made "perfectly holy" (1 Thessalonians 5:23).

CONSIDER/ DISCUSS:
- And you, who are you? How do you think of yourself?
- How does the mystery of God touch your life?
- Do you rejoice always, as Paul calls us to do, and live in gratitude to God?

Responding to the Word

The words of Second Isaiah in the first reading, "The spirit of the Lord God is upon me, / because the Lord has anointed me" (Isaiah 61:1) helped Jesus to know who he was and what his mission was. Pray that God will help you to know who God is and who you are and how God wants to work through you, so that you can make your own the psalm response today: "My soul rejoices in my God" (Isaiah 61:10b).

December 21, 2008

FOURTH SUNDAY OF ADVENT

Today's Focus: The Marriage of Heaven and Earth

The final Sunday of Advent always takes us into the homes of Jesus' family. Last year it was the house of his foster father, Joseph; next year, the home of his kin Elizabeth and Zechariah; and this year that of his mother, Mary. Today's Gospel presents our God committing to an unimaginable relationship with a young girl from Nazareth and through her, all creation.

FIRST READING
2 Samuel 7: 1–5, 8b–12, 14a, 16

When King David was settled in his palace, and the LORD had given him rest from his enemies on every side, he said to Nathan the prophet, "Here I am living in a house of cedar, while the ark of God dwells in a tent!" Nathan answered the king, "Go, do whatever you have in mind, for the LORD is with you." But that night the LORD spoke to Nathan and said: "Go, tell my servant David, 'Thus says the LORD: Should you build me a house to dwell in?

"'It was I who took you from the pasture and from the care of the flock to be commander of my people Israel. I have been with you wherever you went, and I have destroyed all your enemies before you. And I will make you famous like the great ones of the earth. I will fix a place for my people Israel; I will plant them so that they may dwell in their place without further disturbance. Neither shall the wicked continue to afflict them as they did of old, since the time I first appointed judges over my people Israel. I will give you rest from all your enemies. The LORD also reveals to you that he will establish a house for you. And when your time comes and you rest with your ancestors, I will raise up your heir after you, sprung from your loins, and I will make his kingdom firm. I will be a father to him, and he shall be a son to me. Your house and your kingdom shall endure forever before me; your throne shall stand firm forever.'"

PSALM RESPONSE
Psalm 89:2a

For ever I will sing the goodness of the Lord.

SECOND READING
Romans 16: 25–27

Brothers and sisters: To him who can strengthen you, according to my gospel and the proclamation of Jesus Christ, according to the revelation of the mystery kept secret for long ages but now manifested through the prophetic writings and, according to the command of the eternal God, made known to all nations to bring about the obedience of faith, to the only wise God, through Jesus Christ be glory forever and ever. Amen.

GOSPEL
Luke 1:26–38

The angel Gabriel was sent from God to a town of Galilee called Nazareth, to a virgin betrothed to a man named Joseph, of the house of David, and the virgin's name was Mary. And coming to her, he said, "Hail, full of grace! The Lord is with you." But she was greatly troubled at what was said and pondered what sort of greeting this might be. Then the angel said to her, "Do not be afraid, Mary, for you have found favor with God.

"Behold, you will conceive in your womb and bear a son, and you shall name him Jesus. He will be great and will be called Son of the Most High, and the Lord God will give him the throne of David his father, and he will rule over the house of Jacob forever, and of his kingdom there will be no end." But Mary said to the angel, "How can this be, since I have no relations with a man?" And the angel said to her in reply, "The Holy Spirit will come upon you, and the power of the Most High will overshadow you. Therefore the child to be born will be called holy, the Son of God. And behold, Elizabeth, your relative, has also conceived a son in her old age, and this is the sixth month for her who was called barren; for nothing will be impossible for God." Mary said, "Behold, I am the handmaid of the Lord. May it be done to me according to your word." Then the angel departed from her.

Understanding the Word

The Gospel today presents the annunciation to Mary in relation to the annunciation to Zechariah and the one much earlier to Abraham and Sarah. It does this in order to demonstrate that Mary's immersion in the scriptural witness empowers her acceptance of God into her life. It is the angel Gabriel who announces to both Mary and Zechariah the birth of a son. Both are troubled by these annunciations, and Gabriel reassures each with the same words: "Do not be afraid."

The major difference is that Mary believes the message of Gabriel and Zechariah expresses disbelief. This is reflected in their questions. Zechariah asks how he can know that what Gabriel says is true, whereas Mary, whose similar words convey a very different meaning, asks how this will be because she does not know man. Zechariah suspends belief until there is further proof. Mary wants to know what she is to do. Thus, the angel criticizes the response of Zechariah, but instructs Mary about how Jesus will be conceived.

The annunciation to Mary requires us to look not only to the annunciation to Zechariah that is beside it, but also to look at an older annunciation that is behind it as well. There is a clear connection to the annunciation to Abram and Sarah that Sarah, although apparently beyond the age of childbearing, would conceive and have a son (Genesis 18:1–15). The last thing that Gabriel tells Mary is that "nothing will be impossible for God" (Luke 1:37). This is a reference to Genesis 18:14: "Is anything too marvelous for the LORD to do?" Mary's response to the angel, "May it be done to me according to your word" (Luke 1:38), demonstrates her belief in these words about Abram and Sarah to which Gabriel refers. Unlike Zechariah, Mary believed that God would act in the face of her own weakness because she remained rooted in the scriptural witness of God acting in such ways.

In our house chapel there is a stained glass window of the Annunciation. I must confess that I have always thought it a little silly—until recently. Mary is dressed in a lovely white gown with beautiful stars embroidered on it. She is kneeling in what looks like a house chapel. Next to her is a single potted lily. Through the window, one can glimpse a charming village. Behind her a book is opened and you can see but not read words printed on it. And, most dramatically, hovering above her is a very handsome angel, his hair wreathed with flowers. It is all so syrupy, so preposterously romantic.

Besides, all this is quite impossible. Mary was a peasant woman, unlikely to have had any reading skills; her clothing would have been very simple; and she certainly would not have had a house chapel to pray in. The form of an angel can be debated, but this one looks more like a flower child from the Sixties.

Nevertheless, what this stained glass window captures so beautifully through its romantic imagery is that the story we heard today is a love story. God has come wooing the virgin Mary, and in her "yes" we hear the beginning of the marriage of heaven and earth, of divinity with humanity.

God has chosen to dwell with us, not merely in a grand temple of stone and marble like David wanted to build, but in our flesh and blood. God has chosen to reveal a divinely passionate love for humankind. Nothing else will do but that this word of love not only be spoken but that the Word become flesh.

CONSIDER/ DISCUSS:
- How do you imagine Mary reacted to the words of the angel?
- Do you see the story of the Annunciation as part of a love story between God and humanity?
- How does this story offer hope and peace and comfort to our world, our Church, our families, our individual hearts?

Responding to the Word

The English mystic Caryll Houselander once wrote that we know so very little about Mary, Mother of Jesus, but we do know the one essential fact that we are all called to imitate: she bore him in her body and gave him to the world. Ask God to open your heart to receive this mystery of faith and incorporate it into your being, so the Word will continue to become flesh, our flesh.

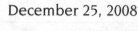

December 25, 2008

THE NATIVITY OF THE LORD
CHRISTMAS VIGIL MASS

Today's Focus: Joseph, God's Quiet Man

When we approach the manger scene on Christmas, our eyes usually go the infant Jesus. Then, perhaps, they move to Mary, his mother. And then, to the shepherds and their sheep. If we glance at Joseph, it is only briefly. He slides into the background. Tonight we are invited to contemplate Joseph and learn from him.

FIRST READING
Isaiah 62:1–5

For Zion's sake I will not be silent,
　for Jerusalem's sake I will not be quiet,
until her vindication shines forth like the dawn
　and her victory like a burning torch.

Nations shall behold your vindication,
　and all the kings your glory;
you shall be called by a new name
　pronounced by the mouth of the LORD.
You shall be a glorious crown in the hand of the LORD,
　a royal diadem held by your God.
No more shall people call you "Forsaken, "
　or your land "Desolate, "
but you shall be called "My Delight, "
　and your land "Espoused."
For the LORD delights in you
　and makes your land his spouse.
As a young man marries a virgin,
　your Builder shall marry you;
and as a bridegroom rejoices in his bride
　so shall your God rejoice in you.

PSALM RESPONSE
Psalm 89:2a

For ever I will sing the goodness of the Lord.

SECOND READING
Acts 13:16–17, 22–25

When Paul reached Antioch in Pisidia and entered the synagogue, he stood up, motioned with his hand, and said, "Fellow Israelites and you others who are God-fearing, listen. The God of this people Israel chose our ancestors and exalted the people during their sojourn in the land of Egypt. With uplifted arm he led them out of it. Then he removed Saul and raised up David as king; of him he testified, 'I have found David, son of Jesse, a man after my own heart; he will carry out my every wish.' From this man's descendants God, according to his promise, has brought to Israel a savior, Jesus. John heralded his coming by proclaiming a baptism of repentance to all the people of Israel; and as John was completing his course, he would say, 'What do you suppose that I am? I am not he.Behold, one is coming after me; I am not worthy to unfasten the sandals of his feet.' "

In the shorter form of the reading, the passage in brackets is omitted.

GOSPEL
Matthew 1:1–25
or 1:18–25

[The book of the genealogy of Jesus Christ, the son of David, the son of Abraham.

Abraham became the father of Isaac, Isaac the father of Jacob, Jacob the father of Judah and his brothers. Judah became the father of Perez and Zerah, whose mother was Tamar. Perez became the father of Hezron, Hezron the father of Ram, Ram the father of Amminadab. Amminadab became the father of Nahshon, Nahshon the father of Salmon, Salmon the father of Boaz, whose mother was Rahab. Boaz became the father of Obed, whose mother was Ruth. Obed became the father of Jesse, Jesse the father of David the king.

David became the father of Solomon, whose mother had been the wife of Uriah. Solomon became the father of Rehoboam, Rehoboam the father of Abijah, Abijah the father of Asaph. Asaph became the father of Jehoshaphat, Jehoshaphat the father of Joram, Joram the father of Uzziah. Uzziah became the father of Jotham, Jotham the father of Ahaz, Ahaz the father of Hezekiah. Hezekiah became the father of Manasseh, Manasseh the father of Amos, Amos the father of Josiah. Josiah became the father of Jechoniah and his brothers at the time of the Babylonian exile.

After the Babylonian exile, Jechoniah became the father of Shealtiel, Shealtiel the father of Zerubbabel, Zerubbabel the father of Abiud. Abiud became the father of Eliakim, Eliakim the father of Azor, Azor the father of Zadok. Zadok became the father of Achim, Achim the father of Eliud, Eliud the father of Eleazar. Eleazar became the father of Matthan, Matthan the father of Jacob, Jacob the father of Joseph, the husband of Mary. Of her was born Jesus who is called the Christ.

Thus the total number of generations from Abraham to David is fourteen generations; from David to the Babylonian exile, fourteen generations; from the Babylonian exile to the Christ, fourteen generations.]

Now this is how the birth of Jesus Christ came about. When his mother Mary was betrothed to Joseph, but before they lived together, she was found with child through the Holy Spirit. Joseph her husband, since he was a righteous man, yet unwilling to expose her to shame, decided to divorce her quietly. Such was his intention when, behold, the angel of the Lord appeared to him in a dream and said, "Joseph, son of David, do not be afraid to take Mary your wife into your home. For it is through the Holy Spirit that this child has been conceived in her. She will bear a son and you are to name him Jesus, because he will save his people from their sins." All this took place to fulfill what the Lord had said through the prophet:

Behold, the virgin shall conceive and bear a son,
   and they shall name him Emmanuel,
which means "God is with us."

When Joseph awoke, he did as the angel of the Lord had commanded him and took his wife into his home. He had no relations with her until she bore a son, and he named him Jesus.

For Matthew everything is in its place because God's place is consistently with us. This is the Gospel that begins by speaking about Jesus as "Emmanuel, which means, 'God is with us'" and ends with Jesus telling the eleven disciples, "I am with you always, until the end of the age" (Matthew 1:23; 28:20). God is always active in bringing about a divinely ordered life in what looks like a chaotic jumble of events. Thus, the birth of Jesus is preceded by an orderly sequence of ancestors that stretches all they way back to Abraham. God has been at work to bring about a fulfillment of human life through a welter of events, sometimes very difficult ones. Jesus' ancestors are divided by Matthew into three sets of fourteen generations that culminate in Jesus. The final step in each series of fourteen is a significant one to show that God is moving life toward a goal. So the first set of fourteen generations ends with King David, the second set with those who were deported to Babylon, and the third set with the birth of "Jesus who is called the Christ" (1:16).

Joseph participates in this ordered move toward God's fulfillment of history. All forty-two generations of Jesus' line lead to the identity of the father of the child. Unlike Luke's Gospel, in which the angel Gabriel speaks to Mary, in Matthew's Gospel the angel of the Lord speaks to Joseph in a dream. How Joseph participates in God's consummation of human life is by not fleeing the chaos in his life, but rather by acting mercifully toward others and trusting in God when life appears to be coming undone. Thus, upon learning that Mary is pregnant, he first decides to divorce her quietly rather than put her to shame (1:19). After the revelation that Jesus was conceived of the Holy Spirit, Joseph believes and takes Mary for his wife (1:24). For Matthew the recognition of divine order bolsters compassion and trust.

Reflecting on the Word

So many works of art depict Mary and the infant Jesus. We can trace this tendency back to Luke's Gospel, the first to focus on Mary. If we had only Luke's Gospel, we would know nothing about that other person central to the Christmas story, Joseph, husband of Mary and foster father of Jesus. Thank Matthew for giving Joseph a moment to hold our attention.

Suddenly, he discovered that the young woman to whom he was betrothed was pregnant. Joseph is described as "righteous," one who lives according to the law of Moses. The law was clear on what was to be done in this case: divorce, perhaps even death. But Joseph was also compassionate. He would not publicly humiliate his betrothed. So he decided to divorce her quietly.

Enter the angel of God in a dream. The message was that God is at work here, that God is doing something new here. Joseph was invited to be part of it—not only to take Mary as his wife but to take the child into his family, the family of David. Joseph never speaks in the story. He simply acts, doing as the angel commands him. In the silence, Joseph's heart was moved to put his trust in God.

Sometimes we are asked to let God enter our lives in a new way, one that can only come about through our cooperation, giving life to others. Augustine once said, "The birth of Christ is always happening, but what good is it if it does not happen in me? How can it help me?"

CONSIDER/ DISCUSS:
- What enabled Joseph to decide to obey the angel?
- Is God asking you for help in bringing divine life into to the world?

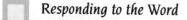

Responding to the Word

Spend a few moments in prayer, asking God to help you enter into the trusting attitude that will allow you to respond positively to the promptings of the Holy Spirit in your life, just as Joseph did.

December 28, 2008

THE HOLY FAMILY
OF JESUS, MARY, AND JOSEPH

Today's Focus: God Wants a Family

The Holy Family is not limited to three people who lived two thousand years ago. While Jesus, Mary, and Joseph can be thought of as the Holy Family, they were only the beginning of a new family, based not on blood but on the working of the Holy Spirit. We are all part of God's holy family.

FIRST READING

Genesis 15:1–6; 21:1–3

The word of the LORD came to Abram in a vision, saying:
"Fear not, Abram!
I am your shield;
I will make your reward very great."
But Abram said, "O Lord GOD, what good will your gifts be, if I keep on being childless and have as my heir the steward of my house, Eliezer?" Abram continued, "See, you have given me no offspring, and so one of my servants will be my heir." Then the word of the LORD came to him: "No, that one shall not be your heir; your own issue shall be your heir." The Lord took Abram outside and said, "Look up at the sky and count the stars, if you can. Just so," he added, "shall your descendants be." Abram put his faith in the LORD, who credited it to him as an act of righteousness.

The LORD took note of Sarah as he had said he would; he did for her as he had promised. Sarah became pregnant and bore Abraham a son in his old age, at the set time that God had stated. Abraham gave the name Isaac to this son of his whom Sarah bore him.

PSALM RESPONSE

Psalm 105:7a, 8a

The Lord remembers his covenant forever.

SECOND READING

Hebrews 11: 8, 11–12, 17–19

Brothers and sisters: By faith Abraham obeyed when he was called to go out to a place that he was to receive as an inheritance; he went out, not knowing where he was to go. By faith he received power to generate, even though he was past the normal age — and Sarah herself was sterile — for he thought that the one who had made the promise was trustworthy. So it was that there came forth from one man, himself as good as dead, descendants as numerous as the stars in the sky and as countless as the sands on the seashore.

By faith Abraham, when put to the test, offered up Isaac, and he who had received the promises was ready to offer his only son, of whom it was said, "Through Isaac descendants shall bear your name." He reasoned that God was able to raise even from the dead, and he received Isaac back as a symbol.

In the shorter form of the reading, the passage in brackets is omitted.

GOSPEL
Luke 2:22–40
or 22, 39–40

When the days were completed for their purification according to the law of Moses, they took him up to Jerusalem to present him to the Lord, [just as it is written in the law of the Lord,

Every male that opens the womb shall be consecrated to the Lord,
and to offer the sacrifice of
a pair of turtledoves or two young pigeons,
in accordance with the dictate in the law of the Lord.
Now there was a man in Jerusalem whose name was Simeon. This man was righteous and devout, awaiting the consolation of Israel, and the Holy Spirit was upon him. It had been revealed to him by the Holy Spirit that he should not see death before he had seen the Christ of the Lord. He came in the Spirit into the temple; and when the parents brought in the child Jesus to perform the custom of the law in regard to him, he took him into his arms and blessed God, saying:

"Now, Master, you may let your servant go
in peace, according to your word,
for my eyes have seen your salvation,
which you prepared in sight of all the peoples,
a light for revelation to the Gentiles,
and glory for your people Israel."

The child's father and mother were amazed at what was said about him; and Simeon blessed them and said to Mary his mother, "Behold, this child is destined for the fall and rise of many in Israel, and to be a sign that will be contradicted — and you yourself a sword will pierce — so that the thoughts of many hearts may be revealed." There was also a prophetess, Anna, the daughter of Phanuel, of the tribe of Asher. She was advanced in years, having lived seven years with her husband after her marriage, and then as a widow until she was eighty-four. She never left the temple, but worshiped night and day with fasting and prayer. And coming forward at that very time, she gave thanks to God and spoke about the child to all who were awaiting the redemption of Jerusalem.]

When they had fulfilled all the prescriptions of the law of the Lord, they returned to Galilee, to their own town of Nazareth. The child grew and became strong, filled with wisdom; and the favor of God was upon him.

Understanding the Word

Our Gospel from Luke today is a tale of God's actions through the devout to produce future hope. The parents of Jesus are presented by Luke as devout observers of the Jewish law who fulfilled what was required of them to do for Jesus. Only in this Gospel do we read about Mary and Joseph taking the infant Jesus to Jerusalem to fulfill the Law (Luke 2:22–24). While there they meet two godly people. Simeon is described as "righteous and devout" and Anna as a prophetess who "never left the temple, but worshiped night and day with fasting and prayer" (2:25, 37).

God responds to these dedicated lives with signs of a rich future opening up for others. Thus, Simeon has a revelation that he would not die until he saw the Christ (2:26). Upon seeing Jesus he proclaims, to the wonderment of Joseph and Mary, that their son would be the means of salvation for all (2:29–35). In turn, Anna acclaims the infant Jesus both to his parents and "to all who were awaiting the redemption of Jerusalem" (2:38). After Joseph and Mary complete all the requirements of the Law for that time and return to Galilee, Luke writes that Jesus grew in strength and was filled with wisdom and the favor of God (2:40). God brings a hope-filled future through devout lives.

Today's Gospel passage is about the initial and long-term maintenance of the relationship with God and the hopes to which such a life leads. Mary and Joseph start their son out on the right foot, and Simeon and Anna have grown old in righteousness and worship. Beginning and maintaining the relationship with God opens one to God's future expansive plans.

Reflecting on the Word

On Christmas we celebrate God becoming human, when the face of creation was changed. We ponder that great mystery of the Incarnation: Jesus is true God and truly human. The divine has entered into communion with the human in the body and soul of Jesus of Nazareth.

Christmas is not a single day, however, but an entire season. Today, the Sunday after Christmas, we ponder the Holy Family. What difference does this mystery of the Incarnation make for families? Jesus came to bring together the children of Israel into a new family, a family united not by blood but by faith in him. So in today's Gospel we see some of the first members of that family.

Luke's Gospel has been called the Gospel of Jesus as the compassion of God, the Gospel of prayer, the Gospel of the Holy Spirit; we can also think of it as the Gospel of family. He first introduces us to Mary's cousin, Elizabeth, and Elizabeth's husband, Zechariah, parents of John the Baptist. Then we meet Mary and Joseph.

Today we meet two other family members, Simeon and Anna, not related by blood, but only by faith in the promises of the God of Israel. Each sees in the child Jesus the glory of Israel and the light for the Gentiles.

Christmas reminds us that by baptism into Christ we are now part of God's family. As God's family, "God's chosen ones," as Paul reminded the Colossians (3:62), we are to put on heartfelt compassion, kindness, gentleness, and patience, bearing with one another and forgiving one another.

CONSIDER/ DISCUSS:

- What does it mean to be "family"?
- Do you see yourself as part of God's family?
- Is there a way that you can help someone feel what it means to be part of God's family?

 Responding to the Word

Spend a few quiet moments in prayer, thanking God for calling us to be part of God's holy family, for giving us at baptism and at confirmation the gift of the Holy Spirit. This Spirit has been poured into our hearts and dwells within us, binding us together, for Christ came as a Savior for all men and women.

January 1, 2009

THE BLESSED VIRGIN MARY, THE MOTHER OF GOD

Today's Focus: Mary, the Woman Who Ponders

Today, God's word calls us to shift our gaze from the baby in the manger to the figure hovering over him, his mother, Mary. On this day of New Year's resolutions, Mary calls us to reflection—not first and foremost on ourselves, but on the meaning of her child for our lives in this new year.

FIRST READING
Numbers 6: 22–27

The LORD said to Moses: "Speak to Aaron and his sons and tell them: This is how you shall bless the Israelites. Say to them:

The LORD bless you and keep you!
The LORD let his face shine upon you, and be gracious to you!
The LORD look upon you kindly and give you peace!

So shall they invoke my name upon the Israelites, and I will bless them."

PSALM RESPONSE
Psalm 67:2a

May God bless us in his mercy.

SECOND READING
Galatians 4:4–7

Brothers and sisters: When the fullness of time had come, God sent his Son, born of a woman, born under the law, to ransom those under the law, so that we might receive adoption as sons. As proof that you are sons, God sent the Spirit of his Son into our hearts, crying out, "Abba, Father!" So you are no longer a slave but a son, and if a son then also an heir, through God.

GOSPEL
Luke 2:16–21

The shepherds went in haste to Bethlehem and found Mary and Joseph, and the infant lying in the manger. When they saw this, they made known the message that had been told them about this child. All who heard it were amazed by what had been told them by the shepherds. And Mary kept all these things, reflecting on them in her heart. Then the shepherds returned, glorifying and praising God for all they had heard and seen, just as it had been told to them. When eight days were completed for his circumcision, he was named Jesus, the name given him by the angel before he was conceived in the womb.

Understanding the Word

The Gospel reading for today is part of a larger Lukan theme of Mary as a woman who takes her experiences of God to heart and acts on them. In this passage the shepherds make known to Mary and Joseph their encounter with the angels and their message concerning Jesus and his significance (Luke 2:17). We next hear of two responses to the shepherds. All who heard them were "amazed," while "Mary kept all these things, reflecting on them in her heart" (2:18–19). Indeed, Mary does more than marvel at the news. She "keeps" it and reflects on it. Similarly, when the angel Gabriel greeted her with the words "Hail, full of grace! The Lord is with you" (1:28) Mary's reaction was to be "greatly troubled at what was said, . . . ponder[ing] what sort of greeting this might be" (1:29). Later, when she and Joseph find the twelve-year-old Jesus in the temple after searching for him for three days, she asks Jesus why he acted this way to his parents. Jesus responds, "Why were you looking for me? Did you not know that I must be in my Father's house?" (2:49). Mary's response is not to push the issue, but rather she "kept all these things in her heart" (2:51).

Because Mary takes the divine message seriously, she responds appropriately to God and to others. Gabriel tells Mary that she will name her son "Jesus," and when Jesus is circumcised Mary so names him (1:31; 2:21). Perhaps because she took to heart the words of the shepherds, she did not overreact to the young Jesus' later disappearance in the temple and, from a parental point of view, his totally unsatisfactory response when she asked him why he did this to them.

Mary does not just hear the message of God; she considers it and incorporates it into her very being so that it provides an impetus for responsible actions and deep feeling.

Reflecting on the Word

Often during this time of year when we honor the Prince of Peace, we encounter incidents of violence. Last year on New Year's Day, Kenya was in the news with images of the violent fighting between the Kikuyu and Lao tribes. That had followed upon the assassination of Benazir Bhutto and the violence it unleashed in Pakistan. In previous years, there were other events of mayhem and chaos among the children of the world.

In the midst of all that might be occurring on the first day of the New Year, the Church continues to place before us the woman whom we honor as the Mother of God. Luke's Gospel presents her several times as the woman who ponders, who listens to what is going on around her, to what others have experienced, and who reflects on these things in her heart.

Today she ponders the message the shepherds received from the angel: "Do not be afraid; for behold, I proclaim to you good news of great joy that will be for all the people. For today in the city of David, a savior has been born for you who is Christ and Lord" (Luke 2:10–11).

We, too, must ponder the angels' message. In a world that needs saving more than ever, Mary calls us to live in hope. The commitment that God has made to us through the birth of Jesus the Son has not been withdrawn. Jesus has come and continues to bring salvation. These remain tidings of great joy.

CONSIDER/
DISCUSS:
- What does it mean to call Jesus our savior? From what do we need saving?
- What events hold you back from entering into the peace of Christ?

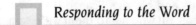

Responding to the Word

Spend a few quiet moments in prayer, reflecting on Jesus as Savior. Pray for deliverance from one thing that weighs down on you outwardly or inwardly, and for one place in our world that needs the peace of Christ.

January 4, 2009

THE EPIPHANY OF THE LORD

Today's Focus: An Ongoing Story

The story of the magi speaks of a God who came for all peoples, then and now, who continues to reveal the divine presence in songs and words, but especially through the Child at the heart of this story. The journey of the magi reminds us that the truly wise are willing to leave behind the familiar to seek a greater treasure.

FIRST READING
Isaiah 60:1–6

Rise up in splendor, Jerusalem! Your light has come,
   the glory of the Lord shines upon you.
See, darkness covers the earth,
   and thick clouds cover the peoples;
but upon you the LORD shines,
   and over you appears his glory.
Nations shall walk by your light,
   and kings by your shining radiance.
Raise your eyes and look about;
   they all gather and come to you:
your sons come from afar,
   and your daughters in the arms of their nurses.

Then you shall be radiant at what you see,
   your heart shall throb and overflow,
for the riches of the sea shall be emptied out before you,
   the wealth of nations shall be brought to you.
Caravans of camels shall fill you,
   dromedaries from Midian and Ephah;
all from Sheba shall come
   bearing gold and frankincense,
   and proclaiming the praises of the LORD.

PSALM RESPONSE
Psalm 72:11

Lord, every nation on earth will adore you.

SECOND READING
Ephesians 3: 2–3a, 5–6

Brothers and sisters: You have heard of the stewardship of God's grace that was given to me for your benefit, namely, that the mystery was made known to me by revelation. It was not made known to people in other generations as it has now been revealed to his holy apostles and prophets by the Spirit: that the Gentiles are coheirs, members of the same body, and copartners in the promise in Christ Jesus through the gospel.

GOSPEL
Matthew 2: 1–12

When Jesus was born in Bethlehem of Judea, in the days of King Herod, behold, magi from the east arrived in Jerusalem, saying, "Where is the newborn king of the Jews? We saw his star at its rising and have come to do him homage." When King Herod heard this, he was greatly troubled, and all Jerusalem with him. Assembling all the chief priests and the scribes of the people, he inquired of them where the Christ was to be born. They said to him, "In Bethlehem of Judea, for thus it has been written through the prophet:

> And you, Bethlehem, land of Judah,
>   are by no means least among the rulers of Judah;
> since from you shall come a ruler,
>   who is to shepherd my people Israel."

Then Herod called the magi secretly and ascertained from them the time of the star's appearance. He sent them to Bethlehem and said, "Go and search diligently for the child. When you have found him, bring me word, that I too may go and do him homage." After their audience with the king they set out. And behold, the star that they had seen at its rising preceded them, until it came and stopped over the place where the child was. They were overjoyed at seeing the star, and on entering the house they saw the child with Mary his mother. They prostrated themselves and did him homage. Then they opened their treasures and offered him gifts of gold, frankincense, and myrrh. And having been warned in a dream not to return to Herod, they departed for their country by another way.

Understanding the Word

Today we hear Matthew's account of the magi coming to pay homage to Jesus. Having recently emphasized the kingly origins of Jesus from the house of David (Matthew 1:1–17), Matthew now addresses how one comes to recognize the kingly power of Jesus in our lives.

This recognition does not come through official channels of power. King Herod is asked by the magi, "Where is the newborn king of the Jews?" (2:2). But Herod does not know, and needs not only the chief priests and scribes but also the magi to inform him where Jesus is to be found (2:4–8). The former rely on their interpretation of prophecy and the latter on their experience of intimations of the supernatural in nature. The magi are wise men who rely on the sighting of a star in the East to lead them. They are also led in their actions by a dream in which they are warned not to return to Herod (2:12).

These types of guidance are consistent with Matthew's treatment of prophecy and dreams elsewhere in his accounts of the birth and infancy of Jesus. In these other passages prophecy and dreams are often the means by which God acts; they also reveal how people should act in response. Thus, an angel of the Lord appears to Joseph three times in dreams and directs his actions (1:20–22, 24–25; 2:13–15, 19–21). Four times prophecies signal Jesus' birth and events that happen in his life (1:23; 2:15, 18, 23).

The kingly power of Jesus is suggested in our lives through subtle perceptions that are not susceptible to logical analysis, in transcendent experiences amid everyday living, and in the word of God that guides us to perceive the divine.

Reflecting on the Word

The feast of the Epiphany has always been the major celebration at this time of year in the Eastern Church, more so than our observance of Christmas in the West. From the earliest days, it was recognized that the Epiphany referred not only to the journey of the three magi to the place where the child was. Epiphany was also found in the events of Jesus being baptized and the miracle of water turned to wine at Cana. All three manifested this Jesus as one in whom the presence of God was to be found in a unique way.

We can say about the Epiphany what Augustine said about the feast of the birth of Jesus: It is always happening. But for it to help us, it must happen for us and in us. The final verse of the lovely Christmas hymn "O Little Town of Bethlehem" boldly recognizes this when we sing:

> O holy Child of Bethlehem! Descend to us we pray;
> Cast out our sin and enter in, Be born in us today.
> We hear the Christmas angels The great glad tidings tell;
> O come to us, abide with us, Our Lord Emmanuel!

We ask God to attune us in these coming days of Epiphany to the many ways that God continues to be revealed to us in Christ—through his words and deeds when we hear the Gospel, through his presence in the sacraments, and through the many gifts of creation, especially one another.

CONSIDER/
DISCUSS:
- Read the story of the magi again and think about how God has been with you on your journey through life.
- Have you had any special experience of God through nature? Through the scriptures?
- The magi brought gifts to the child. Is there a gift you feel prompted to give this Christmas season?

Responding to the Word

Spend a few minutes in quiet prayer reflecting on the importance of the word of God in this story. It was God's word that helped the magi to reach their ultimate destination.

Reflect on the three gifts that the magi gave to the Child: the gold symbolizing his kingship over all creation, the frankincense his dignity as Son of God, and the myrrh his suffering and death by which he would redeem the world.

January 11, 2009

THE BAPTISM OF THE LORD

Today's Focus: The Descent of the Dove

The baptism of Jesus is the beginning of his public ministry. The Christmas season concludes with this feast that calls us to consider how we are given the Spirit at our baptism, a Spirit who leads us into the world so that God's work may be done.

FIRST READING
Isaiah 55:1–11

Thus says the LORD:
All you who are thirsty,
    come to the water!
You who have no money,
    come, receive grain and eat;
come, without paying and without cost,
    drink wine and milk!
Why spend your money for what is not bread,
    your wages for what fails to satisfy?
Heed me, and you shall eat well,
    you shall delight in rich fare.
Come to me heedfully,
    listen, that you may have life.
I will renew with you the everlasting covenant,
    the benefits assured to David.
As I made him a witness to the peoples,
    a leader and commander of nations,
so shall you summon a nation you knew not,
    and nations that knew you not shall run to you,
because of the LORD, your God,
    the Holy One of Israel, who has glorified you.
Seek the LORD while he may be found,
    call him while he is near.
Let the scoundrel forsake his way,
    and the wicked man his thoughts;
let him turn to the LORD for mercy;
    to our God, who is generous in forgiving.
For my thoughts are not your thoughts,
    nor are your ways my ways, says the LORD.
As high as the heavens are above the earth
    so high are my ways above your ways
    and my thoughts above your thoughts.

For just as from the heavens
  the rain and snow come down
and do not return there
  till they have watered the earth,
  making it fertile and fruitful,
giving seed to the one who sows
  and bread to the one who eats,
so shall my word be
  that goes forth from my mouth;
my word shall not return to me void,
  but shall do my will,
  achieving the end for which I sent it.

PSALM RESPONSE
Isaiah 12:3

You will draw water joyfully from the springs of salvation.

SECOND READING
1 John 5:1–9

Beloved: Everyone who believes that Jesus is the Christ is begotten by God, and everyone who loves the Father loves also the one begotten by him. In this way we know that we love the children of God when we love God and obey his commandments. For the love of God is this, that we keep his commandments. And his commandments are not burdensome, for whoever is begotten by God conquers the world. And the victory that conquers the world is our faith. Who indeed is the victor over the world but the one who believes that Jesus is the Son of God? This is the one who came through water and blood, Jesus Christ, not by water alone, but by water and blood. The Spirit is the one who testifies, and the Spirit is truth. So there are three that testify, the Spirit, the water, and the blood, and the three are of one accord. If we accept human testimony, the testimony of God is surely greater. Now the testimony of God is this, that he has testified on behalf of his Son.

GOSPEL
Mark 1:7–11

This is what John the Baptist proclaimed: "One mightier than I is coming after me. I am not worthy to stoop and loosen the thongs of his sandals. I have baptized you with water; he will baptize you with the Holy Spirit."

It happened in those days that Jesus came from Nazareth of Galilee and was baptized in the Jordan by John. On coming up out of the water he saw the heavens being torn open and the Spirit, like a dove, descending upon him. And a voice came from the heavens, "You are my beloved Son; with you I am well pleased."

Mark's account of the baptism of Jesus portrays the inner life of Jesus as one empowered and guided by the Holy Spirit and, as a result, the unique giver of the Spirit who will liberate humanity.

The verses prior to today's scripture present John the Baptist as a composite of Old Testament figures who signal important arrivals of God in human history. John is the messenger whom the prophet Malachi says will come before God, as well as the voice in Second Isaiah that cries in the wilderness to prepare the people (Mark 1:2–3). All in Judea are impressed and are baptized by him in the wilderness (1:4–5).

Despite this scriptural and popular acclaim, John preaches that compared to Jesus, who baptizes with the Holy Spirit, he himself is not even fit to be a servant who unties Jesus' sandal (1:7–8). This greater status of Jesus is based on his relationship to the Father and the Spirit. The Spirit comes upon Jesus and a voice from heaven testifies that Jesus is God's Son. Jesus becomes the Spirit-bearer, and the first thing that this implies is shown right after today's reading: "At once the Spirit drove him out into the desert" (1:12). The verb is a powerful one that is often used to describe Jesus driving out demons. Coming in the power of the Spirit means his complete submission to the way the Spirit works in his life. Out in the wilderness to which the Spirit drives Jesus are Satan and wild animals. But the Spirit and ministering angels also appear there (1:13).

The power by which Jesus drives out the evil that pervades our life and initiates us into God's life has its source in his acceptance of how the Spirit drives him into difficult situations. Completely open to the Spirit's influences in his life, Jesus is the one who baptizes with this Spirit.

Reflecting on the Word

This is one of the key moments in the life of Jesus. He must have heard about John up north in his home town of Nazareth. At some point an inner voice must have said, "Go south, go to the desert. Go listen to this preacher John."

When he came to the desert, he may have stood in a long line before that moment came when he entered the water and John baptized him. Mark gives us only the briefest account of their meeting, but does present John as expecting someone mightier than he who would baptize with the Holy Spirit.

It is this same Holy Spirit who came down on Jesus as he was coming out of the water. At that moment, the heavens were torn open, heaven reached down to touch the Galilean, and the Spirit descended like a dove. Have you ever seen a gull descend to snatch a fish, or a hawk swoop down to seize its prey? By contrast, the image of a descending dove is one of beauty and grace, of gentle alighting.

The words do not announce Jesus to others, as in Matthew's account, but they are spoken only to him: "You are my beloved Son; with you I am well pleased" (1:11) echoing the words the Lord speaks in the first song of the Servant in the book of Isaiah.

The descent of the dove did not mean an easy life for Jesus, but God had penetrated his being in a way that would then drive him into the desert to begin his mission of confronting the powers of sin and death. This gentle dove came—and continues to come—with a mighty power.

CONSIDER/
DISCUSS:
- Why did Jesus undergo John's baptism?
- What did this event mean in the life of Jesus?
- What does your baptism mean to you?

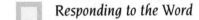

Responding to the Word

At baptism, the Spirit came upon you in the presence of the Christian community, claiming you in Jesus' name, and God said, "You are my beloved son/daughter." Spend some time praying over these words. What do you say to God in return? How does it affect what you do in life?

Notes

The Gospel that is featured in Ordinary Time this year is the Gospel of Mark. The shortest of the Gospels, it nevertheless possesses a number of extraordinary features, some of which begin to be explored in the Sundays of Ordinary Time that we have before Lent this year. The Gospel reading for the Second Sunday, however, is from John, and it highlights by contrast some of the unique features of Mark's Gospel that we will hear about on the following Sundays. In John's Gospel almost all the disciples find Jesus rather than Jesus finding them. This reversal of the order of who finds whom will make profound points about what it means to be a Johannine Christian.

In the Markan account, it is Jesus who finds the disciples, as we hear on the Third Sunday in Ordinary Time. This reading emphasizes that the Father acts decisively through Jesus in our lives, and people must respond willingly and promptly to cooperate with the pace of these divine deeds. This reading and the ones that follow on the next two Sundays are at the beginning of the Gospel of Mark. The next Gospel reading, on the Fourth Sunday in Ordinary Time, builds on the dispatch that Jesus requires of his disciples by showing his own forceful actions performed without delay, and the reasons for this way of acting. Here is where we start to learn about the meaning of the principal Markan message: "This is the time of fulfillment. The kingdom of God is at hand. Repent and believe in the gospel" (Mark 1:15). Something important is happening. Jesus, impelled by the Spirit, confronts the numinous powers that afflict humanity. The question then becomes whether people are open to this liberating power of the Spirit. In developing these ideas, the Gospel readings for the Fourth and Fifth Sundays in Ordinary Time will inaugurate the distinctive Markan emphases on the role of exorcisms and the value Mark places on an apocalyptic perspective in Christian life. In apocalyptic thought, the world can expect some decisive intervention by God in ways that will transform it beyond the reach of human history. In this perspective, forces inimical to humanity have gained such a stranglehold on life that it takes God's decisive power from outside history to liberate us.

On the Sixth and Seventh Sundays in Ordinary Time, we begin to see how the people's response to God's decisive actions—in this case two miraculous healings by Jesus—actually begins to hamper Jesus' ability to get his message of repentance heard. This tension between popular reaction to the effects of God's reign and Jesus' insistence that repentance and belief are necessary is a theme to which Mark will return repeatedly throughout his Gospel.

January 18, 2009

SECOND SUNDAY IN ORDINARY TIME

Today's Focus: "Behold, the Lamb of God"

As we move into Ordinary Time, we leave the celebration of Christmas but not the awareness that God sent this only-begotten Son into the world for our salvation. Today's readings remind us that we bring each other to God by helping one another to see and listen to God at work among us.

FIRST READING
1 Samuel 3: 3b–10, 19

Samuel was sleeping in the temple of the LORD where the ark of God was. The LORD called to Samuel, who answered, "Here I am." Samuel ran to Eli and said, "Here I am. You called me." "I did not call you," Eli said. "Go back to sleep." So he went back to sleep. Again the LORD called Samuel, who rose and went to Eli. "Here I am," he said. "You called me." But Eli answered, "I did not call you, my son. Go back to sleep."

At that time Samuel was not familiar with the LORD, because the LORD had not revealed anything to him as yet. The LORD called Samuel again, for the third time. Getting up and going to Eli, he said, "Here I am. You called me." Then Eli understood that the LORD was calling the youth. So he said to Samuel, "Go to sleep, and if you are called, reply, Speak, LORD, for your servant is listening." When Samuel went to sleep in his place, the LORD came and revealed his presence, calling out as before, "Samuel, Samuel!" Samuel answered, "Speak, for your servant is listening."

Samuel grew up, and the LORD was with him, not permitting any word of his to be without effect.

PSALM RESPONSE
Psalm 40:8a and 9a

Here am I, Lord; I come to do your will.

SECOND READING
1 Corinthians 6: 13c–15a, 17–20

Brothers and sisters: The body is not for immorality, but for the Lord, and the Lord is for the body; God raised the Lord and will also raise us by his power.

Do you not know that your bodies are members of Christ? But whoever is joined to the Lord becomes one Spirit with him. Avoid immorality. Every other sin a person commits is outside the body, but the immoral person sins against his own body. Do you not know that your body is a temple of the Holy Spirit within you, whom you have from God, and that you are not your own? For you have been purchased at a price. Therefore glorify God in your body.

GOSPEL
John 1:35–42 John was standing with two of his disciples, and as he watched Jesus walk by, he said, "Behold, the Lamb of God." The two disciples heard what he said and followed Jesus. Jesus turned and saw them following him and said to them, "What are you looking for?" They said to him, "Rabbi" — which translated means Teacher —, "where are you staying?" He said to them, "Come, and you will see." So they went and saw where Jesus was staying, and they stayed with him that day. It was about four in the afternoon. Andrew, the brother of Simon Peter, was one of the two who heard John and followed Jesus. He first found his own brother Simon and told him, "We have found the Messiah" — which is translated Christ. Then he brought him to Jesus. Jesus looked at him and said, "You are Simon the son of John; you will be called Cephas" — which is translated Peter.

Understanding the Word

Today's Gospel introduces us to the first Johannine disciples. Unlike the Synoptic Gospels (Matthew, Mark, and Luke), in which Jesus finds the first disciples, in John's Gospel (with one exception) they find Jesus. This coming to Jesus is an important example of what, according to John, it takes to be a Christian.

John writes today about the first three disciples: Andrew, an unnamed disciple, and Peter, the brother of Andrew. Having heard John the Baptist's witness to Jesus, Andrew and the unnamed disciple take the initiative and seek him out. They ask Jesus where he is staying, and upon being invited by him to "Come, and you will see," they themselves stay "with him that day" (1:39). On the next day Andrew finds his brother, Simon Peter, tells him about Jesus, and brings Simon to him (1:40–42).

The first disciples set an example for the Johannine community and for those who would be part of it. The Fourth Gospel is the only one with three references to those who confess Jesus being threatened with or actually experiencing expulsion from the synagogue. The community of Johannine Christians is often said to be sectarian in nature, meaning that they existed on the fringes of their larger socio-cultural milieu. To be a Johannine Christian meant having the courage to step out of the dominant culture and enter into an estranged one. It also meant having the resolve to persist in this religious subculture that was scorned and isolated. This is never easy for such social beings as we are. The difficulty of being marginalized for the sake of Jesus is evident in John's story of the parents of a man born blind who will not speak up for their son, who has been healed by Jesus, for fear of being "expelled from the synagogue" (9:22).

The earliest disciples point the way for future disciples by themselves stepping out to find Jesus, by remaining with him, and by drawing others to Jesus though their witness.

Once more we stand with John the Baptist and learn from what he does. Watching Jesus walk by, he says to two of his disciples, "Behold, the Lamb of God." And "[t]he two disciples heard what he said and followed Jesus" (John 1:36–37). One was Andrew, who, in turn, goes to his brother Simon and brings him to Jesus. And Jesus gives him a new name, Cephas, which means "rock."

A new life begins for Andrew and Simon, and most likely for the other disciple as well, possibly either James or John (both were fishermen with Peter and Andrew). It was clear to Jesus that they were searching for something: "What are you looking for?" They answered, "Teacher, where are you staying?" implying that it was going to take more than a few minutes to answer that question. Jesus took them in immediately: "Come, and you will see." And they stayed with him that day (see John 1:38–39).

As we return to Ordinary Time, which comes from the Latin *ordo* ("numbered"), we count the weeks off by numbers: Second Sunday, Third Sunday, and so on. But "ordinary time" is lived in a world touched by God's grace. God continues to come into our lives, if we would notice.

Like John pointing out Jesus to his two disciples, the old priest Eli helps Samuel to understand that the Lord is entering the boy's life and tells him to respond, "Speak, Lord, for your servant is listening" (1 Samuel 3:9). We bring each other to God, to Jesus Christ, by being attentive to how God is at work among us. God continues to work through each of us and that is what makes "ordinary time" continuously extraordinary.

CONSIDER/ DISCUSS:
- Have there been people in your life who helped you to recognize that God was calling?
- How might Jesus be working through you to enter the life of others—your family, friends, fellow workers, acquaintances, even strangers?
- Do you have reason to say, "Speak, Lord, your servant is listening"?

■ *Responding to the* Word

Our prayer can be full of words, giving voice to our plans, our needs, our desires. We can bring a lot of "help, help, help" or "gimme, gimme, gimme" to prayer. Try just listening.

January 25, 2009

THIRD SUNDAY IN ORDINARY TIME

Today's Focus: Called and Collected

Today we return to Mark's Gospel. We hear Jesus' preaching message and Mark's version of the call of Simon, Andrew, James, and John. What is most striking is the immediacy of their response. Not only individuals, but sometimes whole cities respond to the word of the Lord, as the Ninevites do in the story of Jonah.

FIRST READING
Jonah 3:1–5, 10

The word of the LORD came to Jonah, saying: "Set out for the great city of Nineveh, and announce to it the message that I will tell you." So Jonah made ready and went to Nineveh, according to the LORD's bidding. Now Nineveh was an enormously large city; it took three days to go through it. Jonah began his journey through the city, and had gone but a single day's walk announcing, "Forty days more and Nineveh shall be destroyed," when the people of Nineveh believed God; they proclaimed a fast and all of them, great and small, put on sackcloth.

When God saw by their actions how they turned from their evil way, he repented of the evil that he had threatened to do to them; he did not carry it out.

PSALM RESPONSE
Psalm 25:4a

Teach me your ways, O Lord.

SECOND READING
1 Corinthians 7: 29–31

I tell you, brothers and sisters, the time is running out. From now on, let those having wives act as not having them, those weeping as not weeping, those rejoicing as not rejoicing, those buying as not owning, those using the world as not using it fully. For the world in its present form is passing away.

GOSPEL
Mark 1:14–20

After John had been arrested, Jesus came to Galilee proclaiming the gospel of God: "This is the time of fulfillment. The kingdom of God is at hand. Repent, and believe in the gospel."

As he passed by the Sea of Galilee, he saw Simon and his brother Andrew casting their nets into the sea; they were fishermen. Jesus said to them, "Come after me, and I will make you fishers of men." Then they abandoned their nets and followed him. He walked along a little farther and saw James, the son of Zebedee, and his brother John. They too were in a boat mending their nets. Then he called them. So they left their father Zebedee in the boat along with the hired men and followed him.

Understanding the Word

The calling of the first disciples is markedly different in the Gospel of Mark from what we find in the Gospel of John. Mark's account stresses the decisive resolve of Jesus and the necessary willingness of disciples to respond with dispatch to marching orders to undertake a mission for others.

In John's Gospel the first disciples find Jesus. In Mark's Gospel Jesus finds them. Moreover, there is an abruptness to Jesus' call of the disciples that is not found, for example, in Luke's version. Luke has Jesus first get into Simon's boat, next ask him to put out from shore a bit, and then teach the people on the shore. After this Jesus asks Simon to go out into the deep and cast their nets. It is only after they have caught a multitude of fish and Simon has expressed his astonishment that Jesus actually calls him and James and John (Luke 5:1–11). In Mark there is no such preparation for the call. Jesus simply comes upon Simon and Andrew, calls them to follow him, and they do so. The same pattern occurs next with James and John (Mark 1:16–20). Corresponding to the directness of the call, each set of brothers responds right away by joining Jesus and "following" him.

The quickness of Jesus' call and the disciples' response mirrors a sense of urgency in this passage and surrounding ones. At the beginning of today's Gospel story we read that "[a]fter John had been arrested" Jesus came proclaiming, "This is the time of fulfillment. The kingdom of God is at hand. Repent, and believe in the gospel" (1:14–15). The need for repentance is urgent in order to take advantage of the propitious time in which God's reign draws near. Several verses prior to this we read about the Spirit driving Jesus "at once" out into the wilderness (1:12). Jesus and the Spirit realize that the time to capitalize on God's gift has arrived, and they need people with hearts and temperaments that enable them to respond willingly and promptly.

Reflecting on the Word

This week we are back up north in Galilee, where Jesus meets his first disciples "as he passed by the Sea of Galilee." He has been making his way through the countryside, calling people to "repent and believe in the gospel" (Mark 1:16). There is an urgency to this message as Mark records it: "This is the time of fulfillment. The kingdom of God is at hand" (1:15). There is no time to waste! Turn to God—now!

This same urgency permeates the call of the first disciples. Jesus says, "Come after me and I will make you fishers of men" (1:17). And they do—immediately! First, Simon and Andrew, who were casting their nets, instantly "abandoned their nets and followed him" (1:18). The same with James and John, "in a boat mending their nets," who immediately "left their father Zebedee in the boat along with the hired men and followed him" (1:18, 19). Called and collected.

The power of God's word to get attention is affirmed in both the Old Testament and the Gospel today. Both Jonah and Jesus call for repentance in their preaching, a response that demands action now. But Jesus' call to the disciples is an invitation to join in the work of netting others for God.

By our baptism we have been called to join with Jesus in the work of proclaiming God as alive and present, of catching people for the kingdom. This work is especially needed in our day, when people are willing to settle for so much less than the kingdom of God to satisfy their hearts.

CONSIDER/
DISCUSS:
- Do you see yourself as called to join Jesus in "catching others" for God?
- How can you preach by your actions that the kingdom of God is at hand?
- What must you leave behind so that you can follow Jesus more generously?

Responding to the Word

At this time in the life of the Church in the United States, there seems to be a dearth of disciples who hear the call to follow Jesus and respond immediately. Let us pray that the Father will draw more to this important work. Let us pray that we will answer in our own life.

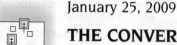

January 25, 2009

THE CONVERSION OF SAINT PAUL, APOSTLE

Some parishes will observe the Year of Saint Paul by celebrating the Conversion of Saint Paul on this Sunday.

Today's Focus: Where Are You Heading?

On this feast of Saint Paul, in this year of Paul, we remember the crucial moment in his life, his conversion. When you know a little about his life, it is strange to think he needed a conversion. But when he heard the voice of Jesus, risen Lord, speak to him, his life changed direction completely. And that's what a conversion is, a 180-degree turnaround.

FIRST READING
Acts 22:3–16

Paul addressed the people in these words: "I am a Jew, born in Tarsus in Cilicia, but brought up in this city. At the feet of Gamaliel I was educated strictly in our ancestral law and was zealous for God, just as all of you are today. I persecuted this Way to death, binding both men and women and delivering them to prison. Even the high priest and the whole council of elders can testify on my behalf. For from them I even received letters to the brothers and set out for Damascus to bring back to Jerusalem in chains for punishment those there as well.

"On that journey as I drew near to Damascus, about noon a great light from the sky suddenly shone around me. I fell to the ground and heard a voice saying to me, 'Saul, Saul, why are you persecuting me?' I replied, 'Who are you, sir?' And he said to me, 'I am Jesus the Nazorean whom you are persecuting.' My companions saw the light but did not hear the voice of the one who spoke to me. I asked, 'What shall I do, sir?' The Lord answered me, 'Get up and go into Damascus, and there you will be told about everything appointed for you to do.' Since I could see nothing because of the brightness of that light, I was led by hand by my companions and entered Damascus.

"A certain Ananias, a devout observer of the law, and highly spoken of by all the Jews who lived there, came to me and stood there and said, 'Saul, my brother, regain your sight.' And at that very moment I regained my sight and saw him. Then he said, 'The God of our ancestors designated you to know his will, to see the Righteous One, and to hear the sound of his voice; for you will be his witness before all to what you have seen and heard. Now, why delay? Get up and have yourself baptized and your sins washed away, calling upon his name.' "

—*or*—

Acts 9:1–22 Saul, still breathing murderous threats against the disciples of the Lord, went to the high priest and asked him for letters to the synagogues in Damascus, that, if he should find any men or women who belonged to the Way, he might bring them back to Jerusalem in chains. On his journey, as he was nearing Damascus, a light from the sky suddenly flashed around him. He fell to the ground and heard a voice saying to him, "Saul, Saul, why are you persecuting me?" He said, "Who are you, sir?" The reply came, "I am Jesus, whom you are persecuting. Now get up and go into the city and you will be told what you must do." The men who were traveling with him stood speechless, for they heard the voice but could see no one. Saul got up from the ground, but when he opened his eyes he could see nothing; so they led him by the hand and brought him to Damascus. For three days he was unable to see, and he neither ate nor drank.

There was a disciple in Damascus named Ananias, and the Lord said to him in a vision, "Ananias." He answered, "Here I am, Lord." The Lord said to him, "Get up and go to the street called Straight and ask at the house of Judas for a man from Tarsus named Saul. He is there praying, and in a vision he has seen a man named Ananias come in and lay his hands on him, that he may regain his sight." But Ananias replied, "Lord, I have heard from many sources about this man, what evil things he has done to your holy ones in Jerusalem. And here he has authority from the chief priests to imprison all who call upon your name." But the Lord said to him, "Go, for this man is a chosen instrument of mine to carry my name before Gentiles, kings, and children of Israel, and I will show him what he will have to suffer for my name."

So Ananias went and entered the house; laying his hands on him, he said, "Saul, my brother, the Lord has sent me, Jesus who appeared to you on the way by which you came, that you may regain your sight and be filled with the Holy Spirit." Immediately things like scales fell from his eyes and he regained his sight. He got up and was baptized, and when he had eaten, he recovered his strength.

He stayed some days with the disciples in Damascus, and he began at once to proclaim Jesus in the synagogues, that he is the Son of God. All who heard him were astounded and said, "Is not this the man who in Jerusalem ravaged those who call upon this name, and came here expressly to take them back in chains to the chief priests?" But Saul grew all the stronger and confounded the Jews who lived in Damascus, proving that this is the Christ.

PSALM RESPONSE
Mark 16:15 Go out to all the world and tell the Good News.

51

SECOND READING
1 Corinthians 7:29–31

I tell you, brothers and sisters, the time is running out. From now on, let those having wives act as not having them, those weeping as not weeping, those rejoicing as not rejoicing, those buying as not owning, those using the world as not using it fully. For the world in its present form is passing away.

GOSPEL
Mark 16:15–18

Jesus appeared to the Eleven and said to them: "Go into the whole world and proclaim the Gospel to every creature. Whoever believes and is baptized will be saved; whoever does not believe will be condemned. These signs will accompany those who believe: in my name they will drive out demons, they will speak new languages. They will pick up serpents with their hands, and if they drink any deadly thing, it will not harm them. They will lay hands on the sick, and they will recover."

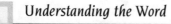 ## Understanding the Word

The conversion of Paul was one of the most radical transformations of a person imaginable. In Acts 22:3–16 the evangelist Luke describes Paul before his conversion as intensely active in his opposition to Christians. Paul is quoted as saying that he bound Christians to hand them over to death (22:4). This included going "from synagogue to synagogue" in order to root out Christians and beat them (22:19). Not flagging in these efforts, Paul enlisted the help of the high priest and the Sanhedrin in an attempt to range even to Antioch in Syria in his attempt to track and capture Christians (22:5).

This past closed some doors for Paul's future but with God's help it opened other doors that were to be both consonant with his character and extremely fruitful for the church. Following Paul's conversion and the return of his eyesight, Luke writes that Paul went back to Jerusalem. In the verses just after today's first reading, the Lord reveals to him that he will not be effective in Jerusalem (22:17–18). This causes Paul emotional pain as he wonders if his former persecution of Christians has made useless his present and future witness to Christ (22:19–20). The Lord responds, however, "Go, I shall send you far away to the Gentiles" (22:21). Paul's drive and his love of going to new areas for new initiatives—in his letters he will himself note as much (Romans 15:20–21)—is used by the Lord to move the message of Jesus out decisively into the Gentile world. Paul's past mistakes did not constrict his mission but rather were used by God to empower the expansion of Christianity.

Our past actions, no matter how harmful, cannot hinder the miraculous deeds that God can work in our future.

Paul was religious, charismatic, dedicated, and zealous, even before his conversion. This feast reminds us that breeding is not enough. Paul was born a Jew in a little town in Asia Minor, Tarsus, but he was raised in the center of the Jewish world, Jerusalem. Education was not enough, nor was a wise mentor; Paul was taught by Gamaliel, a dedicated scholar who educated him strictly in Jewish ancestral law. Zeal was not sufficient, either; Paul's zeal led him to persecute Christians, to the point of going to Damascus to bring them back in chains to be punished. He was a man on fire with zeal.

But he was going in the wrong direction. On his way, a light surrounded him that ended up blinding him. But in that light, Paul heard this voice: "Saul, Saul, why are you persecuting me?" When he inquired who "me" was, he was told: "I am Jesus, whom you are persecuting" (Acts 9:4, 5).

"Faith comes through hearing," he was to write later on in his masterpiece, the Letter to the Romans. Faith in Jesus began with that message he heard on the road to Damascus and then he saw truly, even though he was blinded for a short time. When his sight came back, he didn't forget the message he had heard: Persecute my church, persecute me. The belief in the church as the body of Christ goes back to this event. It is the mystery we continue to live today.

Paul's life changed when he heard the voice of Jesus. It gave him a different way of seeing. And he ran with it for the rest of his life.

CONSIDER/ DISCUSS:
- Have you ever had a conversion event that changed the course of your life?
- In which direction are you heading these days?
- Do you think of the Church as the body of Christ?

Responding to the Word

We pray that we might recognize our role as a people called to witness to Jesus Christ, to call others to conversion by our words and our deeds. By our baptism, we are commissioned as Paul was to go forth to bring the gospel to people who do not know Jesus and to invite them to come to know the church as the body of Christ.

February 1, 2009

FOURTH SUNDAY IN ORDINARY TIME

Today's Focus: War Has Been Declared

Mark's first story of Jesus' ministry presented him as preaching that the kingdom of God is at hand and then calling some fishermen to join him in his work of "catching people." Today we see Jesus going beyond preaching to enacting the kingdom: His first act is to deliver a man from an unclean spirit.

FIRST READING
Deuteronomy 18: 15–20

Moses spoke to all the people, saying: "A prophet like me will the LORD, your God, raise up for you from among your own kin; to him you shall listen. This is exactly what you requested of the LORD, your God, at Horeb on the day of the assembly, when you said, 'Let us not again hear the voice of the LORD, our God, nor see this great fire any more, lest we die.' And the LORD said to me, 'This was well said. I will raise up for them a prophet like you from among their kin, and will put my words into his mouth; he shall tell them all that I command him. Whoever will not listen to my words which he speaks in my name, I myself will make him answer for it. But if a prophet presumes to speak in my name an oracle that I have not commanded him to speak, or speaks in the name of other gods, he shall die.' "

PSALM RESPONSE
Psalm 95:8

If today you hear his voice, harden not your hearts.

SECOND READING
1 Corinthians 7: 32–35

Brothers and sisters: I should like you to be free of anxieties. An unmarried man is anxious about the things of the Lord, how he may please the Lord. But a married man is anxious about the things of the world, how he may please his wife, and he is divided. An unmarried woman or a virgin is anxious about the things of the Lord, so that she may be holy in both body and spirit. A married woman, on the other hand, is anxious about the things of the world, how she may please her husband. I am telling you this for your own benefit, not to impose a restraint upon you, but for the sake of propriety and adherence to the Lord without distraction.

GOSPEL
Mark 1:21–28

Then they came to Capernaum, and on the sabbath Jesus entered the synagogue and taught. The people were astonished at his teaching, for he taught them as one having authority and not as the scribes. In their synagogue was a man with an unclean spirit; he cried out, "What have you to do with us, Jesus of Nazareth? Have you come to destroy us? I know who you are—the Holy One of God!" Jesus rebuked him and said, "Quiet! Come out of him!" The unclean spirit convulsed him and with a loud cry came out of him. All were amazed and asked one another, "What is this? A new teaching with authority. He commands even the unclean spirits and they obey him." His fame spread everywhere throughout the whole region of Galilee.

Understanding the Word

Today we begin to trace the reason for the urgency in Jesus' mission, as told by Mark, and the urgency required of disciples who enter into this mission. The Gospel for today recounts Jesus' first act after calling his initial disciples, and he does it "immediately." (This term, present in the Greek, unfortunately does not appear in the Lectionary translation used in the United States.) Jesus and the disciples go down to Capernaum, "and immediately on the sabbath Jesus entered the synagogue and taught" (Mark 1:21). What happens next also happens "immediately": "and immediately there was in their synagogue a man with an unclean spirit" (1:23). When the unclean spirit cries out, Jesus responds summarily: "Quiet! Come out of him" (1:25). "At once" Jesus' fame spreads everywhere in the surrounding region (1:28).

The explanation for this sense of urgency and immediacy is begun in today's passage. Only in Mark's Gospel is the first miracle by Jesus an exorcism. If "the reign of God is at hand" is for Mark the principal message of Jesus, then this reign begins with the casting out of a malevolent power that has taken control of a person.

God's progressive reign arrives with the Spirit coming upon and impelling Jesus. When God affirms Jesus' sonship at his baptism, the Spirit comes upon him and then "at once" casts Jesus out into the desert (1:10–12). The dispatch with which Jesus acts in the Gospel of Mark resonates with the haste with which the Spirit hurls Jesus into the desert where he confronts Satan (1:13). Jesus is attuned to the fact that God's power to confront and vanquish evil is at hand and operative through him, and so he acts forcefully to be the means through which this power spreads.

Reflecting on the Word

In Jesus' day, demonic possession was not uncommon. Mark presents Jesus as one who takes on the evil spirits, overturning their possession of this man. Jesus has declared war against the kingdom of Satan. Its hour of ascendancy is coming to an end.

The unclean spirit recognizes Jesus as one with greater power, for it asks, "Have you come to destroy us?" Then it confesses Jesus as the "Holy One of God" (1:24). Jesus will battle the forces of evil to the death, his death. But what looks like defeat for Jesus will be changed to victory, because the power of God is at work in him.

In the first reading from Deuteronomy, Moses is speaking to the people before they enter the Promised Land. The entire book is his farewell speech to them. He will not go with them. He consoles them, saying that God promises to raise up a prophet like Moses and will speak through him: "I . . . will put my words into his mouth" (Deuteronomy 18:18).

Jesus is presented to us today as the prophet like Moses, who teaches with the authority of God and whose words are obeyed even by unclean spirits. There is no power on earth or beyond it greater than the power of God at work in him.

- Does the image of Jesus as one who casts out unclean spirits still speak to our own age?
- How do "unclean spirits" show themselves in our world today?
- How are we to respond to them?

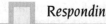 *Responding to the Word*

We pray at every Mass the Lord's Prayer, which concludes: "And lead us not into temptation, but deliver us from evil." The power of evil has been overcome by Jesus' saving death, but we continue to pray that it does not find a home in us, in our Church, or in our society.

February 8, 2009

FIFTH SUNDAY IN ORDINARY TIME

Today's Focus: Getting Through the Day

Today's Gospel presents listeners with a day in the life of Jesus. His ministry includes exorcisms, like the one we heard about last week, and healings of sick people, teaching, and preaching. How did Jesus keep going? The Gospel holds a clue.

FIRST READING
Job 7:1–4, 6–7

Job spoke, saying:
Is not man's life on earth a drudgery?
    Are not his days those of hirelings?
He is a slave who longs for the shade,
    a hireling who waits for his wages.
So I have been assigned months of misery,
    and troubled nights have been allotted to me.
If in bed I say, "When shall I arise?"
    then the night drags on;
    I am filled with restlessness until the dawn.
My days are swifter than a weaver's shuttle;
    they come to an end without hope.
Remember that my life is like the wind;
I shall not see happiness again.

PSALM RESPONSE
Psalm 147:3a

Praise the Lord, who heals the brokenhearted.

SECOND READING
1 Corinthians 9: 16–19, 22–23

Brothers and sisters: If I preach the gospel, this is no reason for me to boast, for an obligation has been imposed on me, and woe to me if I do not preach it! If I do so willingly, I have a recompense, but if unwillingly, then I have been entrusted with a stewardship. What then is my recompense? That, when I preach, I offer the gospel free of charge so as not to make full use of my right in the gospel. Although I am free in regard to all, I have made myself a slave to all so as to win over as many as possible. To the weak I became weak, to win over the weak. I have become all things to all, to save at least some. All this I do for the sake of the gospel, so that I too may have a share in it.

On leaving the synagogue Jesus entered the house of Simon and Andrew with James and John. Simon's mother-in-law lay sick with a fever. They immediately told him about her. He approached, grasped her hand, and helped her up. Then the fever left her and she waited on them.

When it was evening, after sunset, they brought to him all who were ill or possessed by demons. The whole town was gathered at the door. He cured many who were sick with various diseases, and he drove out many demons, not permitting them to speak because they knew him.

Rising very early before dawn, he left and went off to a deserted place, where he prayed. Simon and those who were with him pursued him and on finding him said, "Everyone is looking for you." He told them, "Let us go on to the nearby villages that I may preach there also. For this purpose have I come." So he went into their synagogues, preaching and driving out demons throughout the whole of Galilee.

Understanding the Word

In last Sunday's Gospel we saw that the purpose of Jesus' decisiveness and dispatch in going about his mission was to allow the Spirit the scope to counter evil spiritual forces that plague humanity. Evil spirits for Mark are those nebulous forces that afflict us and that we often struggle to name. They frequently resulted in aberrant forms of behavior that placed people beyond the realm of normal social intercourse.

In this Sunday's Gospel Jesus continues this ministry of exorcisms to show how God is conquering these powers that afflict our inner lives. Three times today we hear of Jesus casting out demons. But his range of activity becomes more expansive in this section, suggesting other means through which the reign of God is expressed. Jesus also engages in healings without exorcisms (Mark 1:30–31, 34). This suggests the comprehensiveness of the reign of God. It extends over all problem areas in life, not simply those that plague the inner life. Still, the focus on exorcising demons continues as this section of Mark concludes with the summary statement that Jesus "went into their synagogues, preaching and driving out demons throughout the whole of Galilee" (1:39). For Mark, preaching and exorcisms are the *raison d'être* for Jesus' ministry. By contrast, Matthew's summary statement at this point has Jesus proceeding to teach, preach, and heal. In Luke's comparable statement Jesus moves on simply to preach (Matt 4:35; Luke 4:44). This emphasis on exorcisms appears for Mark to indicate Jesus' frontal assault on what was considered to be, from an apocalyptic perspective, the basis of all the problems in life: evil spirits.

But something more is afoot. We encounter Jesus' first attempt to silence witness to his exorcisms as he refuses to allow the demons to speak "because they knew him" (1:34). Afterward, he tells his disciples that he must go on to the nearby villages and preach (1:38). The Gospel readings on coming Sundays will clarify why Jesus focuses on preaching and prefers not to advertise his exorcisms in the midst of his mission to establish God's reign.

In his first chapter, Mark gives us a day in the life of Jesus. The day begins with Jesus entering the synagogue and teaching, then casting out an unclean spirit (this was last week's Gospel). Jesus immediately goes into the house of Simon and heals his mother-in-law of a fever. She gets up and waits on them—which indicates perhaps that they took time for a meal—then in the evening Jesus is back with the people, who "brought to him all who were ill or possessed by demons" (1:32). This apparently was not a small group: "The whole town was gathered at the door" (1:33). And Jesus healed "many who were sick . . . and he drove out many demons" (1:34).

The ministry of Jesus was not a few hours now and then. It was an all-day affair, going into the night. He took on the suffering of the world. How did he find the strength to keep up such a pace? The key is in the second part of today's Gospel: "Rising very early before dawn, he left and went off to a deserted place, where he prayed" (1:35). Luke presents Jesus at prayer more than any of the other Gospel writers. Perhaps Mark figured that he only had to say it once or twice (see also Mark 6:46).

Mark doesn't tell us what or how he prayed. Matthew and Luke give us the prayer he taught his disciples. All we know is that he prayed at the beginning of this day in his life, and it seems safe to assume, given his relationship with God, that this was not an isolated occasion. Mark also tells us that Jesus prayed in Gethsemane the night before he died. And he encouraged his disciples to do the same. Jesus' openness to the driving force of the Spirit and the strength of his resolve in confronting demonic powers can be attributed to his persistence in prayer. Perhaps that is the best hint for getting through the day, any day, every day—and getting through a very dark night.

CONSIDER/ DISCUSS:
- How do you get through your busy days?
- Does prayer get "slotted in" or does it "slip through the cracks"?
- What do you pray about/for?

Responding to the Word

As we learn in the other Gospels, the disciples who were with him eventually asked that Jesus teach them to pray. They knew how his habit of prayer provided the sustenance he needed to pursue his mission. He taught them the prayer that we continue to say to this day. Pray the Our Father today. Say it slowly; think about each phrase. Ask Jesus to teach you to really pray this prayer so that you, too, will be empowered for the mission that God has given you.

February 15, 2009

SIXTH SUNDAY IN ORDINARY TIME

Today's Focus: Compassion That Goes Beyond Skin Deep

Mark brings the first chapter of his Gospel to a close with the healing of someone with leprosy, one of the most dreaded diseases at that time because it cut the infected person off from everyone. Even so, there are deeper ruptures that can isolate us from others and from our God.

FIRST READING
Leviticus 13: 1–2, 44–46

The Lord said to Moses and Aaron, "If someone has on his skin a scab or pustule or blotch which appears to be the sore of leprosy, he shall be brought to Aaron, the priest, or to one of the priests among his descendants. If the man is leprous and unclean, the priest shall declare him unclean by reason of the sore on his head.

"The one who bears the sore of leprosy shall keep his garments rent and his head bare, and shall muffle his beard; he shall cry out, 'Unclean, unclean!' As long as the sore is on him he shall declare himself unclean, since he is in fact unclean. He shall dwell apart, making his abode outside the camp."

PSALM RESPONSE
Psalm 32:7

I turn to you, Lord, in time of trouble, and you fill me with the joy of salvation.

SECOND READING
1 Corinthians 10:31 — 11:1

Brothers and sisters, Whether you eat or drink, or whatever you do, do everything for the glory of God. Avoid giving offense, whether to the Jews or Greeks or the church of God, just as I try to please everyone in every way, not seeking my own benefit but that of the many, that they may be saved. Be imitators of me, as I am of Christ.

GOSPEL
Mark 1:40–45

A leper came to Jesus and kneeling down begged him and said, "If you wish, you can make me clean." Moved with pity, he stretched out his hand, touched him, and said to him, "I do will it. Be made clean." The leprosy left him immediately, and he was made clean. Then, warning him sternly, he dismissed him at once.

He said to him, "See that you tell no one anything, but go, show yourself to the priest and offer for your cleansing what Moses prescribed; that will be proof for them."

The man went away and began to publicize the whole matter. He spread the report abroad so that it was impossible for Jesus to enter a town openly. He remained outside in deserted places, and people kept coming to him from everywhere.

Understanding the Word

In last Sunday's Gospel reading, Jesus for the first time prohibited speech about his miracles, forbidding demons whom he had exorcised to speak (Mark 1:34). Today we begin to see what happens when Jesus' miraculous power is proclaimed. After healing a man with leprosy, Jesus enjoins him not to say anything about this healing, but rather to go and offer to the priest what is required for the cleansing. This act, says Jesus, will be a proof for them. In other words, the witness to the miracle that the man is to provide must be the private indirect one of an offering to the priest rather than the public direct one of personal testimony before a multitude. This certainly does not seem prudent from the perspective of advertising. What could account for this seemingly poor marketing plan?

Today's Gospel begins to answer this question in terms of the effects of the message outrunning the message itself. The first words of Mark's Jesus are, "This is the time of fulfillment. The kingdom of God is at hand. Repent, and believe in the gospel" (1:15). The primary message is that in Jesus God's power decisively and effectively expresses itself in this world, and that people are called both to repent and to believe in his message. What happens, however, after the man with leprosy refuses to follow Jesus' instruction and instead "began to publicize the whole matter . . . spread[ing] the report abroad" (1:45)? Jesus can no longer enter towns openly but must remain in deserted places waiting for people to come to him. The mission of Jesus has been compromised by such publicity. The message can no longer spread where most people are congregated. As we progress through Mark's Gospel, we will see that the message necessary to create repentance and belief is in danger of being overshadowed by the effects of the reign of God.

Reflecting on the Word

Sickness tends to exclude a person from life. It can exclude us physically, when we do not feel well enough even to get out of bed; psychologically, when we find it hard to talk or even pay attention to others; and spiritually, when it leads us to wonder whether God cares or even if there is a God.

The disease of leprosy in Jesus' time was devastating. Leprosy cast one out from the community: from one's home, one's family, one's village—in short, from all that was cherished. A person had to wander the land.

Today's Gospel gives us a hint of a leper's desperation. The man with leprosy kneels, begging Jesus: "If you wish, you can make me clean" (Mark 1:40). Jesus is "moved with pity." He reaches out and touches him, saying, "I do will it. Be made clean" (1:41). And immediately the man is made clean.

It can be puzzling, then, to hear Jesus "warning him sternly" (1:43) that he is to tell no one, but must go and do what the law of Moses requires by showing himself to the priest and offering what Moses prescribed. Why wouldn't the man be jumping for joy and wanting to tell everyone—family, friends, total strangers, even enemies—what this healer Jesus had done for him?

Which is precisely why Jesus enjoins him not to tell—Jesus did not come to be merely the Healer. Healings were only a sign of the coming of the kingdom. The deepest healing that Jesus came to bring was not skin deep, but on the level of our relationship with God. Jesus came to heal the breach, to gather all God's children to know the God whom Jesus called Father. That remains his purpose.

**CONSIDER/
DISCUSS:**
- Do Jesus' words to the healed leper surprise you, the transition from compassion to "warning sternly"?
- How do you understand the mission of Jesus during his years of preaching, teaching, healing, and casting out demons?
- Is there a need that you know of for deeper healing in your own life?

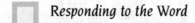

Responding to the Word

When you look at our world, our country, your parish, your family, ask the Lord for the healing that each needs at the deepest level.

February 22, 2009

SEVENTH SUNDAY IN ORDINARY TIME

Today's Focus: The Heart of God: Forgiveness

"See, I am doing something new!" says the God of Isaiah, calling on Israel to forget the sins of their past (Isaiah 43:19). God proclaims: "It is I, I, who wipe out, / for my own sake, your offenses; / your sins I remember no more" (43:25). We glimpse the heart of God in the divine will to forgive sin, enacted by Jesus in the Gospel.

FIRST READING
Isaiah 43: 18–19, 21–22, 24b–25

Thus says the LORD:
Remember not the events of the past,
    the things of long ago consider not;
see, I am doing something new!
    Now it springs forth, do you not perceive it?
In the desert I make a way,
    in the wasteland, rivers.
The people I formed for myself,
    that they might announce my praise.
Yet you did not call upon me, O Jacob,
    for you grew weary of me, O Israel.
You burdened me with your sins,
    and wearied me with your crimes.
It is I, I, who wipe out,
    for my own sake, your offenses;
    your sins I remember no more.

PSALM RESPONSE
Psalm 41:5b

Lord, heal my soul, for I have sinned against you.

SECOND READING
2 Corinthians 1: 18–22

Brothers and sisters: As God is faithful, our word to you is not "yes" and "no." For the Son of God, Jesus Christ, who was proclaimed to you by us, Silvanus and Timothy and me, was not "yes" and "no," but "yes" has been in him. For however many are the promises of God, their Yes is in him; therefore, the Amen from us also goes through him to God for glory. But the one who gives us security with you in Christ and who anointed us is God; he has also put his seal upon us and given the Spirit in our hearts as a first installment.

GOSPEL

Mark 2:1–12

When Jesus returned to Capernaum after some days, it became known that he was at home. Many gathered together so that there was no longer room for them, not even around the door, and he preached the word to them. They came bringing to him a paralytic carried by four men. Unable to get near Jesus because of the crowd, they opened up the roof above him. After they had broken through, they let down the mat on which the paralytic was lying. When Jesus saw their faith, he said to the paralytic, "Child, your sins are forgiven." Now some of the scribes were sitting there asking themselves, "Why does this man speak that way? He is blaspheming. Who but God alone can forgive sins?" Jesus immediately knew in his mind what they were thinking to themselves, so he said, "Why are you thinking such things in your hearts? Which is easier, to say to the paralytic, 'Your sins are forgiven,' or to say, 'Rise, pick up your mat and walk'? But that you may know that the Son of Man has authority to forgive sins on earth" — he said to the paralytic, "I say to you, rise, pick up your mat, and go home." He rose, picked up his mat at once, and went away in the sight of everyone. They were all astounded and glorified God, saying, "We have never seen anything like this."

Understanding the Word

Last Sunday we saw that the effect of the leper's proclamation that Jesus had healed him was that Jesus had to remain away from cities and towns, out in the desert so as to avoid the mad crush. In today's Gospel Jesus returns home to Capernaum. He had just left there recently (Mark 1:39). The need to preach the Good News had occasioned his departure from the city (1:38). The insistent press of all the people of Capernaum who had gathered at the door of the house of Peter's mother-in-law in the evening, bringing with them "all who were ill or who were possessed by demons," had necessitated Jesus' departure into a deserted place (1:33–35). While there he had made his decision to go and preach to other villages. Now he comes in from the desert back to his home town.

The resultant time lapse has diminished the crowds' obsession with his miracles. After a few days, however, we again find a large gathering at the door of the house in which Jesus resides, as when the whole city "gathered at the door" of Peter's mother-in-law's house with all the ill and possessed (1:30). Now, however, Jesus is able to "preach the word to them" (2:2), though the time for such preaching is short. Right away we hear that some bring a man who is paralyzed to Jesus and lower him down through the roof (2:3–4). Jesus uses this opportunity to try to refocus the crowd's fervor. He heals the man as a sign that "the Son of Man has authority to forgive sins" (2:10). But the passage ends in a way that causes doubt as to whether the people will refocus their efforts on repentance and belief rather than on seeking healing. The last we hear is that the people are astounded and say, "We have never seen anything like this," referring to the healing, not to Jesus' ability to forgive sins (2:12).

It is natural to want to be whole, to seek healing. Nevertheless, the Gospel of Mark seems to be saying, "First things first."

Word got around when Jesus returned to Capernaum from preaching in the towns of Galilee. They filled the house, probably Simon Peter's, and he preached to them. His message Mark told us early on: Now is the time of fulfillment; the kingdom of God is at hand (see Mark 1:15). To participate in the reign of God one had to repent of one's sins and believe in the good news of a forgiving God.

Jesus' agenda had to do with bringing people into the kingdom by calling them to repentance. This was his purpose, in fidelity to his Father's will. So when a paralyzed man was lowered through the roof, Jesus' response to the faith he saw exhibited was to announce, "Child, your sins are forgiven" (2:5). The passive voice indicates that God is at work here. Jesus is announcing the forgiveness of the God of Isaiah, who is doing something new through him.

Forgiveness may have come first in Jesus' mind, but what the scribes heard was blasphemy. To forgive sins was the prerogative of God. No human could lay claim to this or assume the authority to do it. Nothing is said, but the heart can communicate without words both love and hatred.

Jesus' response is to confront these scribes and then turn to the man to say, "Pick up your mat and go home" (2:11). The healing came after the forgiving. For Jesus, forgiveness comes first, for it effects the deepest healing. Through forgiveness a new world can come about, for in forgiving God touches and transforms human hearts. Forgiveness heals.

CONSIDER/ DISCUSS:
- Have you experienced the healing that being forgiven brings?
- How might forgiveness transform our world today?
- Is there a need in your heart either to be forgiven or to bring forgiveness to another?

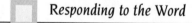

Responding to the Word

Sinning in return is the usual response to being sinned against. Only the spirit of forgiveness can break the cycle and bring about a new world. Pray that the healing forgiveness of God will touch and transform the hearts of all those bent on exacting vengeance.

The Lenten readings inform and energize the members of the community as they prepare to enter into the Church or renew their baptismal commitment. The first reading for the First Sunday of Lent treats the first covenant as one in which only God has responsibilities. Through this binding self-commitment God nurtures the possibility for human growth and development by providing room for failure and subsequent repentance. This covenant with Noah is articulated in such a way as to help people to think beyond themselves by presenting God's concern for all of life.

Such other-focused concern is the topic of the readings for the Second Sunday of Lent. The story from Genesis of God's command to Abraham to bind his son Isaac and sacrifice him is echoed in the second reading from Romans to show the extent of divine self-commitment in giving Jesus to and for humanity.

On the Third Sunday of Lent we read about the beginning of what the Sinai covenant entails. Unlike the covenant with Noah, this covenant does make explicit demands on God's people. In treating the Ten Commandments, this Sunday's reading shows how care for our caregivers supports our concern for the whole human family.

The Year A Gospel reading for the Third Sunday of Lent is the story of Jesus' encounter first with the Samaritan woman and then with her whole village. John places this story in a context that encourages people to see that those we least expect to be "religious" may have much to teach us about how to respond to the divine Word.

The Fourth Sunday of Lent offers us in the Gospel reading the Johannine Jesus' summary of his dialogue with Nicodemus. Here we see that God's saving activity in Jesus manifests God's love for humanity. But this passage builds on an earlier one in the Prologue of John's Gospel to show that this saving love of God is seen as love for a family, as the gathering of family members. Our response to God's love, according to this day's Gospel, should be our belief that Jesus is God's Son. This belief would then express itself in a determination to return to the family of God by turning unambiguously toward Jesus.

The Gospel passsage from John proclaimed for the Fourth Sunday of Lent, Year A, presents an example for all Christians who live where a Christian commitment threatens to isolate them from their larger community. The story of the man born blind portrays a man willing to step out into a world with new sight only to have others consciously refuse to look his way because of his commitment to Jesus.

For the Fifth Sunday of Lent we are presented with Year B and Year A readings from Jeremiah and Ezekiel about the difficulties of reforming character and how this transformation can occur.

Finally, for Palm Sunday of the Lord's Passion, the processional and Gospel readings from the Gospel of Mark treat what is often a dichotomy between how God comes in life and how people expect God to come.

March 1, 2009

FIRST SUNDAY OF LENT

Today's Focus: Lent, Season of the Heart

The word Lent means spring, the season of new life. Every Ash Wednesday we hear, "Rend your hearts, not your garments, / and return to the LORD, your God" (Joel 2:13). We are entreated to peel away the rind around our hearts that insulates us from God's touch. Like Noah during the flood and Jesus in the desert, we, God's beloved, have forty days to turn our hearts to God, who brings us new life in the Spirit.

FIRST READING
Genesis 9:8–15

God said to Noah and to his sons with him: "See, I am now establishing my covenant with you and your descendants after you and with every living creature that was with you: all the birds, and the various tame and wild animals that were with you and came out of the ark. I will establish my covenant with you, that never again shall all bodily creatures be destroyed by the waters of a flood; there shall not be another flood to devastate the earth." God added: "This is the sign that I am giving for all ages to come, of the covenant between me and you and every living creature with you: I set my bow in the clouds to serve as a sign of the covenant between me and the earth. When I bring clouds over the earth, and the bow appears in the clouds, I will recall the covenant I have made between me and you and all living beings, so that the waters shall never again become a flood to destroy all mortal beings."

PSALM RESPONSE
Psalm 25:10

Your ways, O Lord, are love and truth to those who keep your covenant.

SECOND READING
1 Peter 3:18–22

Beloved: Christ suffered for sins once, the righteous for the sake of the unrighteous, that he might lead you to God. Put to death in the flesh, he was brought to life in the Spirit. In it he also went to preach to the spirits in prison, who had once been disobedient while God patiently waited in the days of Noah during the building of the ark, in which a few persons, eight in all, were saved through water. This prefigured baptism, which saves you now. It is not a removal of dirt from the body but an appeal to God for a clear conscience, through the resurrection of Jesus Christ, who has gone into heaven and is at the right hand of God, with angels, authorities, and powers subject to him.

GOSPEL
Mark 1:12–15
The Spirit drove Jesus out into the desert, and he remained in the desert for forty days, tempted by Satan. He was among wild beasts, and the angels ministered to him.

After John had been arrested, Jesus came to Galilee proclaiming the gospel of God: "This is the time of fulfillment. The kingdom of God is at hand. Repent, and believe in the gospel."

 ## Understanding the Word

The reading from the Book of Genesis describes the first covenant in the Bible. The word for "covenant" is *berith*, and it denotes a binding contract. A contract can be unilateral or bilateral. In the former, duties are only required of one party, and in the latter duties are required of both parties in order to fulfill the stipulations of the contract. The Sinai covenant in Exodus 20–24 is an example of a bilateral covenant. God promises what God will do for the people. In turn, in order to live up to their end of the contract, the people have the Ten Commandments and a number of laws specific to certain situations. If either party fails to live up to its obligations, the covenant may become null and void.

This is not the type of covenant we hear about today. The first contract God makes is with Noah, his descendants, and with "every living creature." It is a unilateral contract. Nothing is required of people, only of God. The implication is that this covenant cannot be broken because, unlike what is often the case with people, God is faithful.

This covenant is a pledge never again to destroy the earth by a flood, as had just occurred in the time of Noah. The rainbow is given as a sign of this covenant.

This covenant allows time and space for humanity and all creatures to develop. It is the expression of the commitment of the God who nurtures life. That the animals are also included is noteworthy. Scholars call the authors of today's reading from Genesis the Priestly editors. In other writings in Genesis that are attributed to them, these editors have exhibited a concern that animals be treated with care in recognition that they are also creatures of God. This first covenant in the Bible binds both people and animals in the overarching care of God the Creator.

 ## Reflecting on the Word

We begin Lent with the conclusion to the story of the flood in Genesis. The flood was sent because "the LORD saw how great was man's wickedness on earth, and how no desire that his heart conceived was ever anything but evil, [and] he regretted that he had made man on the earth, and his heart was grieved" (Genesis 6:5–6).

We might not think of God as having a heart that experiences different emotions. But the authors of scripture were not so hesitant. God not only grieves and even repents, God forgives, searches out, and seeks. Most of all, God loves. Indeed, God is love. In Noah's story we see the heart of God change from grieving at human sinfulness to entering once again into a new covenant with humankind through Noah and his family.

Jesus was the man of God's heart, the one who revealed both the heart of God and what the human heart could be. Today we hear that the Spirit drove Jesus into the desert, where he remained for forty days and was tempted by Satan. But the heart of Jesus did not turn from the Father who had called him "beloved son." And so he went from the desert proclaiming God's presence among us—*now*—so that we would turn to God and believe in this good news.

CONSIDER/
DISCUSS:
- What is God asking of you this Lent?
- How does God wish to draw you closer?
- How will you give God a chance?

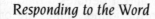

Responding to the Word

Lent's forty days can change our hearts. Three exercises of the heart are appropriate: fasting—to appreciate the hunger of our world and the hungers of our own hearts; prayer—to open our hearts to hear God speak and allow us to respond from the heart; and almsgiving—to open the eyes of our hearts to see those around us most in need. Ask God to transform your heart, turning into flesh what has become stony.

March 8, 2009

SECOND SUNDAY OF LENT

Today's Focus: Have You Been to Moriah?

Mountains usually offer a good view. We find both Abraham and Jesus up on a mountain today. Each sees something about himself. Lent is a time for seeing, for looking beyond the surface into the mystery of life and seeing the traces of our loving God there.

FIRST READING
Genesis 22:1–2, 9a, 10–13, 15–18

God put Abraham to the test. He called to him, "Abraham!" "Here I am!" he replied. Then God said: "Take your son Isaac, your only one, whom you love, and go to the land of Moriah. There you shall offer him up as a holocaust on a height that I will point out to you."

When they came to the place of which God had told him, Abraham built an altar there and arranged the wood on it. Then he reached out and took the knife to slaughter his son. But the LORD's messenger called to him from heaven, "Abraham, Abraham!" "Here I am!" he answered. "Do not lay your hand on the boy," said the messenger. "Do not do the least thing to him. I know now how devoted you are to God, since you did not withhold from me your own beloved son." As Abraham looked about, he spied a ram caught by its horns in the thicket. So he went and took the ram and offered it up as a holocaust in place of his son.

Again the LORD's messenger called to Abraham from heaven and said: "I swear by myself, declares the LORD, that because you acted as you did in not withholding from me your beloved son, I will bless you abundantly and make your descendants as countless as the stars of the sky and the sands of the seashore; your descendants shall take possession of the gates of their enemies, and in your descendants all the nations of the earth shall find blessing — all this because you obeyed my command."

PSALM RESPONSE
Psalm 116:9

I will walk before the Lord, in the land of the living.

SECOND READING
Romans 8: 31b–34

Brothers and sisters: If God is for us, who can be against us? He who did not spare his own Son but handed him over for us all, how will he not also give us everything else along with him?

Who will bring a charge against God's chosen ones? It is God who acquits us. Who will condemn? Christ Jesus it is who died — or, rather, was raised — who also is at the right hand of God, who indeed intercedes for us.

GOSPEL
Mark 9:2–10

Jesus took Peter, James, and John and led them up a high mountain apart by themselves. And he was transfigured before them, and his clothes became dazzling white, such as no fuller on earth could bleach them. Then Elijah appeared to them along with Moses, and they were conversing with Jesus. Then Peter said to Jesus in reply, "Rabbi, it is good that we are here! Let us make three tents: one for you, one for Moses, and one for Elijah." He hardly knew what to say, they were so terrified. Then a cloud came, casting a shadow over them; from the cloud came a voice, "This is my beloved Son. Listen to him." Suddenly, looking around, they no longer saw anyone but Jesus alone with them.

As they were coming down from the mountain, he charged them not to relate what they had seen to anyone, except when the Son of Man had risen from the dead. So they kept the matter to themselves, questioning what rising from the dead meant.

Understanding the Word

The first reading today is often called the *Akedah*, a Hebrew word that means "binding." In this reading God calls upon Abraham to offer his son as a sacrifice in the land of Moriah. Abraham sets out to follow the divine instructions, ultimately binding his son and placing him upon an altar of sacrifice.

The story shocks people. "How could God ask such a horrendous thing of a father?" It is important to realize, however, that God does not allow the sacrifice to occur. The fact that God halts the sacrifice shows that God is not advocating such child sacrifice, which at that time was practiced in the ancient Near East. What, then, is the purpose of the story?

The *Akedah* shows the extent of the commitment of Abraham to follow God's word and the divine blessing that comes through such resolve. The Danish philosopher Søren Kierkegaard wrote two tracts in which he explored the story. Their titles signal the depth of the proposed sacrifice: *Sickness unto Death* and *Fear and Trembling*. To emphasize such commitment this passage speaks the language of divine astonishment. God says, "I swear by myself . . . that because you acted as you did in not withholding from me your beloved son . . ." (Genesis 22:16). In the context of the Lenten readings the *Akedah* helps us begin to appreciate the extent of the love of the Father in sending the Son to make the supreme sacrifice for humanity. To view this divine gift in the context of the family (father and son) helps us to sense the extent of the divine self-emptying for humanity.

The second reading, from Paul's Letter to the Romans, builds on this divine gift of the Father's Son and draws out from this gift the implication of God's great commitment to us. After giving his own Son for us, what will the Father not do to help us?

Moriah means "the place of seeing." God tells Abraham: "Take your son Isaac . . . and go to the land of Moriah. There you shall offer him up as a holocaust" (Genesis 22:2). Abraham listens and obeys. He takes his son and goes to Moriah, prepares the altar of sacrifice, and lays his son upon it. As he lifts the knife, an angel grasps his arm. A ram replaces Isaac.

Isaac had asked, "Where is the sheep for the holocaust?" Abraham answered: "God himself will provide" (22:7, 8). God will see to it. In the end, God not only provides the victim; God sees "how devoted you are to [me]" (22:12). Until then, God did not know, God had not seen. Because Abraham saw God as one who would provide and trusted in God, there is blessing and new life.

Jesus also goes up a mountain, where he is transfigured, allowing his three disciples to see a glimpse of the glory to come, divinity shining through. They see Jesus with Elijah and Moses. Then a voice speaks, "This is my beloved Son. Listen to him" (Mark 9:7). Another story that requires seeing and listening. Jesus then speaks of his coming death, calling them to take up the cross and follow. Whoever hears and obeys will know blessing and new life—resurrection life.

Lent is a time to see: to see what God is calling us to, to see God at work every time we come here—in the bread and in the cup, to see Jesus as one who has given his life for us and calls us to go forth and give our lives for others.

CONSIDER/ • Have you been called to a place of seeing in your life?
DISCUSS: • Have you seen the face of God who provides?
• Have you known dying to self so new life can follow?

□ *Responding to the* Word

Teilhard de Chardin wrote, "[N]othing here below is profane for those who know how to see" (*The Divine Milieu*, New York: Harper & Row, 1960, p. 30). Ask God to help you to see, to deepen your faith in Jesus, and to open your eyes to the wisdom of what God's beloved Son calls us to be and do.

March 15, 2009

THIRD SUNDAY OF LENT, YEAR B

Today's Focus: Jesus Not So Gentle

Today we see an angry Jesus storming through the temple, overturning tables, driving out the sheep, dispersing the doves, and tossing out the merchants. Why is he doing this? What is the reason this Gospel occurs during Lent? What are we to learn from it?

For pastoral reasons, the readings given for Year A may be used in place of these readings. See page 77.

In the shorter form of the reading, the passages in brackets are omitted.

FIRST READING
Exodus 20: 1–17 or 20:1–3, 7–8, 12–17

In those days, God delivered all these commandments:

"I, the LORD, am your God, who brought you out of the land of Egypt, that place of slavery. You shall not have other gods besides me. [You shall not carve idols for yourselves in the shape of anything in the sky above or on the earth below or in the waters beneath the earth; you shall not bow down before them or worship them. For I, the LORD, your God, am a jealous God, inflicting punishment for their fathers' wickedness on the children of those who hate me, down to the third and fourth generation; but bestowing mercy down to the thousandth generation on the children of those who love me and keep my commandments.]

"You shall not take the name of the LORD, your God, in vain. For the LORD will not leave unpunished the one who takes his name in vain.

"Remember to keep holy the sabbath day. [Six days you may labor and do all your work, but the seventh day is the sabbath of the LORD, your God. No work may be done then either by you, or your son or daughter, or your male or female slave, or your beast, or by the alien who lives with you. In six days the LORD made the heavens and the earth, the sea and all that is in them; but on the seventh day he rested. That is why the LORD has blessed the sabbath day and made it holy.]

"Honor your father and your mother, that you may have a long life in the land which the LORD, your God, is giving you.

You shall not kill.
You shall not commit adultery.
You shall not steal.
You shall not bear false witness against your neighbor.
You shall not covet your neighbor's house.
You shall not covet your neighbor's wife,
   nor his male or female slave, nor his ox or ass,
   nor anything else that belongs to him."

PSALM RESPONSE
John 6:68c

Lord, you have the words of everlasting life.

74

SECOND READING
1 Corinthians 1: 22–25 Brothers and sisters: Jews demand signs and Greeks look for wisdom, but we proclaim Christ crucified, a stumbling block to Jews and foolishness to Gentiles, but to those who are called, Jews and Greeks alike, Christ the power of God and the wisdom of God. For the foolishness of God is wiser than human wisdom, and the weakness of God is stronger than human strength.

GOSPEL
John 2:13–25

Since the Passover of the Jews was near, Jesus went up to Jerusalem. He found in the temple area those who sold oxen, sheep, and doves, as well as the money changers seated there. He made a whip out of cords and drove them all out of the temple area, with the sheep and oxen, and spilled the coins of the money changers and overturned their tables, and to those who sold doves he said, "Take these out of here, and stop making my Father's house a marketplace." His disciples recalled the words of Scripture,

Zeal for your house will consume me.

At this the Jews answered and said to him, "What sign can you show us for doing this?" Jesus answered and said to them, "Destroy this temple and in three days I will raise it up." The Jews said, "This temple has been under construction for forty-six years, and you will raise it up in three days?" But he was speaking about the temple of his body. Therefore, when he was raised from the dead, his disciples remembered that he had said this, and they came to believe the Scripture and the word Jesus had spoken.

While he was in Jerusalem for the feast of Passover, many began to believe in his name when they saw the signs he was doing. But Jesus would not trust himself to them because he knew them all, and did not need anyone to testify about human nature. He himself understood it well.

Understanding the Word

The Old Testament reading for today is the beginning of the Sinai covenant—so called because scripture presents it as occurring on Mount Sinai following the Exodus from Egypt and during the wilderness wanderings of the Israelites. Unlike the covenant with Noah that we heard two Sundays ago, the Sinai covenant was a bilateral covenant: duties were required of both God and the people. The passage that we hear today presents the first words of God about what the Sinai covenant entails. The Ten Commandments come first. These laws are called apodictic: they apply throughout life and are not relevant only to certain specific situations.

The Ten Commandments are the beginning of the covenant. There is an order to them that places the commandments pertaining directly to worship of God before those treating one's relationship with others. The first four commandments are about the former and the last six about the latter relationship. The idea behind the order appears to be that a strong relationship with God will buttress one's relationships with others. An even prior recognition of the liberation God has provided in one's life supports one's relationship with God: "I, the LORD, am your God, who brought you out of the land of Egypt, that place of slavery" (Exodus 20:2).

First things first. Attention to those who have cared for us will be a basis for care in other areas of our life. This may be why the first commandment after the four commandments dealing with God, themselves prefaced by what God has done for us, is the commandment to honor our father and mother (20:12). How we treat others is nourished or undernourished by the pattern of care or neglect we show for those who have been our primary caregivers. Care for those who have expended themselves for us promotes, and should lead to, the expense of our own selves for others.

Reflecting on the Word

Anger is not always a bad thing. It is something like cholesterol: some anger is good, some bad. Destructive anger comes boiling to the surface and scalds not only the one angry, but anyone who comes within range. When those who have power let their anger have free rein it can wreak great destruction.

Today's Gospel reading may make some feel uneasy, especially those who only want Jesus to be kind, loving, and gentle—all the time! But scripture tells us that Jesus showed many emotions during his ministry: disappointment, exasperation, sadness, grief, and, yes, even anger. He got angry with the religious leaders and even with his disciples on occasion.

Today we see the anger of Jesus up close—Jesus with whip cutting through the air, Jesus overturning the tables, Jesus sending coins flying all over the place. In a fit of anger, Jesus spits out his words: "Get these things out of there and stop making my Father's house a marketplace!" Why so angry? The moneychangers and those selling animals were performing a necessary service.

Jesus is the prophet here, proclaiming in word and deed that a new age has come. The old temple where God lived among the people is being replaced by a new temple where God dwells in human flesh. Jesus is the place where God has taken up residence and where all can encounter God. No payment is necessary; all is gift. His words are the words of God; his deeds are the deeds of God. It is in the dying and rising of Jesus that we encounter the love of God fully revealed.

CONSIDER/ DISCUSS:
- Do we see Jesus as the new temple where God dwells?
- Do we hear his words calling us to a new identity, grounded in him?

Responding to the Word

God's wisdom and power are shown to us in Jesus, especially in the broken body of Jesus crucified that was raised to new life by the Father. Let us pray that God will continue to be glorified by the Church, we who are Christ's body in the world.

March 15, 2009

THIRD SUNDAY OF LENT, YEAR A

Today's Focus: Thirsty?

Thirst is a common experience. Today's readings present us with a thirsty people and a thirsty woman. God provides in both cases. The Samaritan woman is one of the great witnesses in John's Gospel. Jesus promises her life-giving water, water that will refresh her deep within her being. He promises us the same.

FIRST READING
Exodus 17: 3–7

In those days, in their thirst for water, the people grumbled against Moses, saying, "Why did you ever make us leave Egypt? Was it just to have us die here of thirst with our children and our livestock?" So Moses cried out to the LORD, "What shall I do with this people? A little more and they will stone me!" The LORD answered Moses, "Go over there in front of the people, along with some of the elders of Israel, holding in your hand, as you go, the staff with which you struck the river. I will be standing there in front of you on the rock in Horeb. Strike the rock, and the water will flow from it for the people to drink." This Moses did, in the presence of the elders of Israel. The place was called Massah and Meribah, because the Israelites quarreled there and tested the LORD, saying, "Is the LORD in our midst or not?"

PSALM RESPONSE
Psalm 95:8

If today you hear his voice, harden not your hearts.

SECOND READING
Romans 5: 1–2, 5–8

Brothers and sisters: Since we have been justified by faith, we have peace with God through our Lord Jesus Christ, through whom we have gained access by faith to this grace in which we stand, and we boast in hope of the glory of God.

And hope does not disappoint, because the love of God has been poured out into our hearts through the Holy Spirit who has been given to us. For Christ, while we were still helpless, died at the appointed time for the ungodly. Indeed, only with difficulty does one die for a just person, though perhaps for a good person one might even find courage to die. But God proves his love for us in that while we were still sinners Christ died for us.

In the shorter version of the reading, the three passages in brackets are omitted.

GOSPEL
John 4:5–42 or
4:5–15, 19b–26,
39a, 40–42

Jesus came to a town of Samaria called Sychar, near the plot of land that Jacob had given to his son Joseph. Jacob's well was there. Jesus, tired from his journey, sat down there at the well. It was about noon.

A woman of Samaria came to draw water. Jesus said to her, "Give me a drink." His disciples had gone into the town to buy food. The Samaritan woman said to him, "How can you, a Jew, ask me, a Samaritan woman, for a drink?" — For Jews use nothing in common with Samaritans. — Jesus answered and said to her, "If you knew the gift of God and who is saying to you, 'Give me a drink,' you would have asked him and he would have given you living water." The woman said to him, "Sir, you do not even have a bucket and the cistern is deep; where then can you get this living water? Are you greater than our father Jacob, who gave us this cistern and drank from it himself with his children and his flocks?" Jesus answered and said to her, "Everyone who drinks this water will be thirsty again; but whoever drinks the water I shall give will never thirst; the water I shall give will become in him a spring of water welling up to eternal life." The woman said to him, "Sir, give me this water, so that I may not be thirsty or have to keep coming here to draw water."

[Jesus said to her, "Go call your husband and come back." The woman answered and said to him, "I do not have a husband." Jesus answered her, "You are right in saying, 'I do not have a husband.' For you have had five husbands, and the one you have now is not your husband. What you have said is true." The woman said to him, "Sir,] I can see that you are a prophet. Our ancestors worshiped on this mountain; but you people say that the place to worship is in Jerusalem." Jesus said to her, "Believe me, woman, the hour is coming when you will worship the Father neither on this mountain nor in Jerusalem. You people worship what you do not understand; we worship what we understand, because salvation is from the Jews. But the hour is coming, and is now here, when true worshipers will worship the Father in Spirit and truth; and indeed the Father seeks such people to worship him. God is Spirit, and those who worship him must worship in Spirit and truth."

The woman said to him, "I know that the Messiah is coming, the one called the Christ; when he comes, he will tell us everything." Jesus said to her, "I am he, the one speaking with you."

[At that moment his disciples returned, and were amazed that he was talking with a woman, but still no one said, "What are you looking for?" or "Why are you talking with her?" The woman left her water jar and went into the town and said to the people, "Come see a man who told me everything I have done. Could he possibly be the Christ?" They went out of the town and came to him. Meanwhile, the disciples urged him, "Rabbi, eat." But he said to them, "I have food to eat of which you do not know." So the disciples said to one another, "Could someone have brought him something to eat?" Jesus said to them, "My food is to do the will of the one who sent me and to finish his work. Do you not say, 'In four months the harvest will be here'? I tell you, look up and see the fields ripe for the harvest. The reaper is already receiving payment and gathering crops for eternal life, so that the sower and reaper can rejoice together. For here the saying is verified that 'One sows and another reaps.' I sent you to reap what you have not worked for; others have done the work, and you are sharing the fruits of their work."]

Many of the Samaritans of that town began to believe in him [because of the word of the woman who testified, "He told me everything I have done."] When the Samaritans came to him, they invited him to stay with them; and he stayed there two days. Many more began to believe in him because of his word, and they said to the woman, "We no longer believe because of your word; for we have heard for ourselves, and we know that this is truly the savior of the world."

Understanding the Word

Today's Gospel reading from Saint John recounts Jesus' encounter with the Samaritan woman and the outpouring of faith that flows from it. The story is situated at this point in the Gospel of John to caution readers about judging the religious attitudes of others.

Right before this story John wrote about a Jewish leader, a teacher named Nicodemus, coming to Jesus at night and failing miserably in his attempt to understand Jesus' message (John 3:1–21). This occurred in the holiest place in the Jewish world, Jerusalem. Then we read about Jesus going off and baptizing people. The result, as the disciples of John the Baptist tell John, is that "everyone is coming to him" (3:26). Apparently Jesus' message is gaining more support on the periphery than in the religious center of the Jewish world, Jerusalem. Following the cleansing of the temple, John does write that many in Jerusalem believe in Jesus because of the signs that he did (2:23). "But," John also says, "Jesus would not trust himself to them because he knew them all, and did not need anyone to testify about human nature" (2:24–25). So those in Jerusalem are not looked on all too favorably. Nicodemus, who did not understand what Jesus was saying, is seen as a representative of this Jerusalem group of believers. This is why, right after writing that Jesus "did not need anyone to testify about human nature. He himself understood it well," John continues, "Now there was a Pharisee named Nicodemus, a ruler of the Jews" (2:25; 3:1).

The story about the Samaritan woman continues the Johannine emphasis on those on the outside coming to the message sooner than those on the inside, the established religious figures, do. As with those who "believed" in him in Jerusalem, Jesus knows about the Samaritan woman's life (4:16–18), and yet it is the Samaritan woman who brings many Samaritans to Jesus (4:42). The same cannot be said about any of the Jerusalem "believers," including the teacher Nicodemus.

Those on the societal periphery may be in the religious center in terms of their reception of the Christian message.

Reflecting on the Word

When you are really thirsty, there is no more satisfying drink than a glass of cold, clear water. I can remember drinking from a well at my great-aunt's farm when I was a boy. It was cold and clear and tasted so pure.

When Israel was in the desert, the dry wind and hot, barren landscape could shrivel not just their bodies but their hearts. So they began to grumble. They were thirsty.

In today's Gospel story, the woman who came to the well that day also was thirsty, in many ways. She needed water to stay alive, but her soul was also thirsting. Jesus came with his thirst; perhaps that is where they first connected. Both were thirsty. She gave him water to quench his thirst.

Then he tended to her thirst—for companionship and for God. After five husbands and now living with another man, something was not working. Perhaps she had a deeper thirst than she realized, one for God. Jesus spoke of a time when all would worship together in spirit and truth.

Jesus came to the woman with a thirst, not just for water but for her. Jesus brought with him God's thirst for all God's children, that all would come to God and be with God, worshiping in spirit and in truth.

CONSIDER/ DISCUSS:
- What does Jesus thirst for in our day?
- Which of God's children does God wish to bring together?
- What does your own heart thirst for?

Responding to the Word

The Samaritan woman moved from seeing Jesus simply as a Jewish man to seeing him as a prophet and, finally, as the Messiah. She proclaimed this to others and they ended up calling him the Savior of the world. Let us pray that this holy season may bring us a deeper knowledge of who Jesus is for us and what this means for our lives.

March 22, 2009

FOURTH SUNDAY OF LENT, YEAR B

Today's Focus: God Wishes Us Life

Today's first reading traces the sinfulness of Israel and how God's anger engulfed them, bringing death and destruction and the loss of all that was precious. But, as before, God would make a new beginning with Israel, using the Gentile king of Persia. God is rich in mercy and has never ceased bringing new life to the world. This new life is gained by all who look on Jesus with faith.

For pastoral reasons, the readings given for Year A may be used in place of these readings. See page 84.

FIRST READING
2 Chronicles 36:14–16, 19–23

In those days, all the princes of Judah, the priests, and the people added infidelity to infidelity, practicing all the abominations of the nations and polluting the LORD's temple which he had consecrated in Jerusalem.

Early and often did the LORD, the God of their fathers, send his messengers to them, for he had compassion on his people and his dwelling place. But they mocked the messengers of God, despised his warnings, and scoffed at his prophets, until the anger of the LORD against his people was so inflamed that there was no remedy. Their enemies burnt the house of God, tore down the walls of Jerusalem, set all its palaces afire, and destroyed all its precious objects. Those who escaped the sword were carried captive to Babylon, where they became servants of the king of the Chaldeans and his sons until the kingdom of the Persians came to power. All this was to fulfill the word of the LORD spoken by Jeremiah: "Until the land has retrieved its lost sabbaths, during all the time it lies waste it shall have rest while seventy years are fulfilled."

In the first year of Cyrus, king of Persia, in order to fulfill the word of the LORD spoken by Jeremiah, the LORD inspired King Cyrus of Persia to issue this proclamation throughout his kingdom, both by word of mouth and in writing: "Thus says Cyrus, king of Persia: All the kingdoms of the earth the LORD, the God of heaven, has given to me, and he has also charged me to build him a house in Jerusalem, which is in Judah. Whoever, therefore, among you belongs to any part of his people, let him go up, and may his God be with him!"

PSALM RESPONSE
Psalm 137:6ab

Let my tongue be silenced, if I ever forget you!

SECOND
READING
*Ephesians 2:
4–10*
Brothers and sisters: God, who is rich in mercy, because of the great love he had for us, even when we were dead in our transgressions, brought us to life with Christ — by grace you have been saved —, raised us up with him, and seated us with him in the heavens in Christ Jesus, that in the ages to come he might show the immeasurable riches of his grace in his kindness to us in Christ Jesus. For by grace you have been saved through faith, and this is not from you; it is the gift of God; it is not from works, so no one may boast. For we are his handiwork, created in Christ Jesus for the good works that God has prepared in advance, that we should live in them.

GOSPEL
John 3:14–21
Jesus said to Nicodemus: "Just as Moses lifted up the serpent in the desert, so must the Son of Man be lifted up, so that everyone who believes in him may have eternal life."

For God so loved the world that he gave his only Son, so that everyone who believes in him might not perish but might have eternal life. For God did not send his Son into the world to condemn the world, but that the world might be saved through him. Whoever believes in him will not be condemned, but whoever does not believe has already been condemned, because he has not believed in the name of the only Son of God. And this is the verdict, that the light came into the world, but people preferred darkness to light, because their works were evil. For everyone who does wicked things hates the light and does not come toward the light, so that his works might not be exposed. But whoever lives the truth comes to the light, so that his works may be clearly seen as done in God.

Understanding the Word

Today's Gospel reading, the conclusion of the dialogue between Jesus and Nicodemus in John's Gospel, becomes a monologue in which Jesus speaks about the purpose of his coming and what is expected of the believer.

In the Prologue to the Gospel of John we read that the coming of Jesus is a coming "to his own" (John 1:11). The tragedy was that not all received Jesus. God's response, however, was to empower those who did receive Jesus through belief "to become children of God" (1:12). Thus, the offer of salvation is a divine attempt to find and bring back lost children. When in today's reading we find the familiar words, "For God so loved the world that he gave his only Son, that everyone who believes in him might not perish but might have eternal life" (3:16), we are reading about the divine Father and Son going to the extremes of love to bring back those close to them.

82

Now let us consider the belief that welcomes the Father and Son and agrees to come home. For John belief is an active state. It involves the courage to come out of the crowd and return home with Jesus. This is why right after speaking about those who believe as being saved, John writes about the actions of God and people in terms of light and darkness. God comes as light into the darkness. People, however, prefer darkness to the light because of their evil deeds, and so they do not come to the light (3:18–20). Only the one who acts in truth comes to the light (3:21). These sayings remind us that Nicodemus has just come to Jesus at night (3:2). Belief as a coming to the light means announcing by one's Christian affiliation to whose family one belongs, even if it is safer to remain in the dark and not be so known.

 ## Reflecting on the Word

We become what we behold. If we grow up seeing goodness and kindness and mercy and forgiveness, we shall become that. But if we grow up seeing anger and hatred and selfishness and a refusal to forgive others, that will leave its mark on us. The old belief was that what a person looked at was stamped indelibly on the soul.

Now, God of course can reverse that, as God did with Israel in the desert. The very thing that had brought them death became under God's direction a power for life. When the Israelites were out in the desert and tested God, they were punished with serpents that bit them. When they finally turned to Moses for help in their affliction and Moses turned to God, God relented and told Moses to make a serpent of bronze and all who looked on it would be saved. The very thing that had brought death became a source of life.

One may say the same thing of the cross. The startling image that begins today's Gospel calls us to look with faith at the Son of Man who has been lifted up, both on the cross and by his resurrection. When we look with faith at Christ crucified on the cross, we see not death, but the love of God expressed in this total gift of the Son, even unto death. We behold this divine love for us, accept it in faith, and allow it to flood into our hearts and we are saved. Truly the love of God has been poured into our hearts.

CONSIDER/ DISCUSS:
- Have you had moments when you have known the love of God for you?
- Have you had an experience of realizing that God wishes only our love in return?

 ## Responding to the Word

During these forty days, the traditional disciplines of fasting, praying, and sharing with others—not just money, but whatever there is a need for—are meant to lead us to know in a most intimate way the love of God. Ask God to reveal this love for you, that you may know the peace that comes from this knowledge.

March 22, 2009

FOURTH SUNDAY OF LENT, YEAR A

Today's Focus: "I Once Was Blind But Now I See"

Being blind is not simply being unable to see. We can see perfectly well, yet still be blind. Samuel in today's first reading confirms this. And while we call today's Gospel the story of the man born blind, it is equally the story of people who choose to be blind. We might also find that it is our story.

FIRST READING
1 Samuel 16: 1b, 6–7, 10–13a

The LORD said to Samuel: "Fill your horn with oil, and be on your way. I am sending you to Jesse of Bethlehem, for I have chosen my king from among his sons."

As Jesse and his sons came to the sacrifice, Samuel looked at Eliab and thought, "Surely the Lord's anointed is here before him." But the LORD said to Samuel: "Do not judge from his appearance or from his lofty stature, because I have rejected him. Not as man sees does God see, because man sees the appearance but the LORD looks into the heart." In the same way Jesse presented seven sons before Samuel, but Samuel said to Jesse, "The LORD has not chosen any one of these." Then Samuel asked Jesse, "Are these all the sons you have?" Jesse replied, "There is still the youngest, who is tending the sheep." Samuel said to Jesse, "Send for him; we will not begin the sacrificial banquet until he arrives here." Jesse sent and had the young man brought to them. He was ruddy, a youth handsome to behold and making a splendid appearance. The LORD said, "There — anoint him, for this is the one!" Then Samuel, with the horn of oil in hand, anointed David in the presence of his brothers; and from that day on, the spirit of the LORD rushed upon David.

PSALM RESPONSE
Psalm 23:1

The Lord is my shepherd; there is nothing I shall want.

SECOND READING
Ephesians 5: 8–14

Brothers and sisters: You were once darkness, but now you are light in the Lord. Live as children of light, for light produces every kind of goodness and righteousness and truth. Try to learn what is pleasing to the Lord. Take no part in the fruitless works of darkness; rather expose them, for it is shameful even to mention the things done by them in secret; but everything exposed by the light becomes visible, for everything that becomes visible is light. Therefore, it says:

"Awake, O sleeper,
and arise from the dead,
and Christ will give you light."

GOSPEL
John 9:1–41 or
9:1, 6–9, 13–17,
34–38

As Jesus passed by he saw a man blind from birth. [His disciples asked him, "Rabbi, who sinned, this man or his parents, that he was born blind?" Jesus answered,

"Neither he nor his parents sinned;
it is so that the works of God might be made visible through him.

We have to do the works of the one who sent me while it is day. Night is coming when no one can work. While I am in the world, I am the light of the world." When he had said this,] he spat on the ground and made clay with the saliva, and smeared the clay on his eyes, and said to him, "Go wash in the Pool of Siloam" — which means Sent —. So he went and washed, and came back able to see.

His neighbors and those who had seen him earlier as a beggar said, "Isn't this the one who used to sit and beg?" Some said, "It is, " but others said, "No, he just looks like him." He said, "I am." [So they said to him, "How were your eyes opened?" He replied, "The man called Jesus made clay and anointed my eyes and told me, 'Go to Siloam and wash.' So I went there and washed and was able to see." And they said to him, "Where is he?" He said, "I don't know."]

They brought the one who was once blind to the Pharisees. Now Jesus had made clay and opened his eyes on a sabbath. So then the Pharisees also asked him how he was able to see. He said to them, "He put clay on my eyes, and I washed, and now I can see." So some of the Pharisees said, "This man is not from God, because he does not keep the sabbath." But others said, "How can a sinful man do such signs?" And there was a division among them. So they said to the blind man again, "What do you have to say about him, since he opened your eyes?" He said, "He is a prophet."

[Now the Jews did not believe that he had been blind and gained his sight until they summoned the parents of the one who had gained his sight. They asked them, "Is this your son, who you say was born blind? How does he now see?" His parents answered and said, "We know that this is our son and that he was born blind. We do not know how he sees now, nor do we know who opened his eyes. Ask him, he is of age; he can speak for himself." His parents said this because they were afraid of the Jews, for the Jews had already agreed that if anyone acknowledged him as the Christ, he would be expelled from the synagogue. For this reason his parents said, "He is of age; question him."]

So a second time they called the man who had been blind and said to him, "Give God the praise! We know that this man is a sinner." He replied, "If he is a sinner, I do not know. One thing I do know is that I was blind and now I see." So they said to him, "What did he do to you? How did he open your eyes?" He answered them, "I told you already and you did not listen.

85

Why do you want to hear it again? Do you want to become his disciples, too?" They ridiculed him and said, "You are that man's disciple; we are disciples of Moses! We know that God spoke to Moses, but we do not know where this one is from." The man answered and said to them, "This is what is so amazing, that you do not know where he is from, yet he opened my eyes. We know that God does not listen to sinners, but if one is devout and does his will, he listens to him. It is unheard of that anyone ever opened the eyes of a person born blind. If this man were not from God, he would not be able to do anything."] They answered and said to him, "You were born totally in sin, and are you trying to teach us?" Then they threw him out.

When Jesus heard that they had thrown him out, he found him and said, "Do you believe in the Son of Man?" He answered and said, "Who is he, sir, that I may believe in him?" Jesus said to him, "You have seen him, the one speaking with you is he." He said, "I do believe, Lord, " and he worshiped him. [Then Jesus said, "I came into this world for judgment, so that those who do not see might see, and those who do see might become blind."

Some of the Pharisees who were with him heard this and said to him, "Surely we are not also blind, are we?" Jesus said to them, "If you were blind, you would have no sin; but now you are saying, 'We see,' so your sin remains."]

Understanding the Word

In the story of the healing of the man born blind and his ensuing entanglements we find a sterling example of someone courageous enough to proclaim belief in the face of intense opposition.

There is an escalating tension in this story. This man has been healed on the Sabbath, and the Pharisees are not at all pleased (John 9:13). They ask him twice how he regained his sight and once where Jesus is (9:10, 12, 13). The man twice confesses that Jesus healed him. When the Pharisees ask him what he thinks of Jesus, he confesses Jesus as a prophet (9:17). This is already a somewhat bold acclamation because John has just written that some of the Pharisees have already said that Jesus cannot be from God (9:16a).

The situation soon becomes a more dangerous one in which to confess Jesus. The next thing the Pharisees do is bring in the man's parents to see if he was really born blind and if so how he can now see. Now the man's own parents throw him to the sharks. They refuse to answer how he can now see. Their refusal stems from fear; they had heard that the Pharisees would expel from the synagogue any who confessed Jesus as the Christ (9:22).

When the man is brought back before the Pharisees, they are now united in proclaiming Jesus a sinner and in this context they ask the man to "give God the praise" (9:24). He is being pressured to agree with them that Jesus is a sinner, but he steadfastly refuses to do so. Rather he defends Jesus and culminates his defense with the claim that Jesus is "from God" (9:25–33). This leads the Pharisees to expel him from the synagogue. For the Johannine Christians who had experienced a rupture from their Jewish heritage for the sake of confessing Christ, the man born blind was an inspiring example.

Reflecting on the Word

Today we meet John's second of three witnesses presented this Lent: the man born blind. Last week's witness was a Samaritan woman, transformed by an intimate encounter with Jesus. Today, Jesus is only center stage for a few moments. He heals the blind man, then walks off, leaving the man to shift for himself—which he does quite well. The rest of the time we witness the encounters between him and various seeing people who are presented by the Gospel writer as really quite "blind"!

The man's own neighbors refuse to believe their eyes, saying, "No, he just looks like him." When the Pharisees are told what happened, they refuse to see God at work: "No, it's a Sabbath and God forbids work on the Sabbath." In the midst of all this, the man born blind comes to see with the eyes of faith.

At first, he calls Jesus "a man," then "a prophet." But when the Pharisees say that the one who healed him must be a sinner, the man asserts: "We know that God does not listen to sinners, but if one is devout and does his will, [God] listens to him. . . . If this man were not from God, he would not be able to do anything" (John 9:31, 33). For him, Jesus is "from God."

And so, they throw him out of the synagogue! Coming upon Jesus, who asks if he believes in the Son of Man, the man confesses, "I do believe, Lord," and he worships Jesus (9:38).

CONSIDER/ DISCUSS: Seeing is a complex matter. In John's Gospel, to see is to believe.

• Do we see who Jesus is?

• Do we confess what we see?

• Do we back away from being too public about our faith?

Responding to the Word

God corrects the prophet Samuel for seeing only skin-deep and not seeing with the heart. The author of Ephesians calls us to live as children of light, producing every kind of goodness and righteousness and truth. Let us pray that we might see with the heart, that we will come to know what is pleasing to God. Ask Christ for the light to walk in his way.

March 29, 2009

FIFTH SUNDAY OF LENT, YEAR B

Today's Focus: The Hour of Power

John's Gospel moves toward "the hour." Throughout the Gospel, Jesus talks about this "hour." At Cana he tells his mother, "My hour has not come." In today's Gospel he finally says: "The hour has come for the Son of Man to be glorified." At this hour we shall see the power of God and the wisdom of God revealed.

> *For pastoral reasons, the readings given for Year A may be used in place of these readings. See page 91.*

FIRST READING
Jeremiah 31: 31–34

The days are coming, says the LORD, when I will make a new covenant with the house of Israel and the house of Judah. It will not be like the covenant I made with their fathers the day I took them by the hand to lead them forth from the land of Egypt; for they broke my covenant, and I had to show myself their master, says the LORD. But this is the covenant that I will make with the house of Israel after those days, says the LORD. I will place my law within them and write it upon their hearts; I will be their God, and they shall be my people. No longer will they have need to teach their friends and relatives how to know the LORD. All, from least to greatest, shall know me, says the LORD, for I will forgive their evildoing and remember their sin no more.

PSALM RESPONSE
Psalm 51:12a

Create a clean heart in me, O God.

SECOND READING
Hebrews 5:7–9

In the days when Christ Jesus was in the flesh, he offered prayers and supplications with loud cries and tears to the one who was able to save him from death, and he was heard because of his reverence. Son though he was, he learned obedience from what he suffered; and when he was made perfect, he became the source of eternal salvation for all who obey him.

GOSPEL
John 12:20–33

Some Greeks who had come to worship at the Passover Feast came to Philip, who was from Bethsaida in Galilee, and asked him, "Sir, we would like to see Jesus." Philip went and told Andrew; then Andrew and Philip went and told Jesus. Jesus answered them, "The hour has come for the Son of Man to be glorified. Amen, amen, I say to you, unless a grain of wheat falls to the ground and dies, it remains just a grain of wheat; but if it dies, it produces much fruit. Whoever loves his life loses it, and whoever hates his life in this world will preserve it for eternal life. Whoever serves me must follow me, and where I am, there also will my servant be. The Father will honor whoever serves me.

"I am troubled now. Yet what should I say? 'Father, save me from this hour'? But it was for this purpose that I came to this hour. Father, glorify your name." Then a voice came from heaven, "I have glorified it and will glorify it again." The crowd there heard it and said it was thunder; but others said, "An angel has spoken to him." Jesus answered and said, "This voice did not come for my sake but for yours. Now is the time of judgment on this world; now the ruler of this world will be driven out. And when I am lifted up from the earth, I will draw everyone to myself." He said this indicating the kind of death he would die.

Understanding the Word

The first reading today describes the new covenant that Jeremiah sees as the one effective answer to the human condition. What can be done, the prophet laments, when sinful behavior has become so crystallized by habit that reform seems impossible?

Jeremiah is not sanguine about humanity's ability to follow unaided the dictates of the law. In image after vivid image throughout his book he has shown how set in their sinful ways the people have become. They seem to have lost all ability to change. Thus, he says, "Can the Ethiopian change his skin? / the leopard his spots? / As easily would you be able to do good, / accustomed to evil as you are" (13:23). Jeremiah calls the people evil, refusing to hear God's word and instead "walk[ing] in the stubbornness of their hearts" (13:10; cf. 18:12). It is this recalcitrance that causes God to mourn the "pernicious thoughts" within the people and to claim that their conversions are half-hearted (4:14; 3:10). Their heart remains "stubborn and rebellious" with the result that "they turn and go away" (5:23). The sorry state of the people's continued bad behavior leads Jeremiah to conclude: "More tortuous than all else is the human heart, / beyond remedy" (17:9).

Today's passage from the book of Jeremiah is God's response to this desperate state of affairs. God speaks of days that are coming in which God will give the people a new covenant unlike the one that they broke in the past. This covenant will be unbreakable because it will be written not on tablets of stone but rather on the hearts of the people. The image conveys a realignment of the orientation that so perverts their actions; they will be aligned now with God's orientation.

Today we hear of the inner transformation that God can accomplish even when our dispositions themselves are our worst enemies.

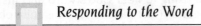

Reflecting on the Word

Several years ago a good friend gave me a book of poems by a twelve-year-old boy, Matty Stepanek, who was afflicted with muscular dystrophy. He had been writing poems since he was three. There was one poem that I have gone back to again and again called "Heartsongs." It is about the songs we can hear in our hearts, the songs that God has placed there.

Today we hear the heart song of Jesus as the Gospel of John presents him. He is the seed that will die so others might have life, the grain of wheat that will be crushed and made into bread that feeds us. He is the one who came to glorify his Father's name, the one who came to witness to the Father. He is the one who came to draw us to himself.

Lent is about a change of heart. Where do we go to get a new heart? Where do we go to have our stony hearts turned once more into hearts of flesh? Where do we go that the Father might write the law of love not on stony tablets but on our hearts? We go to Jesus, who lifts us up so the Father can write on our hearts not with ink, but with the blood of the Son.

CONSIDER/ DISCUSS:
- What does God write on our hearts?
- What do we ask the Father to write on our hearts?
- What is the song we wish to sing?

Responding to the Word

Jesus tells us that he has come to bring life to the world, to be living water, to be light in the darkness, to be the resurrection and the life. So we pray to our Father that we may be given this living water, this light, this new life as we near the great feast that draws us into the paschal mystery, into the life made possible by the saving death and rising of Jesus.

March 29, 2009

FIFTH SUNDAY OF LENT, YEAR A

Today's Focus: The Really Big Question

Another woman is center stage with Jesus today. In the encounter with the Samaritan woman Jesus revealed himself as Living Water. In the healing of the man born blind Jesus showed himself to be the Light of the World. Now in the meeting with Martha, sister of the recently deceased Lazarus, Jesus utters this magnificent claim: "I am the resurrection and the life" (John 11:25).

FIRST READING
Ezekiel 37: 12–14

Thus says the LORD GOD: O my people, I will open your graves and have you rise from them, and bring you back to the land of Israel. Then you shall know that I am the LORD, when I open your graves and have you rise from them, O my people! I will put my spirit in you that you may live, and I will settle you upon your land; thus you shall know that I am the LORD. I have promised, and I will do it, says the LORD.

PSALM RESPONSE
Psalm 130:7

With the Lord there is mercy and fullness of redemption.

SECOND READING
Romans 8:8–11

Brothers and sisters: Those who are in the flesh cannot please God. But you are not in the flesh; on the contrary, you are in the spirit, if only the Spirit of God dwells in you. Whoever does not have the Spirit of Christ does not belong to him. But if Christ is in you, although the body is dead because of sin, the spirit is alive because of righteousness. If the Spirit of the one who raised Jesus from the dead dwells in you, the one who raised Christ from the dead will give life to your mortal bodies also, through his Spirit dwelling in you.

GOSPEL
John 11:1–45 or 11:3–7, 17, 20–27, 33b–45

In the shorter version of the reading, the five passages in brackets are omitted.

[Now a man was ill, Lazarus from Bethany, the village of Mary and her sister Martha. Mary was the one who had anointed the Lord with perfumed oil and dried his feet with her hair; it was her brother Lazarus who was ill. So] the sisters sent word to Jesus saying, "Master, the one you love is ill." When Jesus heard this he said,

"This illness is not to end in death,
but is for the glory of God,
that the Son of God may be glorified through it."

Now Jesus loved Martha and her sister and Lazarus. So when he heard that he was ill, he remained for two days in the place where he was. Then after this he said to his disciples, "Let us go back to Judea." [The disciples said to him, "Rabbi, the Jews were just trying to stone you, and you want to go back there?" Jesus answered,

91

"Are there not twelve hours in a day?
If one walks during the day, he does not stumble,
   because he sees the light of this world.
But if one walks at night, he stumbles,
   because the light is not in him."

He said this, and then told them, "Our friend Lazarus is asleep, but I am going to awaken him." So the disciples said to him, "Master, if he is asleep, he will be saved." But Jesus was talking about his death, while they thought that he meant ordinary sleep. So then Jesus said to them clearly, "Lazarus has died. And I am glad for you that I was not there, that you may believe. Let us go to him." So Thomas, called Didymus, said to his fellow disciples, "Let us also go to die with him."]

When Jesus arrived, he found that Lazarus had already been in the tomb for four days. [Now Bethany was near Jerusalem, only about two miles away. And many of the Jews had come to Martha and Mary to comfort them about their brother.] When Martha heard that Jesus was coming, she went to meet him; but Mary sat at home. Martha said to Jesus, "Lord, if you had been here, my brother would not have died. But even now I know that whatever you ask of God, God will give you." Jesus said to her, "Your brother will rise." Martha said to him, "I know he will rise, in the resurrection on the last day." Jesus told her,

"I am the resurrection and the life;
   whoever believes in me, even if he dies, will live,
   and everyone who lives and believes in me will never die.

Do you believe this?" She said to him, "Yes, Lord. I have come to believe that you are the Christ, the Son of God, the one who is coming into the world."

[When she had said this, she went and called her sister Mary secretly, saying, "The teacher is here and is asking for you." As soon as she heard this, she rose quickly and went to him. For Jesus had not yet come into the village, but was still where Martha had met him. So when the Jews who were with her in the house comforting her saw Mary get up quickly and go out, they followed her, presuming that she was going to the tomb to weep there. When Mary came to where Jesus was and saw him, she fell at his feet and said to him, "Lord, if you had been here, my brother would not have died." When] Jesus [saw her weeping and the Jews who had come with her weeping, he] became perturbed and deeply troubled, and said, "Where have you laid him?" They said to him, "Sir, come and see." And Jesus wept. So the Jews said, "See how he loved him." But some of them said, "Could not the one who opened the eyes of the blind man have done something so that this man would not have died?"

So Jesus, perturbed again, came to the tomb. It was a cave, and a stone lay across it. Jesus said, "Take away the stone." Martha, the dead man's sister, said to him, "Lord, by now there will be a stench; he has been dead for four days." Jesus said to her, "Did I not tell you that if you believe you will see the glory of God?" So they took away the stone. And Jesus raised his eyes and said,

"Father, I thank you for hearing me.
I know that you always hear me;
but because of the crowd here I have said this,
that they may believe that you sent me."

And when he had said this, He cried out in a loud voice, "Lazarus, come out!" The dead man came out, tied hand and foot with burial bands, and his face was wrapped in a cloth. So Jesus said to them, "Untie him and let him go."

Now many of the Jews who had come to Mary and seen what he had done began to believe in him.

Understanding the Word

The reading from Ezekiel builds upon last week's reading from Jeremiah. We saw that Jeremiah envisioned God acting to transform people from the inside out by providing them with a will that enabled them to know God. "Knowledge" is often an active concept in biblical literature, implying not only cognition but also living in certain ways. For Jeremiah, knowing God is explained in terms of practicing "kindness, justice and uprightness" (Jeremiah 9:23–24). So Jeremiah's plan for the law written on people's hearts has practical effects.

Ezekiel picks up on this idea of inner renewal leading to relational justice. The reading today is from the famous chapter 37, in which the prophet narrates his vision of a valley full of dry bones. God tells Ezekiel to prophesy to the bones so that they come together, sinews and flesh are added to them, and finally breath comes into them so that they live. Then God explains that the dry bones represent the hopeless Israelites in exile in Babylon in the sixth century BC. The reconnected bones, flesh, sinews, and the breath represent the new life God gives to them by returning them from the Exile back to their home.

For Ezekiel inner renewal begins with the restoration of hope. The image of the reknitting of matter and spirit into human beings represents first of all the construction of reasons to hope for effective change. Without such hope Ezekiel sees the potential for reform as a pipe dream. Expectations grounded in God are the means for preparing the inner person for radical reform. Hope keeps open our capacity for change. The structure of the book of Ezekiel suggests, however, that hope itself must be well grounded in a recognition of the need for change, a perception of those aspects of our behavior that are inimical to just behavior. This is why the oracles proclaiming the sinfulness of the people come in the first part of the book of Ezekiel and the oracles of proffered salvation in the latter part of the book.

Reflecting on the Word

For the third week we turn to the Gospel of John for one of the most dramatic encounters in its pages. Jesus had been sent for with an anguished message: "Master, the one you love is ill" (John 11:3). But he allowed several days to pass before he arrived in the town of Bethany, outside of Jerusalem.

We can hear both the sorrow and the anger in Martha's voice when she says, "Lord, if you had been here, my brother would not have died" (11:21). And then the hope against all hope as she continues, "But even now I know that whatever you ask of God, God will give you" (11:22). That mixture of anguish and hope in the face of death is the inheritance of any believer who has suffered the loss of a loved one. Having faith does not lessen the pain of death.

Jesus assures Martha that her brother will arise, and Martha acknowledges that will happen on the last day. Then we have one of those Johannine statements that rings as boldly now as it did when it was first heard: "I am the resurrection and the life; / whoever believes in me, even if he dies, will live, / and everyone who lives and believes in me will never die." Then the great challenge, "Do you believe this?" (11:25–26).

The God of Israel spoke through Ezekiel to a people deadened by exile far from their home: "I will open your graves and have you rise from them, and bring you back to the land of Israel" (Ezekiel 37:12). These listeners were the living dead. Jesus, son of the Father, speaks not only to Martha but to all who acknowledge him as Lord and God: "I am the resurrection and the life. . . . Do you believe this?"

CONSIDER/ DISCUSS:
- Do we believe not just that there will be life after death, not just that death will not have the final word, but that Jesus Christ is the resurrection and the life?

- Are we willing to profess that belief by renewing our baptismal vows on Easter Sunday?

- Do you believe that resurrection life started when you were baptized?

Responding to the Word

Take some time this week and read through this story of Jesus and the two sisters. Reflect on your own experience of the death of a loved one. Is there anyone who has died whom you have not handed over to the God of the living? Make that act of trust today.

April 5, 2009

PALM SUNDAY OF THE LORD'S PASSION

Today's Focus: A Sad Story, But Not Hopeless

The Passion in Mark's Gospel is the saddest of the four, unrelenting in its portrayal of abuse and abandonment. Everyone leaves Jesus, even God. Or so it seems: "My God, my God, why have you forsaken me?" are Jesus' last and only words on the cross, according to Mark 15:35. Yet even here, hope seeps through in surprising ways. That is why we wave the palms on a day when we listen to the Passion.

FIRST READING
Isaiah 50:4–7

The Lord GOD has given me
  a well-trained tongue,
that I might know how to speak to the weary
  a word that will rouse them.
Morning after morning
  he opens my ear that I may hear;
and I have not rebelled,
  have not turned back.
I gave my back to those who beat me,
  my cheeks to those who plucked my beard;
my face I did not shield
  from buffets and spitting.

The Lord GOD is my help,
  therefore I am not disgraced;
I have set my face like flint,
  knowing that I shall not be put to shame.

PSALM RESPONSE
Psalm 22:2a

My God, my God, why have you abandoned me?

SECOND READING
Philippians 2: 6–11

Christ Jesus, though he was in the form of God,
  did not regard equality with God
  something to be grasped.
Rather, he emptied himself,
  taking the form of a slave,
  coming in human likeness;
  and found human in appearance,
  he humbled himself,
  becoming obedient to the point of death,
  even death on a cross.
Because of this, God greatly exalted him
  and bestowed on him the name
  which is above every name,
  that at the name of Jesus
  every knee should bend,
  of those in heaven and on earth and under the earth,
  and every tongue confess that
  Jesus Christ is Lord,
  to the glory of God the Father.

GOSPEL
Mark
14:1 — 15:47
or 15:1–39

[The Passover and the Feast of Unleavened Bread were to take place in two days' time. So the chief priests and the scribes were seeking a way to arrest him by treachery and put him to death. They said, "Not during the festival, for fear that there may be a riot among the people."

When he was in Bethany reclining at table in the house of Simon the leper, a woman came with an alabaster jar of perfumed oil, costly genuine spikenard. She broke the alabaster jar and poured it on his head. There were some who were indignant. "Why has there been this waste of perfumed oil? It could have been sold for more than three hundred days' wages and the money given to the poor." They were infuriated with her. Jesus said, "Let her alone. Why do you make trouble for her? She has done a good thing for me. The poor you will always have with you, and whenever you wish you can do good to them, but you will not always have me. She has done what she could. She has anticipated anointing my body for burial. Amen, I say to you, wherever the gospel is proclaimed to the whole world, what she has done will be told in memory of her."

Then Judas Iscariot, one of the Twelve, went off to the chief priests to hand him over to them. When they heard him they were pleased and promised to pay him money. Then he looked for an opportunity to hand him over.

On the first day of the Feast of Unleavened Bread, when they sacrificed the Passover lamb, his disciples said to him, "Where do you want us to go and prepare for you to eat the Passover?" He sent two of his disciples and said to them, "Go into the city and a man will meet you, carrying a jar of water. Follow him. Wherever he enters, say to the master of the house, 'The Teacher says, "Where is my guest room where I may eat the Passover with my disciples?"' Then he will show you a large upper room furnished and ready. Make the preparations for us there." The disciples then went off, entered the city, and found it just as he had told them; and they prepared the Passover.

When it was evening, he came with the Twelve. And as they reclined at table and were eating, Jesus said, "Amen, I say to you, one of you will betray me, one who is eating with me." They began to be distressed and to say to him, one by one, "Surely it is not I?" He said to them, "One of the Twelve, the one who dips with me into the dish. For the Son of Man indeed goes, as it is written of him, but woe to that man by whom the Son of Man is betrayed. It would be better for that man if he had never been born."

While they were eating, he took bread, said the blessing, broke it, and gave it to them, and said, "Take it; this is my body." Then he took a cup, gave thanks, and gave it to them, and they all drank from it. He said to them, "This is my blood of the covenant, which will be shed for many. Amen, I say to you, I shall not drink again the fruit of the vine until the day when I drink it new in the kingdom of God." Then, after singing a hymn, they went out to the Mount of Olives.

Then Jesus said to them, "All of you will have your faith shaken, for it is written:

> I will strike the shepherd,
>   and the sheep will be dispersed.

But after I have been raised up, I shall go before you to Galilee." Peter said to him, "Even though all should have their faith shaken, mine will not be." Then Jesus said to him, "Amen, I say to you, this very night before the cock crows twice you will deny me three times." But he vehemently replied, "Even though I should have to die with you, I will not deny you." And they all spoke similarly.

Then they came to a place named Gethsemane, and he said to his disciples, "Sit here while I pray." He took with him Peter, James, and John, and began to be troubled and distressed. Then he said to them, "My soul is sorrowful even to death. Remain here and keep watch." He advanced a little and fell to the ground and prayed that if it were possible the hour might pass by him; he said, "Abba, Father, all things are possible to you. Take this cup away from me, but not what I will but what you will." When he returned he found them asleep. He said to Peter, "Simon, are you asleep? Could you not keep watch for one hour? Watch and pray that you may not undergo the test. The spirit is willing but the flesh is weak." Withdrawing again, he prayed, saying the same thing. Then he returned once more and found them asleep, for they could not keep their eyes open and did not know what to answer him. He returned a third time and said to them, "Are you still sleeping and taking your rest? It is enough. The hour has come. Behold, the Son of Man is to be handed over to sinners. Get up, let us go. See, my betrayer is at hand."

Then, while he was still speaking, Judas, one of the Twelve, arrived, accompanied by a crowd with swords and clubs who had come from the chief priests, the scribes, and the elders. His betrayer had arranged a signal with them, saying, "The man I shall kiss is the one; arrest him and lead him away securely." He came and immediately went over to him and said, "Rabbi." And he kissed him. At this they laid hands on him and arrested him. One of the bystanders drew his sword, struck the high priest's servant, and cut off his ear. Jesus said to them in reply, "Have you come out as against a robber, with swords and clubs, to seize me? Day after day I was with you teaching in the temple area, yet you did not arrest me; but that the Scriptures may be fulfilled." And they all left him and fled. Now a young man followed him wearing nothing but a linen cloth about his body. They seized him, but he left the cloth behind and ran off naked.

They led Jesus away to the high priest, and all the chief priests and the elders and the scribes came together. Peter followed him at a distance into the high priest's courtyard and was seated with the guards, warming himself at the fire. The chief priests and the entire Sanhedrin kept trying to obtain testimony against Jesus in order to put him to death, but they found none. Many gave false witness against him, but their testimony did not agree. Some took the stand and testified falsely against him, alleging, "We heard him say, 'I will destroy this temple made with hands and within three days I will build another not made with hands.'" Even so their testimony did not agree. The high priest rose before the assembly and questioned Jesus, saying, "Have you no answer? What are these men testifying against you?" But he was silent and answered nothing. Again the high priest asked him and said to him, "Are you the Christ, the son of the Blessed One?" Then Jesus answered, "I am;

and 'you will see the Son of Man
    seated at the right hand of the Power
    and coming with the clouds of heaven.'"

At that the high priest tore his garments and said, "What further need have we of witnesses? You have heard the blasphemy. What do you think?" They all condemned him as deserving to die. Some began to spit on him. They blindfolded him and struck him and said to him, "Prophesy!" And the guards greeted him with blows.

While Peter was below in the courtyard, one of the high priest's maids came along. Seeing Peter warming himself, she looked intently at him and said, "You too were with the Nazarene, Jesus." But he denied it saying, "I neither know nor understand what you are talking about." So he went out into the outer court. Then the cock crowed. The maid saw him and began again to say to the bystanders, "This man is one of them." Once again he denied it. A little later the bystanders said to Peter once more, "Surely you are one of them; for you too are a Galilean." He began to curse and to swear, "I do not know this man about whom you are talking." And immediately a cock crowed a second time. Then Peter remembered the word that Jesus had said to him, "Before the cock crows twice you will deny me three times." He broke down and wept.]

As soon as morning came, the chief priests with the elders and the scribes, that is, the whole Sanhedrin, held a council. They bound Jesus, led him away, and handed him over to Pilate. Pilate questioned him, "Are you the king of the Jews?" He said to him in reply, "You say so." The chief priests accused him of many things. Again Pilate questioned him, "Have you no answer? See how many things they accuse you of." Jesus gave him no further answer, so that Pilate was amazed.

Now on the occasion of the feast he used to release to them one prisoner whom they requested. A man called Barabbas was then in prison along with the rebels who had committed murder in a rebellion. The crowd came forward and began to ask him to do for them as he was accustomed. Pilate answered, "Do you want me to release to you the king of the Jews?" For he knew that it was out of envy that the chief priests had handed him over. But the chief priests stirred up the crowd to have him release Barabbas for them instead. Pilate again said to them in reply, "Then what do you want me to do with the man you call the king of the Jews?" They shouted again, "Crucify him." Pilate said to them, "Why? What evil has he done?" They only shouted the louder, "Crucify him." So Pilate, wishing to satisfy the crowd, released Barabbas to them and, after he had Jesus scourged, handed him over to be crucified.

The soldiers led him away inside the palace, that is, the praetorium, and assembled the whole cohort. They clothed him in purple and, weaving a crown of thorns, placed it on him. They began to salute him with, "Hail, King of the Jews!" and kept striking his head with a reed and spitting upon him. They knelt before him in homage. And when they had mocked him, they stripped him of the purple cloak, dressed him in his own clothes, and led him out to crucify him.

They pressed into service a passer-by, Simon, a Cyrenian, who was coming in from the country, the father of Alexander and Rufus, to carry his cross.

They brought him to the place of Golgotha—which is translated Place of the Skull—. They gave him wine drugged with myrrh, but he did not take it. Then they crucified him and divided his garments by casting lots for them to see what each should take. It was nine o'clock in the morning when they crucified him. The inscription of the charge against him read, "The King of the Jews." With him they crucified two revolutionaries, one on his right and one on his left. Those passing by reviled him, shaking their heads and saying, "Aha! You who would destroy the temple and rebuild it in three days, save yourself by coming down from the cross." Likewise the chief priests, with the scribes, mocked him among themselves and said, "He saved others; he cannot save himself. Let the Christ, the King of Israel, come down now from the cross that we may see and believe." Those who were crucified with him also kept abusing him.

At noon darkness came over the whole land until three in the afternoon. And at three o'clock Jesus cried out in a loud voice, "Eloi, Eloi, lema sabachthani?" which is translated, "My God, my God, why have you forsaken me?" Some of the bystanders who heard it said, "Look, he is calling Elijah." One of them ran, soaked a sponge with wine, put it on a reed and gave it to him to drink, saying, "Wait, let us see if Elijah comes to take him down." Jesus gave a loud cry and breathed his last.

The veil of the sanctuary was torn in two from top to bottom. When the centurion who stood facing him saw how he breathed his last he said, "Truly this man was the Son of God!" [There were also women looking on from a distance. Among them were Mary Magdalene, Mary the mother of the younger James and of Joses, and Salome. These women had followed him when he was in Galilee and ministered to him. There were also many other women who had come up with him to Jerusalem.

When it was already evening, since it was the day of preparation, the day before the sabbath, Joseph of Arimathea, a distinguished member of the council, who was himself awaiting the kingdom of God, came and courageously went to Pilate and asked for the body of Jesus. Pilate was amazed that he was already dead. He summoned the centurion and asked him if Jesus had already died. And when he learned of it from the centurion, he gave the body to Joseph. Having bought a linen cloth, he took him down, wrapped him in the linen cloth, and laid him in a tomb that had been hewn out of the rock. Then he rolled a stone against the entrance to the tomb. Mary Magdalene and Mary the mother of Joses watched where he was laid.]

Understanding the Word

The processional reading and the Gospel reading today together express the idea in the Gospel of Mark that Jesus takes pains to ensure that his message will be received as he intends it to be heard. His elaborate plans are attempts to secure a hearing of the divine word unfiltered by our preconceptions and expectations.

Thus, in the processional reading Jesus tells two of his disciples where they will find a colt in Jerusalem, and that should anyone question their taking it they are to respond, "The Master has need of it" (Mark 11:1–3). The idea is that Jesus has arranged with someone in Jerusalem to place the colt at a certain location. By way of contrast, although Jesus gives basically the same instructions in the Gospel of Luke, it is the owners themselves who question why their colt is being taken (Luke 19:33). One should not be surprised that the Markan Jesus arranged this secret plan upon entering Jerusalem because he has been especially accustomed to the necessity for secrecy from the beginning of his ministry, when the failure to observe secrecy led to his being unable to "enter a town openly" (Mark 1:45).

The same secret arrangement for his entering Jerusalem occurs again in today's Gospel reading. When Jesus, who has gone to Bethany, plans to reenter Jerusalem, he again tells two disciples to go into the city, where they will meet a man carrying a water jar. This man will take them to a householder who will know what they mean when they say to him, "The Teacher says, 'Where is my guest room where I may eat the Passover with my disciples?' " (14:14).

The reason for these precautions is to give the message a chance to be expressed and heard accurately. People's preconceptions about what the message should be necessitate such secrecy. Thus, upon entering Jerusalem the first time the people incorrectly expect Jesus to bring back the Davidic kingdom (11:10). The specific reason for the secrecy upon entering Jerusalem the second time was Judas' arrangement to betray Jesus, an account that immediately precedes the second entry (14:10–11).

Our steadfast adherence to our own ideas of what salvation entails may be influenced by cultural conceptions that obstruct the true content of the salvific message. The Jesus of Mark's Gospel wants to help us overcome such obstacles.

The Passion in Mark begins with a conspiracy, a scene foreshadowing Jesus' death, and then a promise of betrayal: "He looked for an opportunity to hand him over" (Mark 14:11). The story of the Passion then moves swiftly from the Last Supper to the arrest in Gethsemane to the trials before religious and civil authorities to the execution, and finally, to Jesus being laid in a stranger's grave, a large stone rolled in front of the tomb, and two of his followers "watched where he was laid" (15:47). Even in death, no loving hand can touch him.

The Passion is a story of total abandonment. The disciples first fall asleep while Jesus prays; Judas betrays him with a kiss, the perversion of that intimate sign of love, and the disciples flee; Peter denies ever having known the man; the chief priests and the ruling body, the Sanhedrin, put up false witnesses against him; Pilate, knowing the charges were trumped up, caves in to the rabble, releasing a notorious prisoner; the soldiers mock, spit upon, and strike him, and, once crucified, even the two crucified with him revile him along with all those passing by. Jesus' final words ring down through the centuries: "My God, my God, why have you forsaken me?" (15:35). The story is one of unrelenting cruelty, dishonesty, abuse of power, failure of those who knew better, and silence on the part of the One who could have done something. No one gets off the hook in Mark's Gospel.

CONSIDER/ DISCUSS: And yet . . . there is that tear in the veil of the Temple, signaling a new access. And a centurion and his men who whispered, "Truly this man was the Son of God!" (15:39).

- What was it that brought these words forth?
- Do we continue to accept them as the truth?
- Why are you taking that piece of palm home—wall decoration or declaration of faith?

Responding to the Word

Read the story aloud. Listen to it carefully. Stop and pray when the Spirit moves you. Let the Passion of Mark put its mark on your soul and move you to . . . wonder, faith, hope, love . . .

Notes

The Easter readings from the period of the Resurrection through Pentecost invite us to reflect on how we Christians may share in the divine life that leads to resurrection and living in the Spirit. The reading from Mark's Gospel for Easter Sunday stresses that the human concern for power is an obstacle to attaining resurrected life. The resurrected power operates through the participation in weakness and in suffering before leading to glory. Weakness, however, is antithetical to the perceived experiences of power in the world. Therefore, the Gospel of Mark portrays both a different path to the ultimate manifestation of divine power and a shocking original ending to this Gospel, which warns against letting the culturally sanctioned perceptions of authority blur the recognition of the way divine power operates.

The First Letter of John, proclaimed throughout the Sundays of the Easter season, stresses the way that the divine life that raised Jesus may continue to be operative in the world through individual Christians. The love that characterizes the divine life is an expansive reality that flows through the world when Christians exhibit a correct perception of the One whose life they share and a generous response to those in need.

The reading from the Acts of the Apostles on the third Sunday of Easter focuses on another type of human behavior that is necessary for Christians to be good witnesses to the Resurrection: the willingness to proclaim the divine life where we can do the most good. This reading is part of a larger Lukan concern that no place be impermeable, by means of opposition to the word of God, to having this word spoken there. Christians must exhibit the fortitude to speak no matter what the costs.

The Gospel for the Fourth Sunday of Easter is part of the Good Shepherd discourse in the Gospel of John. If the previous three Sunday readings have asked Christians to manifest behavior that enables them to be means through which the divine life continually reveals itself, the Gospel reading today assures Christians of who God is for them when they themselves are in difficulties.

The readings from the Fifth Sunday of Easter through Pentecost highlight the continual presence of God to us and how we receive this presence. Thus, the Gospels from John 15 and John 17 on the Fifth, Sixth, and Seventh Sundays of Easter stress the necessity to remain part of the divine life through continuing in the love that characterizes it, as expressed in the Johannine perspective on that divine love. The readings heard on the celebrations of the Ascension of the Lord and Pentecost Sunday convey that the movement of Jesus away from us is always accompanied by a concomitant powerful presence with us.

April 12, 2009

EASTER SUNDAY
THE RESURRECTION OF THE LORD

Today's Focus: Looking with Easter Eyes

All the Easter stories proclaim that Christ is risen. Matthew, Mark, and Luke offer us angels or men dressed in dazzling white, and even the risen Christ on occasion. John is more subtle. He places one sign before us, but you have to have Easter eyes, the eyes of faith, to "get" the message.

FIRST READING
Acts 10:34a, 37–43

Peter proceeded to speak and said: "You know what has happened all over Judea, beginning in Galilee after the baptism that John preached, how God anointed Jesus of Nazareth with the Holy Spirit and power. He went about doing good and healing all those oppressed by the devil, for God was with him. We are witnesses of all that he did both in the country of the Jews and in Jerusalem. They put him to death by hanging him on a tree. This man God raised on the third day and granted that he be visible, not to all the people, but to us, the witnesses chosen by God in advance, who ate and drank with him after he rose from the dead. He commissioned us to preach to the people and testify that he is the one appointed by God as judge of the living and the dead. To him all the prophets bear witness, that everyone who believes in him will receive forgiveness of sins through his name.

PSALM RESPONSE
Psalm 118:24

This is the day the Lord has made; let us rejoice and be glad.

SECOND READING
Colossians 3:1–4

Brothers and sisters: If then you were raised with Christ, seek what is above, where Christ is seated at the right hand of God. Think of what is above, not of what is on earth. For you have died, and your life is hidden with Christ in God. When Christ your life appears, then you too will appear with him in glory.

– or –

1 Corinthians 5:6b–8

Brothers and sisters: Do you not know that a little yeast leavens all the dough? Clear out the old yeast, so that you may become a fresh batch of dough, inasmuch as you are unleavened. For our paschal lamb, Christ, has been sacrificed. Therefore, let us celebrate the feast, not with the old yeast, the yeast of malice and wickedness, but with the unleavened bread of sincerity and truth.

GOSPEL
John 20:1–9

On the first day of the week, Mary of Magdala came to the tomb early in the morning, while it was still dark, and saw the stone removed from the tomb. So she ran and went to Simon Peter and to the other disciple whom Jesus loved, and told them, "They have taken the Lord from the tomb, and we don't know where they put him." So Peter and the other disciple went out and came to the tomb. They both ran, but the other disciple ran faster than Peter and arrived at the tomb first; he bent down and saw the burial cloths there, but did not go in. When Simon Peter arrived after him, he went into the tomb and saw the burial cloths there, and the cloth that had covered his head, not with the burial cloths but rolled up in a separate place. Then the other disciple also went in, the one who had arrived at the tomb first, and he saw and believed. For they did not yet understand the Scripture that he had to rise from the dead.

– or –

Mark 16:1–7

When the sabbath was over, Mary Magdalene, Mary, the mother of James, and Salome bought spices so that they might go and anoint him. Very early when the sun had risen, on the first day of the week, they came to the tomb. They were saying to one another, "Who will roll back the stone for us from the entrance to the tomb?" When they looked up, they saw that the stone had been rolled back; it was very large. On entering the tomb they saw a young man sitting on the right side, clothed in a white robe, and they were utterly amazed. He said to them, "Do not be amazed! You seek Jesus of Nazareth, the crucified. He has been raised; he is not here. Behold the place where they laid him. But go and tell his disciples and Peter, 'He is going before you to Galilee; there you will see him, as he told you.' "

Understanding the Word

The alternate Gospel reading today, also used as the Gospel reading at the Easter Vigil, is from the original ending of the Gospel of Mark (16:1–8). In this ending there is no account of the women who were at the tomb spreading the message of Jesus' resurrection. They hear it from a young man "clothed in a white robe," and they are enjoined by this man to tell the disciples that the risen Lord will meet them in Galilee. But out of fear "[t]hey said nothing to anyone" (16:8). (This last verse is not included in the passage chosen for proclamation on Easter.)

People are much more accustomed to hearing Gospels—including the Gospel of Mark with its "longer ending" added to it (16:9–20)—end with the announcement of the Resurrection and actual Resurrection appearances.

This is not the only time that Mark writes about fear standing between people and Jesus. When the Gerasenes see that Jesus has healed the man possessed by demons, they are afraid and ask Jesus to depart from them (5:16–17). The power of Jesus is something that overwhelms them, as is the case also with the women at the tomb.

The experience of Jesus' power has overwhelmed others in this Gospel. It is Mark who writes that a leper's announcement of his healing leads people to so throng Jesus as to make it impossible for him to enter towns openly (1:45). Later Mark will structure a large section of his Gospel around three foretellings by Jesus of his passion and death, the consequent inability of his own disciples to understand these sayings, and their opting instead for positions of power rather than weakness (8:27 — 10:45).

Perhaps the hold that power in this world has on the human psyche leads people away from the experience of a greater power that operates first through suffering but ultimately through resurrection.

Reflecting on the Word

Today's reading from John's Gospel offers us three different witnesses to the Resurrection. Mary Magdalene arrives at the tomb and sees it is empty, but concludes that somebody stole the body. Peter and the beloved disciple run to the tomb. When Peter gets there he looks in and sees the burial cloths, but we are not told anything further, only that the "other disciple"—who had outraced Simon Peter but waited so he could enter first—"saw and believed" (John 20:8).

What did he see? What did he believe? It is something like a detective story. When that other disciple first arrived, scripture says he poked his head in and saw the burial cloths there, but did not go in. Only later, after Simon Peter had gone in, did the other disciple go in and see what Simon Peter had seen but apparently had left little impression: "the cloth that had covered his head, not with the burial cloths but rolled up in a separate place" (20:7).

Remember, the Gospel of John is a Gospel of signs. All the miracles Jesus performed were a series of signs: water turned to wine, a blind man given sight, a multitude fed with little food. What is the sign here? The head cloth, lying folded, in a separate place. The beloved disciple did not see it until he entered the tomb. The cloth goes back to Moses, whose face would shine after speaking face to face with God. When he left God's presence, others were afraid to come near him, so he covered his face with a cloth. Jesus had put on a veil of flesh, concealing his divinity. Now, no veil was needed. He had returned to the Father. The beloved disciple read the sign; he had begun to see with Easter eyes.

CONSIDER/ DISCUSS:
- Do you see with Easter eyes?
- What signs of Resurrection life have you noticed today?
- Is there anything that prevents you from seeing with the eyes of faith?

Responding to the Word

To see with Easter eyes means to look at all God's children as being just that, to recognize the world as entrusted to our care, and most of all, to live in the awareness that the risen Christ is with us even now. Let us pray for the gift of Easter eyes.

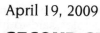

April 19, 2009

SECOND SUNDAY OF EASTER

Today's Focus: Getting in Touch with Faith Means
Living in Love

On Easter we renewed our baptismal profession of faith in Jesus Christ as the risen crucified Lord, the Son of God. The fifty days after Easter continue the work of allowing our faith to penetrate our lives more deeply, reminding us how the risen Lord continues to work in and through us as individuals and as a community that believes.

FIRST READING
Acts 4:32–35

The community of believers was of one heart and mind, and no one claimed that any of his possessions was his own, but they had everything in common. With great power the apostles bore witness to the resurrection of the Lord Jesus, and great favor was accorded them all. There was no needy person among them, for those who owned property or houses would sell them, bring the proceeds of the sale, and put them at the feet of the apostles, and they were distributed to each according to need.

PSALM RESPONSE
Psalm 118:1

Give thanks to the Lord for he is good, his love is everlasting.

SECOND READING
1 John 5:1–6

Beloved: Everyone who believes that Jesus is the Christ is begotten by God, and everyone who loves the Father loves also the one begotten by him. In this way we know that we love the children of God when we love God and obey his commandments. For the love of God is this, that we keep his commandments. And his commandments are not burdensome, for whoever is begotten by God conquers the world. And the victory that conquers the world is our faith. Who indeed is the victor over the world but the one who believes that Jesus is the Son of God?

This is the one who came through water and blood, Jesus Christ, not by water alone, but by water and blood. The Spirit is the one that testifies, and the Spirit is truth.

GOSPEL
John 20:19–31

On the evening of that first day of the week, when the doors were locked, where the disciples were, for fear of the Jews, Jesus came and stood in their midst and said to them, "Peace be with you." When he had said this, he showed them his hands and his side. The disciples rejoiced when they saw the Lord. Jesus said to them again, "Peace be with you. As the Father has sent me, so I send you." And when he had said this, he breathed on them and said to them, "Receive the Holy Spirit. Whose sins you forgive are forgiven them, and whose sins you retain are retained."

Thomas, called Didymus, one of the Twelve, was not with them when Jesus came. So the other disciples said to him, "We have seen the Lord." But he said to them, "Unless I see the mark of the nails in his hands and put my finger into the nailmarks and put my hand into his side, I will not believe."

Now a week later his disciples were again inside and Thomas was with them. Jesus came, although the doors were locked, and stood in their midst and said, "Peace be with you." Then he said to Thomas, "Put your finger here and see my hands, and bring your hand and put it into my side, and do not be unbelieving, but believe." Thomas answered and said to him, "My Lord and my God!" Jesus said to him, "Have you come to believe because you have seen me? Blessed are those who have not seen and have believed."

Now Jesus did many other signs in the presence of his disciples that are not written in this book. But these are written that you may come to believe that Jesus is the Christ, the Son of God, and that through this belief you may have life in his name.

Understanding the Word

The second reading today is from the First Letter of John. In it the writer speaks about how the overcoming of the world that was made possible through Jesus' resurrection becomes a daily reality in the lives of Christians.

The divine life has been given to us through Jesus Christ (1 John 5:1; 1:3). The divine life is one of immense love. This is the love by which the Father sent the only-begotten Son "as an expiation for our sins" (4:10). This great act of love is meant to be an inspiration for our love of others (4:11). In fact, one of the two tests of whether we are part of the divine family is whether we share the characteristic divine family life, which is love (4:7–8; 3:9). It is this type of life that brings light to the world (2:7–11). But First John is very specific about what a loving life entails. It means providing practical help to those who are in need (3:17–18). Love expresses itself in generosity where there is lack. Such love enables our continuation in and spreading of the divine life. The practical result in terms of prayer is that those who live in such a way can be confident in their prayer, which is heard and answered (3:22; 5:13–15). The underlying image seems to be that of one who remains in the family by living the type of life the family lives and so is in position to receive the benefits of family life.

The second test of whether one is part of the divine family is a proper recognition of family members. Concretely, this entails an acknowledgment that Jesus came from God and took on a fleshly human existence (3:23; 4:2–3). It is this belief in the incarnation of Jesus that proclaims the extent of God's love for us as expressed through Jesus' death.

How, for First John, is resurrected life manifested in a daily conquering of the world? Through the belief and love that profess, continue, and spread the divine life that wishes to course through us toward resurrection.

Reflecting on the Word

God's word calls us to be a community whose faith is visible. Though the presentation in Acts is a rather idealized one, living together united in heart and mind and sharing what we have challenges all Christian communities to greater generosity and a more profound unity. We have a long way to go to achieve this. Anyone looking at the Christian churches from the outside can see groups divided not only into various denominations, but into bickering factions within the same denomination.

The First Letter of John reminds us that the basis for living in unity is to be found within the heart of each person: our belief that Jesus is the Christ, the Son of God. Such faith in Jesus draws us into the communion of the Son with the Father and the Holy Spirit, and then into living together in love. Love is the fruit of faith in Jesus, uniting us into a family of faith and love. If love is not to be found, is faith really present?

Thomas exemplifies someone who came to be united with the community through his coming to faith in Jesus. It is instructive that the community of apostles gave him the time to come to faith. Indeed, Jesus gave him the time to come to faith, even offering to meet Thomas' requirements of touching his wounds and putting his hand into his side. We don't know if Thomas did this or not; we do know by his acclamation that Thomas was moved to faith: "My Lord and my God!" (John 20:28). Growing in faith then flows into living in love.

CONSIDER/ DISCUSS:
- How has God given you time to "see," shown patience to you?
- What does it mean for you to say, "My Lord and my God"?
- How does this confession of faith carry over into a life of loving service in the world?

Responding to the Word

Consider what it means to proclaim before others that Jesus is "My Lord and my God." Make that your prayer today. Use it as a mantra throughout the day, repeating it often when the opportunity allows. Let the words carry you into the heart of the risen Lord.

109

April 26, 2009

THIRD SUNDAY OF EASTER

Today's Focus: Is That You?

What does it take to recognize Jesus? In the Easter stories, the followers of Jesus are too caught up in the past to see the present and what it brings. What Jesus Christ does in these Resurrection stories to make himself known continues to happen in our lives today—if we are attentive.

FIRST READING
Acts 3:13–15, 17–19

Peter said to the people: "The God of Abraham, the God of Isaac, and the God of Jacob, the God of our fathers, has glorified his servant Jesus, whom you handed over and denied in Pilate's presence when he had decided to release him. You denied the Holy and Righteous One and asked that a murderer be released to you. The author of life you put to death, but God raised him from the dead; of this we are witnesses. Now I know, brothers, that you acted out of ignorance, just as your leaders did; but God has thus brought to fulfillment what he had announced beforehand through the mouth of all the prophets, that his Christ would suffer. Repent, therefore, and be converted, that your sins may be wiped away."

PSALM RESPONSE
Psalm 4:7a

Lord, let your face shine on us.

SECOND READING
1 John 2:1–5a

My children, I am writing this to you so that you may not commit sin. But if anyone does sin, we have an Advocate with the Father, Jesus Christ the righteous one. He is expiation for our sins, and not for our sins only but for those of the whole world. The way we may be sure that we know him is to keep his commandments. Those who say, "I know him," but do not keep his commandments are liars, and the truth is not in them. But whoever keeps his word, the love of God is truly perfected in him.

GOSPEL
Luke 24:35–48

The two disciples recounted what had taken place on the way, and how Jesus was made known to them in the breaking of bread.

While they were still speaking about this, he stood in their midst and said to them, "Peace be with you." But they were startled and terrified and thought that they were seeing a ghost. Then he said to them, "Why are you troubled? And why do questions arise in your hearts? Look at my hands and my feet, that it is I myself. Touch me and see, because a ghost does not have flesh and bones as you can see I have." And as he said this, he showed them his hands and his feet. While they were still incredulous for joy and were amazed, he asked them, "Have you anything here to eat?" They gave him a piece of baked fish; he took it and ate it in front of them.

He said to them, "These are my words that I spoke to you while I was still with you, that everything written about me in the law of Moses and in the prophets and psalms must be fulfilled." Then he opened their minds to understand the Scriptures. And he said to them, "Thus it is written that the Christ would suffer and rise from the dead on the third day and that repentance, for the forgiveness of sins, would be preached in his name to all the nations, beginning from Jerusalem. You are witnesses of these things."

Understanding the Word

In today's reading from the Acts of the Apostles, Luke develops the theme of the need for courageous witness where such witness can do the most good. The passage contains a portion of the preaching of Peter to a crowd following the healing of a lame man. It is the location of the healing and subsequent witness that are the means through which the Lukan theme unfolds.

Both occur in the temple, a feature that is significant when considered in conjunction with the Lukan portrayal of Jesus in Jerusalem during the final days of his ministry. It is the Lukan Jesus who confines his whole ministry in Jerusalem to teaching in the temple (Luke 19:47; 20:1; 21:37–38). This is in marked contrast to other Gospels. For example, in the Gospel of Mark, during Jesus' final days in Jerusalem he teaches inside the temple, outside the temple, and outside Jerusalem on the Mount of Olives, and he performs a miracle. In Luke's Gospel the comment that "the chief priests, the scribes, and the leaders of the people, meanwhile, were seeking to put him to death" comes after the distinctly Lukan notice that "every day [Jesus] was teaching in the temple area," suggesting that it was this activity of Jesus in this place that provoked their plan (19:47).

The apostles continue this focused ministry of Jesus. It is in Luke-Acts that Jesus twice commands the apostles to wait in Jerusalem for the Holy Spirit (Luke 24:49; Acts 1:4–5). When the Spirit does come to them the first thing they do is preach in Jerusalem (Acts 2:36). In today's passage they move into the temple and teach and preach. This is a return to the place and the action in this place that precipitated Jesus' death.

The temple is where the message will be able to reach the most people. By presenting the apostles as mirroring Jesus' ministry in this locale, Luke portrays the necessity for courage in going where the most can be done.

Resurrection stories do not start out on a happy note. People are either consumed by grief, as we find with the weeping Magdalene; or they are locked away in fear, as the apostles were in the upper room, cowering behind bolted doors; or they are imprisoned in their doubt, as Thomas was for a full week after Jesus had appeared to the others; or they are going back home in a downcast and hopeless state, like the two disciples on the road to Emmaus.

And when Jesus does make an appearance, they don't recognize him. Magdalene thinks he is the gardener, the two on the road to Emmaus relate to him as a stranger, and today the apostles think he is a ghost and are terrified. It is instructive to remember what it is that allows them to make the connection: for Magdalene it is his calling her name; for the twelve in the upper room on Easter evening it is his greeting of peace and his showing his hands and his side—and this holds for Thomas a week later; for the two on the road, it is the breaking of the bread; and here in today's Gospel it is his showing his wounds and then his eating with them.

A certain pattern emerges concerning where the risen Lord was first recognized and where he continues to be found in our own day. It happens when his voice is heard and his words are apprehended, as well as at the table where the community gathers to eat. We continue to meet the risen Lord when we come to hear God's living word address us in the scriptures, and we continue to know his touch when we eat the bread of life and drink from the cup of salvation.

CONSIDER/ DISCUSS:
- Have you met Jesus Christ at either table recently—at the table of the word or the table of the Eucharist?
- Have you met him in his body, the Church?
- Have you met him in other places in your life?

■ *Responding to the Word*

Let us pray to the Lord to open our eyes that we may see with Easter eyes, to open our ears to hear with Easter ears, and to open our minds to be receptive to the joy of the presence of the risen Lord.

May 3, 2009

FOURTH SUNDAY OF EASTER

Today's Focus: Jesus, Our Shepherd

The image of the Good Shepherd is at the heart of the biblical tradition. "I myself will look after and tend my sheep," the Lord God tells Ezekiel (34:11–16), expressing dismay at the religious leaders for their failure to guide Israel in the way of the law. Later Jesus takes up this same image in the Gospel of John, saying, "I am the good shepherd," and goes on to explain what that means.

FIRST READING
Acts 4:8–12

Peter, filled with the Holy Spirit, said: "Leaders of the people and elders: If we are being examined today about a good deed done to a cripple, namely, by what means he was saved, then all of you and all the people of Israel should know that it was in the name of Jesus Christ the Nazarene whom you crucified, whom God raised from the dead; in his name this man stands before you healed. He is

the stone rejected by you, the builders,
which has become the cornerstone.

There is no salvation through anyone else, nor is there any other name under heaven given to the human race by which we are to be saved."

PSALM RESPONSE
Psalm 118:22

The stone rejected by the builders has become the cornerstone.

SECOND READING
1 John 3:1–2

Beloved: See what love the Father has bestowed on us that we may be called the children of God. Yet so we are. The reason the world does not know us is that it did not know him. Beloved, we are God's children now; what we shall be has not yet been revealed. We do know that when it is revealed we shall be like him, for we shall see him as he is.

GOSPEL
John 10:11–18

Jesus said: "I am the good shepherd. A good shepherd lays down his life for the sheep. A hired man, who is not a shepherd and whose sheep are not his own, sees a wolf coming and leaves the sheep and runs away, and the wolf catches and scatters them. This is because he works for pay and has no concern for the sheep. I am the good shepherd, and I know mine and mine know me, just as the Father knows me and I know the Father; and I will lay down my life for the sheep. I have other sheep that do not belong to this fold. These also I must lead, and they will hear my voice, and there will be one flock, one shepherd. This is why the Father loves me, because I lay down my life in order to take it up again. No one takes it from me, but I lay it down on my own. I have power to lay it down, and power to take it up again. This command I have received from my Father."

Understanding the Word

The Gospel reading today is part of an extended discourse by the Johannine Jesus about how he acts toward the Johannine Christians and those who follow in their footsteps. These present and future disciples are portrayed as sheep. In the part of the discourse heard today Jesus communicates who he is to Christians who are most in need.

The image of sheep is an apt one for Christians who are being threatened with expulsion from the synagogue, because the Johannine Christians appear to be largely Jewish Christians for whom synagogue represents fellowship with their larger community (9:22; 12:42; 16:2). Ostracism is extremely difficult because humans are thoroughly social creatures. Losing the associations of a lifetime can be traumatic. This is why the image of the Johannine Christians as sheep is so appropriate.

Ethologists (scientists who study animal behavior) tell us that dogs and sheep were two of the first kinds of animals to be domesticated. This occurred thousands of years ago in the case of sheep. We are also told that sheep have lost any possibility for survival out in the wild. They have no natural defenses.

Today's Gospel reading shows who Jesus is when people are most vulnerable. Jesus meets them in their high degree of vulnerability with a higher degree of commitment to them. Four times in the course of the short nine verses of today's Gospel Jesus declares that he will lay down his life for his sheep (10: 11, 13, 17, 18). The result will be eternal life for Christians exposed to danger. The repetitions of the assurance that Jesus gives his life freely for the safety and welfare of his sheep are soothing for those in difficult situations. Some things need to be said again and again in order to provide relief from daily rebuffs.

The world most of us live in is far from the world of which Jesus speaks in today's Gospel. Few of us have ever had any contact with sheep and shepherds. A good shepherd was one who took care to lead his sheep to safe and green pastures. He would also be sure to clear the ground of thorns and be on the lookout for any nests of scorpions and snakes. He would not only bind up wounds but would bring medicinal herbs to make a drink to help heal them. The good shepherd cares for his sheep.

Jesus claims this title for himself in the Gospel of John, emphasizing in the passage we heard today three characteristics. First is his willingness to lay down his life for his sheep. These words are spoken to us by the crucified risen Lord; it is not a matter of merely hyperbolic language. Secondly, he knows his sheep and his sheep know him. And he quickly adds: "just as the Father knows me and I know the Father" (John 10:15). Jesus is the shepherd who is our mediator, our bridge leading into the presence of God the Father. Finally, the Good Shepherd is one who has sheep that do not belong to "this fold" (10:16). His love embraces all peoples.

CONSIDER/ DISCUSS:
- Does the image of Jesus as Good Shepherd speak to your life?
- Are there times when he has come searching for you when you were lost?
- Do you recognize that his love goes beyond you and yours to others you might not consider "of the fold"?

◻ *Responding to the Word*

In the First Letter of John today we are told that we are God's children now and while we don't know what we shall be in the future with any exactitude, we do know "that when it is revealed we shall be like him, for we shall see him as he is" (1 John 3:2). This must surely include seeing ourselves as shepherds also. Let us pray that we are good shepherds.

May 10, 2009

FIFTH SUNDAY OF EASTER

Today's Focus: My Father, the Vine Grower

At baptism we were grafted onto Christ, the source of life for all who believe in him, as a vine feeds its branches. This relationship with the risen Lord is so intimate that we share now in his life, a relationship that is both gift and responsibility. The will—and work—of God is that we bear fruit.

FIRST READING
Acts 9:26–31

When Saul arrived in Jerusalem he tried to join the disciples, but they were all afraid of him, not believing that he was a disciple. Then Barnabas took charge of him and brought him to the apostles, and he reported to them how he had seen the Lord, and that he had spoken to him, and how in Damascus he had spoken out boldly in the name of Jesus. He moved about freely with them in Jerusalem, and spoke out boldly in the name of the Lord. He also spoke and debated with the Hellenists, but they tried to kill him. And when the brothers learned of this, they took him down to Caesarea and sent him on his way to Tarsus.

The church throughout all Judea, Galilee, and Samaria was at peace. It was being built up and walked in the fear of the Lord, and with the consolation of the Holy Spirit it grew in numbers.

PSALM RESPONSE
Psalm 22:26a

I will praise you, Lord, in the assembly of your people.

SECOND READING
1 John 3:18–24

Children, let us love not in word or speech but in deed and truth.

Now this is how we shall know that we belong to the truth and reassure our hearts before him in whatever our hearts condemn, for God is greater than our hearts and knows everything. Beloved, if our hearts do not condemn us, we have confidence in God and receive from him whatever we ask, because we keep his commandments and do what pleases him. And his commandment is this: we should believe in the name of his Son, Jesus Christ, and love one another just as he commanded us. Those who keep his commandments remain in him, and he in them, and the way we know that he remains in us is from the Spirit he gave us.

GOSPEL
John 15:1–8 Jesus said to his disciples: "I am the true vine, and my Father is the vine grower. He takes away every branch in me that does not bear fruit, and every one that does he prunes so that it bears more fruit. You are already pruned because of the word that I spoke to you. Remain in me, as I remain in you. Just as a branch cannot bear fruit on its own unless it remains on the vine, so neither can you unless you remain in me. I am the vine, you are the branches. Whoever remains in me and I in him will bear much fruit, because without me you can do nothing. Anyone who does not remain in me will be thrown out like a branch and wither; people will gather them and throw them into a fire and they will be burned. If you remain in me and my words remain in you, ask for whatever you want and it will be done for you. By this is my Father is glorified, that you bear much fruit and become my disciples."

Understanding the Word

Today's Gospel reading is the beginning of Jesus' discourse about the vine and the branches. Its purpose is to show how effective prayer keeps the resurrected Lord and his followers in an organic living connection.

The Father is represented as the vine grower, Jesus as the vine, and Jesus' followers as the branches. The Father prunes all fruitful branches so that they will bear more fruit and casts out the unfruitful branches (John 15:1–2). So what keeps people pruned so that they may remain fruitful? Jesus' word (15:3). This word takes away what is extraneous and enables the vital sap to flow most efficiently. Jesus' exhortation in 15:4 that his followers remain rooted in him implies that we do so by remaining rooted in his word.

Why does the word of Jesus keep us fruitful? John suggests that listening to the word keeps the dialogue open between us and God and sustains the relationship. By showing Jesus repeating the instruction that we are to remain in the word, together with the claim that if we do so then whatever we ask for in prayer will be granted (15:7), John demonstrates that our relationship with God primarily involves dialogue. In other words, speaking—specifically, asking—must be grounded in listening, that is, keeping in touch with Jesus' words. The relationship is nourished by listening.

The result of this attending to the word of God (listening) in conjunction with prayer (asking) is that God is glorified by people bearing "much fruit" and so becoming Jesus' disciples (15:8). The divine life is carried on when dialogue between us and God keeps us aware of the characteristics of a godly life. If we care, we listen. If we listen, we learn. If we learn, we are incorporated into Christ, the vine. Listening shows us what matters and opens us to the life of the One to whom we listen.

Reflecting on the Word

Hearing Jesus' words, "I am the vine, you are the branches," sounds comforting at first. But then comes "and my Father is the vine grower" (John 15:1). The task of the vine grower is to prune and pruning can be tricky. The danger is cutting the main vine and not the branches, or cutting the branches that carry this year's fruit and not the old ones from last year. But Jesus tells us that it is the Father who is out there with the pruning shears, not some careless hired hand. He is cutting away the dead wood, and cutting back the good branches so they bear even more fruit.

Nevertheless, you might think, who wants to be pruned, even metaphorically? Who wants God snipping away? It's hard to be pruned. There is a dying in that. But that is the ongoing story of Easter: dying and rising, pruning and bearing more fruit. God is there pruning us to bring out life, to make us life bearers and life givers. The Father continues snipping away, separating us from our selfishness, our self-centeredness, and all those things we hold on to that do not give us life: resentments, old grievances, desires for getting even.

God is about life, committed to an abundance of life—not just life today but eternal life. That's the divine plan. Are we part of it?

CONSIDER/ DISCUSS:
- Do I see Jesus as the Vine whose life flows in me and in those who have faith in him?
- What in my life needs pruning? What needs to be cut away so that new growth can come about?
- Have I known occasions when what seemed like death has proven to open out into life?

Responding to the Word

Jesus tells us: "If you remain in me and my words remain in you, ask for whatever you want and it will be done for you" (John 15:7). Which words of his are calling you to life? Ask him to help you to trust in the Father and surrender to what the Father wills for you.

May 17, 2009

SIXTH SUNDAY OF EASTER

Today's Focus: Settling Down

Today we continue listening to what Jesus said to his disciples at the Last Supper in the Gospel of John. This is part of the longest speech Jesus gives in the New Testament. Here on the night before he dies, Jesus instructs his disciples to "remain in my love" (John 15:9). He goes on to tell us how we can do this, why we should do this, and what we will gain by doing this.

FIRST READING
Acts 10:25–26, 34–35, 44–48

When Peter entered, Cornelius met him and, falling at his feet, paid him homage. Peter, however, raised him up, saying, "Get up. I myself am also a human being."

Then Peter proceeded to speak and said, "In truth, I see that God shows no partiality. Rather, in every nation whoever fears him and acts uprightly is acceptable to him."

While Peter was still speaking these things, the Holy Spirit fell upon all who were listening to the word. The circumcised believers who had accompanied Peter were astounded that the gift of the Holy Spirit should have been poured out on the Gentiles also, for they could hear them speaking in tongues and glorifying God. Then Peter responded, "Can anyone withhold the water for baptizing these people, who have received the Holy Spirit even as we have?" He ordered them to be baptized in the name of Jesus Christ.

PSALM RESPONSE
Psalm 98:2b

The Lord has revealed to the nations his saving power.

SECOND READING
1 John 4:7–10

Beloved, let us love one another, because love is of God; everyone who loves is begotten by God and knows God. Whoever is without love does not know God, for God is love. In this way the love of God was revealed to us: God sent his only Son into the world so that we might have life through him. In this is love: not that we have loved God, but that he loved us and sent his Son as expiation for our sins.

Jesus said to his disciples: "As the Father loves me, so I also love you. Remain in my love. If you keep my commandments, you will remain in my love, just as I have kept my Father's commandments and remain in his love.

"I have told you this so that my joy may be in you and your joy might be complete. This is my commandment: love one another as I love you. No one has greater love than this, to lay down one's life for one's friends. You are my friends if you do what I command you. I no longer call you slaves, because a slave does not know what his master is doing. I have called you friends, because I have told you everything I have heard from my Father. It was not you who chose me, but I who chose you and appointed you to go and bear fruit that will remain, so that whatever you ask the Father in my name he may give you. This I command you: love one another."

Understanding the Word

The Gospel today is the second part of the vine and branches discourse, the first part of which we heard last Sunday. Then we learned that remaining in the word of Jesus is necessary in order to play an integral role in the transmission of divine life for others. The image for such a transmission is fruitfulness (15:8). Fruitfulness is also the point of today's reading, which concludes with Jesus' command "to go and bear fruit that will remain" (John 15:16).

Today we are provided with the key to understanding the word of God in which we are to remain in order to be pruned and fruitful. The word "remain" leads us to this key. Last week we were exhorted to "remain" in Jesus' word (15:3–4, 7). This week we are encouraged to "remain" in Jesus' love (15:9). Immediately we are provided with instructions on how to do so: by keeping Jesus' commandments (15:10).

Then Jesus simplifies all the commandments into one: "love one another as I love you" (15:12). The key to interpreting Jesus' words in the Gospel of John is what they show us about how to love as Jesus loves. And to sharpen the perspective for us, Jesus immediately clarifies this type of love: "No one has greater love than this, to lay down one's life for one's friends" (15:13). Thus, remaining in the word prunes us and nourishes others through us. This happens when the word about self-giving love takes root in us.

When we approach the word from the perspective of love, God's life flows through us so freely that "whatever you ask the Father in my name" the Father will give you (15:16). The lesson of John's Gospel about self-giving love is that we are to align our hearts with the attitude of Jesus, through whom God worked to such great effect.

Reflecting on the Word

As a nation, we are a mobile people. Not only do we travel around during vacations, for special events, and for visiting family and friends, but we readily move from one place to another for college, work, health reasons, and finally retirement. While previous generations usually stayed with one job and in one house for practically all of their lives, today it is common to move from one place to another, to a different state or even to a different country. This mobility carries over into our relationships. We can find that our lives take us from one set of friends to another, from one close relationship to another.

So Jesus' admonition to remain in his love can sound quite challenging to people whose lives are characterized by change and impermanence. The word "remain" is sometimes translated as "abide." The meaning of this invitation is to "take up permanent residence." Last week Jesus called us to "remain" in his word; this week, to "remain in my love" (John 15:9).

Jesus tells us how to do this (by keeping his commandments), why we should do this (so that his joy might be in us and our joy complete), what specifically we should do (love one another as I have loved you, that is, by laying down my life for you), and what is to be gained by doing this (an ongoing friendship with him that bears fruit and gains whatever we ask the Father in his name).

Not a bad exchange for settling down . . . in his love.

CONSIDER/ DISCUSS:
- How can I remain in Jesus' love by loving as he loved?
- How does this command play a part in my relationships with family, friends, spouse, children, those most in need in my world?

Responding to the Word

Sometimes we may feel that we are not particularly loving, not even capable of loving as Jesus loved. The first reading today has a wonderful moment near the end. While Peter is still preaching, the Holy Spirit falls upon those listening, even though they have not yet been baptized. God is that eager to enter our hearts and enable us to love. Ask God to help you in one particular relationship to love as Jesus loves.

May 21, 2009

THE ASCENSION OF THE LORD

Many archdioceses and dioceses celebrate the Ascension on May 24, replacing the Seventh Sunday of Easter

Today's Focus: Moving On Out

Ascension evokes the image of Jesus floating up into the clouds and the disciples looking up at the soles of his feet, rather wistfully perhaps, as he drifts farther and farther away from them. The only one moving is Jesus, and he's heading up and out. But the solemnity calls us to get moving, confident in the One who is both with us and interceding for us.

FIRST READING
Acts 1:1–11

In the first book, Theophilus, I dealt with all that Jesus did and taught until the day he was taken up, after giving instructions through the Holy Spirit to the apostles whom he had chosen. He presented himself alive to them by many proofs after he had suffered, appearing to them during forty days and speaking about the kingdom of God. While meeting with them, he enjoined them not to depart from Jerusalem, but to wait for "the promise of the Father about which you have heard me speak; for John baptized with water, but in a few days you will be baptized with the Holy Spirit."

When they had gathered together they asked him, "Lord, are you at this time going to restore the kingdom to Israel?" He answered them, "It is not for you to know the times or seasons that the Father has established by his own authority. But you will receive power when the Holy Spirit comes upon you, and you will be my witnesses in Jerusalem, throughout Judea and Samaria, and to the ends of the earth." When he had said this, as they were looking on, he was lifted up, and a cloud took him from their sight. While they were looking intently at the sky as he was going, suddenly two men dressed in white garments stood beside them. They said, "Men of Galilee, why are you standing there looking at the sky? This Jesus who has been taken up from you into heaven will return in the same way as you have seen him going into heaven."

PSALM RESPONSE
Psalm 47:6

God mounts his throne to shouts of joy: a blare of trumpets for the Lord.

Brothers and sisters: May the God of our Lord Jesus Christ, the Father of glory, give you a Spirit of wisdom and revelation resulting in knowledge of him. May the eyes of your hearts be enlightened, that you may know what is the hope that belongs to his call, what are the riches of glory in his inheritance among the holy ones, and what is the surpassing greatness of his power for us who believe, in accord with the exercise of his great might, which he worked in Christ, raising him from the dead and seating him at his right hand in the heavens, far above every principality, authority, power, and dominion, and every name that is named not only in this age but also in the one to come. And he put all things beneath his feet and gave him as head over all things to the church, which is his body, the fullness of the one who fills all things in every way.

– or –

In the shorter form of the reading, the passage in brackets is omitted.

Brothers and sisters, I, a prisoner for the Lord, urge you to live in a manner worthy of the call you have received, with all humility and gentleness, with patience, bearing with one another through love, striving to preserve the unity of the spirit through the bond of peace: one body and one Spirit, as you were also called to the one hope of your calling; one Lord, one faith, one baptism; one God and Father of all, who is over all and through all and in all.

But grace was given to each of us according to the measure of Christ's gift. [Therefore, it says:

He *ascended on high and took prisoners captive;*
he gave gifts to men.

What does "he ascended" mean except that he also descended into the lower regions of the earth? The one who descended is also the one who ascended far above all the heavens, that he might fill all things.]

And he gave some as apostles, others as prophets, others as evangelists, others as pastors and teachers, to equip the holy ones for the work of ministry, for building up the body of Christ, until we all attain to the unity of faith and knowledge of the Son of God, to mature manhood, to the extent of the full stature of Christ.

Jesus said to his disciples: "Go into the whole world and proclaim the gospel to every creature. Whoever believes and is baptized will be saved; whoever does not believe will be condemned. These signs will accompany those who believe: in my name they will drive out demons, they will speak new languages. They will pick up serpents with their hands, and if they drink any deadly thing, it will not harm them. They will lay hands on the sick, and they will recover."

So then the Lord Jesus, after he spoke to them, was taken up into heaven and took his seat at the right hand of God. But they went forth and preached everywhere, while the Lord worked with them and confirmed the word through accompanying signs.

Understanding the Word

The first reading today is the account of the Ascension at the very beginning of the Acts of the Apostles, in which Jesus redirects the expectations of his disciples about how God's power is expressed in the world.

For forty days Jesus has been speaking to them about the kingdom of God (Acts 1:3). In conjunction with this teaching, he has enjoined them not to leave Jerusalem but to wait there for a baptism with the Holy Spirit (1:4–5).

The disciples have interpreted this speech of Jesus in terms of a restoration of "the kingdom to Israel." So they ask him if this is the time in which this kingdom will be restored (1:6). He replies that it is not for them to know "times or seasons." Rather, they are to concentrate on being witnesses throughout the earth when the Spirit comes upon them (1:7–8). This Spirit will give them a power, but one that is to be used for witness, not for restoring a Jewish kingdom. As Richard Dillon notes in his article on this section of Acts in the *Jerome Biblical Commentary*, the Spirit will send them out throughout the world to others rather than have them focus on the kingdom in Israel.

"Kingdom" in the phrase "kingdom of God" is a very active concept conveyed by the word "reign." It designates God's active power. After hearing so much about this power during the forty days in which the resurrected Lord appeared *to* them, Jesus' disciples conceived of it in terms of what would be manifested *for* them. In today's passage, however, the Lord reconfigures their understanding of the power of God's reign as something operative principally *through* them.

Given this perspective on divine power, the passage concludes with two men in white exhorting Jesus' followers to stop staring into the heavens (1:11). They have to prepare to do something for others rather than await what will happen to themselves.

Reflecting on the Word

Most dioceses in the United States have moved the solemnity of the Ascension from Thursday to Sunday. Too many American Catholics were missing an important celebration in the Church year. Observing the feast forty days after Easter is not central to the celebration. Only Luke has Jesus ascending to heaven forty days after his resurrection. Matthew has an ascension but doesn't indicate when, only where: in Galilee; and John has Jesus ascending immediately on Easter Sunday after speaking to Mary Magdalene and before appearing to the apostles. Mark puts his ascension right on Easter Sunday night after he appears to the Eleven.

What is important for us and common to all four events is the point that the risen Lord sent out his disciples to preach the gospel right before he ascended. In Mark's Gospel today we hear him say, "Go into the whole world and proclaim the gospel to every creature" (Mark 16:15). I am reminded of those Westerns in which a wagon train is traveling across the country. Early each morning, the cry would come, "Move on out!" Our annual celebration of the Ascension reminds us once again that we are called to "move on out."

The Ascension is an important part of the story of a new creation that began with Jesus' death and resurrection. These events signaled a new era. The Ascension advances that story by telling us that Jesus ascended to the Father where he now intercedes for us. But not only that! As Mark reminds us in the final words of his Gospel, "they went forth and preached everywhere, while the Lord worked with them" (Mark 16:20). This presence of the Lord remains with us to this day when we proclaim the gospel through our words and deeds.

So as Luke's angels said two millennia ago, "Why are you standing there looking at the sky?" (Acts 1:11). Move on out. There is work to be done.

CONSIDER/
DISCUSS:
- Do you think of the feast of the Ascension as Jesus leaving us on our own?
- Does the feast challenge all of us to find new ways to bring the gospel into our world, a challenge no easier now than it was in the beginning?
- How can you respond to the command of Jesus to go out and preach the gospel to every creature?

Responding to the Word

We can pray to God in thanksgiving for the work that we have been given of drawing others into the faith. And we can thank God for this feast that reminds us that we are not alone, but the risen Lord himself is with us, both praying for us and working with us.

May 24, 2009

SEVENTH SUNDAY OF EASTER

Today's Focus: That We May Be One in Christ

Many churches no longer hear today's Gospel during the Easter season since the observance of the Ascension has been moved to the Seventh Sunday of Easter. John's Gospel today allows us to overhear Jesus at the Last Supper, praying to his Father for his disciples, then and now.

FIRST READING
Acts 1:15–17, 20a, 20c–26

Peter stood up in the midst of the brothers — there was a group of about one hundred and twenty persons in the one place —. He said, "My brothers, the Scripture had to be fulfilled which the Holy Spirit spoke beforehand through the mouth of David, concerning Judas, who was the guide for those who arrested Jesus. He was numbered among us and was allotted a share in this ministry.

"For it is written in the Book of Psalms:
May another take his office.

"Therefore, it is necessary that one of the men who accompanied us the whole time the Lord Jesus came and went among us, beginning from the baptism of John until the day on which he was taken up from us, become with us a witness to his resurrection." So they proposed two, Judas called Barsabbas, who was also known as Justus, and Matthias. Then they prayed, "You, Lord, who know the hearts of all, show which one of these two you have chosen to take the place in this apostolic ministry from which Judas turned away to go to his own place." Then they gave lots to them, and the lot fell upon Matthias, and he was counted with the eleven apostles.

PSALM RESPONSE
Psalm 103:19a

The Lord has set his throne in heaven.

SECOND READING
1 John 4:11–16

Beloved, if God so loved us, we also must love one another. No one has ever seen God. Yet, if we love one another, God remains in us, and his love is brought to perfection in us.

This is how we know that we remain in him and he in us, that he has given us of his Spirit. Moreover, we have seen and testify that the Father sent his Son as savior of the world. Whoever acknowledges that Jesus is the Son of God, God remains in him and he in God. We have come to know and to believe in the love God has for us.

God is love, and whoever remains in love remains in God and God in him.

GOSPEL
John 17:11b–19

Lifting up his eyes to heaven, Jesus prayed, saying: "Holy Father, keep them in your name that you have given me, so that they may be one just as we are one. When I was with them I protected them in your name that you gave me, and I guarded them, and none of them was lost except the son of destruction, in order that the Scripture might be fulfilled. But now I am coming to you. I speak this in the world so that they may share my joy completely. I gave them your word, and the world hated them, because they do not belong to the world any more than I belong to the world. I do not ask that you take them out of the world but that you keep them from the evil one. They do not belong to the world any more than I belong to the world. Consecrate them in the truth. Your word is truth. As you sent me into the world, so I sent them into the world. And I consecrate myself for them, so that they also may be consecrated in truth."

Understanding the Word

The Gospel reading for today is part of John 17, which itself is part of the prolonged final discourse of Jesus to his disciples before his death. In the part of the discourse that we hear today Jesus prays on behalf of his disciples for the courage and protection they will need to bear joyful, steadfast witness a hostile world.

One of the greatest stressors that any of us can face is the experience of hostility. Antagonism abrades our thoroughly social natures. We need each other. This we feel deeply even if we may not admit it or idealize the one who goes it alone. Jesus knows this when he first prays that the Father "keep them in your name that you have given me so that they may be one just as we are one" (17:11b). The disciples are promised a community. This is important because the world will "hate" the Johannine Christians (17:14). Their faith places them in opposition to the views of their larger society. That they might be reassured by Jesus' prayer for the Father's protection of them, Jesus reminds them of how he himself protected them during his ministry (17:12). Assurance is grounded in past experience.

Finally, Jesus enables the disciples to see value in their painful separation from the larger society. In the Old Testament consecration implied setting someone or something apart for holy service. The Father consecrated Jesus and sent Jesus into the world (10:36). Jesus now asks the Father to consecrate the disciples (17:17). In other words, their separation from the world is a sign that they perform holy service. Since their consecration is "in the truth" (v. 17), this service is speaking the truth in a world that often wishes to follow other paths. Their separation is a sign that they are saying what needs to be said for those who do not wish but need to hear it.

Reflecting on the Word

There is a beautiful song in Stephen Sondheim's musical *Into the Woods*. It comes at the end of the show, when many of the characters have suffered the loss of loved ones at the hands (or more literally, at the feet) of a giant's wife. She has gone on a rampage and trampled to death half of the inhabitants of this fairy-tale world. The few survivors, including a baker with his infant child, Cinderella, Red Riding Hood, and Jack (of beanstalk fame), gather together and sing a haunting song, "No One Is Alone."

That could be the theme of this Sunday's Gospel from John 17. The author puts a prayer on Jesus' lips, the longest prayer found in the New Testament. As he is facing death, Jesus prays for himself, for his disciples, and for all who will hear his disciples. It is the great prayer for unity, that all may be one, that no one be alone.

Jesus doesn't want anyone to be alone. In this prayer he brings together his Father, his disciples, and all who will hear them preach the gospel. He wants his Father to be glorified, his disciples to be consecrated, that is, "made holy," by the truth that is Jesus himself; and finally, he wants all who hear their preaching to be united with the Father and him. The last words of Jesus addressed to God are a prayer that all find communion through him.

"It is not good for the man to be alone," are among the first words God speaks in Genesis (2:18). The message of the Easter season is that God has acted on this awareness in ways beyond expectation. God loved the world so much that God sent the Son that we might have eternal life, alive in God, alive with each other.

CONSIDER/ DISCUSS:
- Do you take seriously the idea that Jesus continues to pray for us, for you?
- What does it mean to be "consecrated in the truth," considering that Jesus said a little earlier: "I am the way, the truth, and the life" (John 14:6)?
- How do you think about "eternal life"?

Responding to the Word

The prayer of Jesus is to be our prayer: that God be glorified, that we believers be transformed by the power and truth of the gospel, and that others come to believe through us and how we witness to the gospel in word and deed. It takes courage to witness. For this courage we must pray.

May 31, 2009

PENTECOST SUNDAY

Today's Focus: The Spirit Who Guides Us

The readings of Pentecost this year focus on what happens when the Holy Spirit guides us. In his letter to the Galatians, Paul writes that "if you are guided by the Spirit, you are not under the law" (Galatians 5:18). At the Last Supper in John's Gospel, Jesus tells his disciples that when the Spirit of truth comes, he will guide them to all truth.

FIRST READING
Acts 2:1–11

When the time for Pentecost was fulfilled, they were all in one place together. And suddenly there came from the sky a noise like a strong driving wind, and it filled the entire house in which they were. Then there appeared to them tongues as of fire, which parted and came to rest on each one of them. And they were all filled with the Holy Spirit and began to speak in different tongues, as the Spirit enabled them to proclaim.

Now there were devout Jews from every nation under heaven staying in Jerusalem. At this sound, they gathered in a large crowd, but they were confused because each one heard them speaking in his own language. They were astounded, and in amazement they asked, "Are not all these people who are speaking Galileans? Then how does each of us hear them in his native language? We are Parthians, Medes, and Elamites, inhabitants of Mesopotamia, Judea and Cappadocia, Pontus and Asia, Phrygia and Pamphylia, Egypt and the districts of Libya near Cyrene, as well as travelers from Rome, both Jews and converts to Judaism, Cretans and Arabs, yet we hear them speaking in our own tongues of the mighty acts of God."

PSALM RESPONSE
Psalm 104:30

Lord, send out your Spirit, and renew the face of the earth.

SECOND READING
1 Corinthians 12: 3b–7, 12–13

Brothers and sisters: No one can say, "Jesus is Lord," except by the Holy Spirit. There are different kinds of spiritual gifts but the same Spirit; there are different forms of service but the same Lord; there are different workings but the same God who produces all of them in everyone. To each individual the manifestation of the Spirit is given for some benefit.

As a body is one though it has many parts, and all the parts of the body, though many, are one body, so also Christ. For in one Spirit we were all baptized into one body, whether Jews or Greeks, slaves or free persons, and we were all given to drink of one Spirit.

– or –

Galatians 5: 16–25 Brothers and sisters, live by the Spirit and you will certainly not gratify the desire of the flesh. For the flesh has desires against the Spirit, and the Spirit against the flesh; these are opposed to each other, so that you may not do what you want. But if you are guided by the Spirit, you are not under the law. Now the works of the flesh are obvious: immorality, impurity, lust, idolatry, sorcery, hatreds, rivalry, jealousy, outbursts of fury, acts of selfishness, dissensions, factions, occasions of envy, drinking bouts, orgies, and the like. I warn you, as I warned you before, that those who do such things will not inherit the kingdom of God. In contrast, the fruit of the Spirit is love, joy, peace, patience, kindness, generosity, faithfulness, gentleness, self-control. Against such there is no law. Now those who belong to Christ Jesus have crucified their flesh with its passions and desires. If we live in the Spirit, let us also follow the Spirit.

GOSPEL
John 20:19–23 On the evening of that first day of the week, when the doors were locked, where the disciples were, for fear of the Jews, Jesus came and stood in their midst and said to them, "Peace be with you." When he had said this, he showed them his hands and his side. The disciples rejoiced when they saw the Lord. Jesus said to them again, "Peace be with you. As the Father has sent me, so I send you." And when he had said this, he breathed on them and said to them, "Receive the Holy Spirit. Whose sins you forgive are forgiven them, and whose sins you retain are retained."

– or –

John 15:26–27; 16:12–15 Jesus said to his disciples: "When the Advocate comes whom I will send you from the Father, the Spirit of truth that proceeds from the Father, he will testify to me. And you also testify, because you have been with me from the beginning.

"I have much more to tell you, but you cannot bear it now. But when he comes, the Spirit of truth, he will guide you to all truth. He will not speak on his own, but he will speak what he hears, and will declare to you the things that are coming. He will glorify me, because he will take from what is mine and declare it to you. Everything that the Father has is mine; for this reason I told you that he will take from what is mine and declare it to you."

 Understanding the Word

One of the choices for the second reading today is from Galatians 5:16–25, but it must be understood in the context of the preceding verses 13–15. The themes of freedom and the flesh that figure so prominently in today's reading begin in these earlier verses.

Paul's purpose in this passage is to provide concrete guidelines for how to love and how to be inspired to submit to the rigors that love often entails. There are four steps in this process. First, Paul claims that the purpose of life is to "serve one another through love" (5:13). Thus, love involves service. Second, he clarifies that one serves by loving one's neighbor as oneself (5:14).

Third, Paul shows his readers how to tell whether or not they are serving others through love. He does this by setting up an opposition between living in the flesh and living in the Spirit, making it clear that it is by living in the Spirit that one loves: "the fruit of the Spirit is love" (5:22). Then he writes about the concrete characteristics by which one can know if one is living in the flesh or in the Spirit. When one looks at the characteristics of living in the flesh one can see why they are inimical to "serv[ing] one another through love" (5:13). Among them are "hatreds, rivalry, jealousy, outbursts of fury, acts of selfishness, dissensions, factions, occasions of envy, drinking bouts, orgies, and the like" (5:20–21). On the other hand, living by the Spirit produces "love, joy, peace, patience, kindness, generosity, faithfulness, gentleness, self-control" (5:22–23).

Finally, having provided his readers with increasingly specific ways to determine if they are loving others, Paul turns to inspiring them to such a way of life. He paints an image of their internal lives, showing the moral choices to be made between activating the flesh or the Spirit: "For the flesh has desires against the Spirit, and the Spirit against the flesh: they are opposed to each other" (5:17). Opting against life in the flesh makes one follow Christ in his crucifixion: "those who belong to Christ have crucified their flesh with its passions and desires" (5:24). This enables one to live in the Spirit (5:25).

Reflecting on the Word

A friend told me that he loves the GPS device in cars that gives directions after you type in your destination. "It's wonderful!" he said. "It never complains; it never criticizes. Even when you ignore what it's saying, it simply recalculates and speaks so sweetly. It has only one purpose: to guide you safely home."

Pentecost offers us some helpful images of the Holy Spirit. In the Acts of the Apostles, the Holy Spirit is presented as a mighty wind, then as tongues of fire resting on the disciples who had gathered together. Both images are fitting for the One who literally blows them out of the house and into the world to begin the work of proclaiming the gospel.

The image in the Letter to the Galatians and in the Gospel of John complements this first image nicely. The disciples are not sent out alone. They have been given a guide to help them to "live by the Spirit." One commentary on this fiery letter of Paul noted that this is better translated as "walk by the Spirit," suggesting a path. Paul clearly articulates two ways of walking: the way of the flesh, which leads to all kinds of destructive behavior, and the way of the Spirit, which brings us to the kingdom of God—and which brings the kingdom of God to earth even now.

The Spirit who guides us along the way is the gift of the risen Lord Jesus Christ. Coming from the Father, the Spirit's purpose is to bring us to the One who is the Truth, to bring us safely home.

Look at Paul's description in Galatians 5:16–25 of what results from either living by the flesh or living by the Spirit and ask yourself:

- Have you had times in your life when you chose to go "the way of the flesh," resulting in days characterized by "hatreds, rivalry, jealousy, outbursts of fury, acts of selfishness, dissensions" and their ilk?

- And have there also been times of "living by the Spirit," that brought into your life love, joy, peace, patience, kindness, and so on?

Responding to the Word

Today is a good day to pray the words of the Pentecost Sequence, asking the Spirit: "Bend the stubborn heart and will; / Melt the frozen, warm the chill; / Guide the steps that go astray. /. . . Give [us] virtue's sure reward; / Give [us] your salvation, Lord; / Give [us] joys that never end. Amen."

Notes

The solemnity of the Most Holy Trinity begins this section of the liturgical year. In Paul's Letter to the Romans the life of the Trinity is characterized by God's sharing of this life with us. God gives the Holy Spirit so that we can become children of God. By our participation in this close relationship with God, we share in the indestructible nature of the Trinity's union and become more open to the future freedom of life that is our heart's desire.

The Gospel of Mark is the focus of Year B of the three-year Lectionary cycle. During this liturgical season the Gospel readings are from Mark 4:35 — 13:32. This block of material starts after the first prolonged teaching of Jesus in this Gospel. The teaching itself is an extended reflection in Mark 4:1–34 on who receives the word of God in such a way that the word may be fruitful in and through them. The Gospel of Mark progresses by exploring what discipleship entails. It begins by exploring the relationship between (1) chaos and faith and (2) rejection and discipleship. It continues through Mark's own unique theological perspectives related to various geographical features and groups of people. Each different place is associated with a different type of experience in people's lives. Assorted groups of people are portrayed as being closer to or farther away from Jesus with consequent distinctions in the type of teaching provided for each group. As the story progresses, however, those on the inside suprisingly appear to be on the outside, and those on the outside seem to be moving into a closer relationship with Jesus. In this light, Mark 8:22 — 10:52 especially represents this inversion and provides both underlying reasons for it and consequent cautions for Christians.

In the Markan account of Jesus' final days in Jerusalem, the cleansing of the temple is explained in light of the cursing of the fig tree, and the significance of Jesus' crucifixion is clarified by means of pointing back to the Sinai covenant and to the suffering servant of the book of Isaiah. Finally, Mark depicts the betrayal, denials, and dispersion by Jesus' closest followers in the face of his own steadfast resolve to offer himself as a sacrifice for his disciples, an offering that will make possible their own future sacrifices for others.

June 7, 2009

THE MOST HOLY TRINITY

Today's Focus: Be Who You Are—God's Beloved Children

The solemnity of the Most Holy Trinity can make preachers want to take the weekend off. Is there a more daunting feast in the liturgical year than this one that calls us to preach about this mystery of the three persons in one God? Yet our readings today offer us a way to consider this mystery. God has called us to be a family as the Trinity is a family.

FIRST READING
Deuteronomy 4: 32–34, 39–40

Moses said to the people: "Ask now of the days of old, before your time, ever since God created man upon the earth; ask from one end of the sky to the other: Did anything so great ever happen before? Was it ever heard of? Did a people ever hear the voice of God speaking from the midst of fire, as you did, and live? Or did any god venture to go and take a nation for himself from the midst of another nation, by testings, by signs and wonders, by war, with strong hand and outstretched arm, and by great terrors, all of which the LORD, your God, did for you in Egypt before your very eyes? This is why you must now know, and fix in your heart, that the LORD is God in the heavens above and on earth below, and that there is no other. You must keep his statutes and commandments that I enjoin on you today, that you and your children after you may prosper, and that you may have long life on the land which the LORD, your God, is giving you forever."

PSALM RESPONSE
Psalm 33:12b

Blessed the people the Lord has chosen to be his own.

SECOND READING
Romans 8: 14–17

Brothers and sisters: Those who are led by the Spirit of God are sons of God. For you did not receive a spirit of slavery to fall back into fear, but you received a Spirit of adoption, through whom we cry, "Abba, Father!" The Spirit himself bears witness with our spirit that we are children of God, and if children, then heirs, heirs of God and joint heirs with Christ, if only we suffer with him so that we may also be glorified with him.

GOSPEL
Matthew 28: 16–20

The eleven disciples went to Galilee, to the mountain to which Jesus had ordered them. When they all saw him, they worshiped, but they doubted. Then Jesus approached and said to them, "All power in heaven and on earth has been given to me. Go, therefore, and make disciples of all nations, baptizing them in the name of the Father, and of the Son, and of the Holy Spirit, teaching them to observe all that I have commanded you. And behold, I am with you always, until the end of the age."

Understanding the Word

Last Sunday we looked at how the Letter to the Galatians provided guidelines for how to live in the Spirit, and not in the flesh, in order to love others. The reading concluded by saying that such a life in the Spirit is a participation in Christ's crucifixion (Galatians 5:24–25). Today we look at the reading from the Letter to the Romans. It builds on the thought expressed last week in the Letter to the Galatians by showing the implications of living in the Spirit.

The disciplined life in the Spirit makes people into "children of God" (Romans 8:14). The one who lives like Christ shares the divine life by becoming an adopted child of God (8:15). The implication of this childhood is that we are co-heirs with Christ, which means that while currently sharing his sufferings we will also share his glory as well (8:17).

For Paul, two facts follow from this sharing in the divine life. First, the glorification that we will share will be a freedom from all the sufferings and unrealized hopes that people now experience (8:23). All of creation will be affected; people who live in the Spirit will live into a world freed from futility and made for the "glorious freedom of the children of God" (8:20–21). Life in the Spirit, which currently involves checks to many passions and desires, opens up into a glorious freedom. Second, being children of God means that we can be confident that God will conquer everything that stands in the way of our final life with God (8:28–39). The closeness of this relationship guarantees the ultimate exertion of God's power for us.

Reflecting on the Word

It is not always easy to be family. Good parents, the old saying goes, give their children roots and wings, a sense of security and freedom to live their lives. But achieving such a balance is often accomplished only after years of working at it. Sometimes children feel smothered by their parents, that they are trying to control their lives; at other times, children feel neglected, that they are not important, even not loved.

The readings today remind us that God wishes us to know that we can find our roots in the divine love of the Father, Son, and Holy Spirit, and that we can also find our freedom there. Paul's words to the Romans pick up first on the purpose of the gift of the Spirit that we celebrated last Sunday. The Spirit has been given us to lead us more deeply into the mystery of God, into the love of God, so that we recognize that we are God's beloved children.

This same message is found in Moses' words to the people as they are about to enter into the Promised Land. Has anyone ever had a God like our God? Moses marvels. Has any God ever shown a people how dear they are by such signs and wonders as our God has shown us? Moses is moving them to know who they are as God's beloved family and to "fix in your heart, that the LORD is God . . . and that there is no other" (Deuteronomy 4:39).

But we are not to stay all curled up in the divine embrace. We have been sent forth to proclaim to others this good news, to "[g]o, therefore, and make disciples of all nations" (Matthew 28:19). We do this when we allow the Spirit to lead us, to guide us in witnessing to God who is Father, Son, and Holy Spirit.

- What does it mean to bless yourself at the beginning and end of every Mass? Are you conscious of what you are saying?

- Does freedom given by the Holy Spirit differ from what those around you consider to be freedom?

Responding to the Word

We can pray that we may continue to live in the freedom of the children of God, to be led by God's Spirit, to go forth to draw others into this family of God by showing the joy of being disciples.

June 14, 2009

THE MOST HOLY BODY AND BLOOD OF CHRIST

Today's Focus: Take Up the Cup of His Blood, the Blood of the New Covenant

This year the solemnity of the Most Holy Body and Blood of Christ draws our attention to the blood of the new covenant. When we eat the flesh of the Son of Man and drink his blood we have eternal life within us. We are not only washed clean by the blood of the Lamb, but we enter into communion through the blood of the Lamb.

FIRST READING
Exodus 24:3–8

When Moses came to the people and related all the words and ordinances of the LORD, they all answered with one voice, "We will do everything that the LORD has told us." Moses then wrote down all the words of the LORD and, rising early the next day, he erected at the foot of the mountain an altar and twelve pillars for the twelve tribes of Israel. Then, having sent certain young men of the Israelites to offer holocausts and sacrifice young bulls as peace offerings to the LORD, Moses took half of the blood and put it in large bowls; the other half he splashed on the altar. Taking the book of the covenant, he read it aloud to the people, who answered, "All that the LORD has said, we will heed and do." Then he took the blood and sprinkled it on the people, saying, "This is the blood of the covenant that the LORD has made with you in accordance with all these words of his."

PSALM RESPONSE
Psalm 116:13

I will take the cup of salvation, and call on the name of the Lord.

SECOND READING
Hebrews 9: 11–15

Brothers and sisters: When Christ came as high priest of the good things that have come to be, passing through the greater and more perfect tabernacle not made by hands, that is, not belonging to this creation, he entered once for all into the sanctuary, not with the blood of goats and calves but with his own blood, thus obtaining eternal redemption. For if the blood of goats and bulls and the sprinkling of a heifer's ashes can sanctify those who are defiled so that their flesh is cleansed, how much more will the blood of Christ, who through the eternal Spirit offered himself unblemished to God, cleanse our consciences from dead works to worship the living God.

For this reason he is mediator of a new covenant: since a death has taken place for deliverance from transgressions under the first covenant, those who are called may receive the promised eternal inheritance.

On the first day of the Feast of Unleavened Bread, when they sacrificed the Passover lamb, Jesus' disciples said to him, "Where do you want us to go and prepare for you to eat the Passover?" He sent two of his disciples and said to them, "Go into the city and a man will meet you, carrying a jar of water. Follow him. Wherever he enters, say to the master of the house, 'The Teacher says, "Where is my guest room where I may eat the Passover with my disciples?" ' Then he will show you a large upper room furnished and ready. Make the preparations for us there." The disciples then went off, entered the city, and found it just as he had told them; and they prepared the Passover.

While they were eating, he took bread, said the blessing, broke it, gave it to them, and said, "Take it; this is my body." Then he took a cup, gave thanks, and gave it to them, and they all drank from it. He said to them, "This is my blood of the covenant, which will be shed for many. Amen, I say to you, I shall not drink again the fruit of the vine until the day when I drink it new in the kingdom of God." Then, after singing a hymn, they went out to the Mount of Olives.

Understanding the Word

The institution of the Eucharist is treated by Mark in a profound way that leads readers to realize the transformative power at work in them through the sacrifice of Christ.

Mark presents the meal by which Christ shares his body and blood as a Passover meal (14:14). Passover is a celebration of God's liberation of the Exodus generation from Egypt and the oppressive hand of Pharaoh. The ceremony involved sprinkling the blood of a sacrificed lamb upon the door lintels of the homes of the Israelites and eating a lamb and unleavened bread (Exodus 12). In the course of the meal, Jesus identifies the bread that they eat as his body and the wine that they drink as his blood. Thus, the meal presents a sharing in the life of Jesus that liberates his followers.

The meal also presents Jesus as the one who is sacrificing himself in order that the disciples may share in his life. The words "blood of the covenant" (Mark 14:24) are a reference to Exodus 24:8. In Exodus 24:6, 8 Moses throws blood of "sacrificed young bulls" on the altar and on the people to symbolize the covenant. The ancient Jews considered the life force to be in the blood. In the Exodus passage the people will declare three times in reference to the covenant, "we will do everything that the LORD has told us" (24:3, 7; cf. 19:8). Very soon, however, the wilderness generation will utterly break the covenant (Exodus 32). Jesus' sacrifice of himself is presented as an effective covenant because by it he himself lives in his disciples. This sacrifice also alludes to the sacrifice of the suffering servant in Isaiah 53:10–12: Jesus' blood will be "shed for many" (Mark 14:24). The function of the servant's suffering in Isaiah is to "take away the sins of many" (Isaiah 53:12).

Finally, the sacrifice of Jesus is surrounded by his predictions of betrayal, desertion, and denial, and then the actual betrayal by Judas, the desertion by all the disciples, and the denial by Peter (Mark 14:17–72). The sacrifice of Jesus, however, will take away the offenses of the desertions and denials and enable the disciples to live fully by completely sharing in Jesus' sacrifice for others.

Going to movies these days can be an immersion in blood. I go to movies fairly regularly and friends in the parish will ask me my reactions now and again. Often over the years, I have found myself responding, "It's well made, but . . . it's pretty bloody." Or "I'm not sure if you want to see all this bloodshed."

It might be surprising to listen to the three readings that all have to do not just with shedding blood, but sprinkling it on people, as Moses did out in the desert, and presenting Jesus as the great high priest who goes into the sanctuary bearing his own blood, which will "cleanse our consciences from dead works" (Hebrews 9:14) so we can worship the living God.

And then there is the more familiar reading of Mark's account of the Last Supper, where Jesus tells his disciples to drink his blood. Perhaps we have gotten used to hearing these words since they are spoken at every Mass. But if you stop and think about it they are rather shocking.

In the biblical world blood is sacred, blood is life. From the beginning animals were offered in sacrifice. But with the offering of the body and blood of Christ, a new relationship has been entered with our God. Through Jesus' gift of his body and blood, salvation was won for us and is present to us when we gather in his name to praise the Father.

CONSIDER/ DISCUSS:
- Does the gift of new life, given to all who drink the blood of the Son of Man, speak of God's great desire to share with us the life of the Son?

- In a world where millions struggle for food and drink, what does it mean to go forth from the church after receiving the body and blood of the risen Lord? How does this sign of sacrifice speak to our lives in the world?

Responding to the Word

We acknowledge that we are "not worthy to receive" the Lord, but with confidence we go on to pray, "only say the word and I shall be healed." We pray for deep-down healing so that we may give ourselves wholeheartedly to the work of bringing about the kingdom.

June 21, 2009

TWELFTH SUNDAY IN ORDINARY TIME

Today's Focus: Don't Fear—He's Here!

Jesus asleep in the boat as it is tossed about by a violent storm is one of the most interesting images presented in the Gospel. The disciples are in terror, fearing for their lives as waves sweep over the boat. But on being awakened, Jesus brings order to the chaos. "Quiet! Be still!"(Mark 4:39). And then he turns to his disciples . . .

FIRST READING
Job 38:1, 8–11

The Lord addressed Job out of the storm and said:
    Who shut within doors the sea,
      when it burst forth from the womb;
  when I made the clouds its garment
    and thick darkness its swaddling bands?
When I set limits for it
    and fastened the bar of its door,
  and said: Thus far shall you come but no farther,
    and here shall your proud waves be stilled!

PSALM RESPONSE
Psalm 107:1b

Give thanks to the Lord, his love is everlasting.

SECOND READING
2 Corinthians 5: 14–17

Brothers and sisters: The love of Christ impels us, once we have come to the conviction that one died for all; therefore, all have died. He indeed died for all, so that those who live might no longer live for themselves but for him who for their sake died and was raised.

Consequently, from now on we regard no one according to the flesh; even if we once knew Christ according to the flesh, yet now we know him so no longer. So whoever is in Christ is a new creation: the old things have passed away; behold, new things have come.

GOSPEL
Mark 4:35–41

On that day, as evening drew on, Jesus said to his disciples: "Let us cross to the other side." Leaving the crowd, they took Jesus with them in the boat just as he was. And other boats were with him. A violent squall came up and waves were breaking over the boat, so that it was already filling up. Jesus was in the stern, asleep on a cushion. They woke him and said to him, "Teacher, do you not care that we are perishing?" He woke up, rebuked the wind, and said to the sea, "Quiet! Be still!" The wind ceased and there was great calm. Then he asked them, "Why are you terrified? Do you not yet have faith?" They were filled with great awe and said to one another, "Who then is this whom even wind and sea obey?"

The reading from the Gospel of Mark about Jesus stilling the storm that erupted on the Sea of Galilee is part of a larger Markan treatment of the fear that stands in the way of receiving Jesus' word in a way that may be fruitful in us. The section that just preceded today's Gospel was an extended discourse that addressed how one is fruitful by accepting the word of Jesus (Mark 4:1–34). Mark is noteworthy in this respect. Whereas Matthew writes that it is necessary to understand the word and Luke says that one must "embrace it with a generous and good heart and bear fruit through perseverance," Mark writes simply that accepting Jesus' word makes one fruitful (Mark 4:20; Matthew 13:23; Luke 8:15).

Unlike Matthew and Luke, Mark does not record much teaching of Jesus before this passage calls for the acceptance of his word in order to be fruitful. There are brief rejoinders by him, defenses both of those who believe (1:8b–9; 2:17, 19–22; 3:33–35) and of the priority that the coming of the reign of God takes over everything else (2:25–28; 3:4). One finds no large block of teaching material before this point in Mark, however, as one finds, for example, in the Sermon on the Mount in Matthew and the Sermon on the Plain in Luke. The one exception, and it is a brief one, is Jesus' contradiction of the claim that he is possessed by Beelzebul (3:23–29). The reason for this exception is clear. The only teaching that Jesus has initiated in Mark's Gospel is the claim, "This is the time of fulfillment. The kingdom of God is at hand. Repent and believe in the gospel" (1:15). The claim that Beelzebul controls Jesus asserts instead that Beelzebul's reign continues unabated.

The "violent squall" (4:37) at sea provokes terror in the disciples. Jesus' response implies that if they had faith they would not be terrified (4:40). Similarly, when they arrive on the other side of the sea the people will exhibit a fear that causes them to ask Jesus to leave them (5:15). This is caused by Jesus' exorcising from a man a large number of demons. When they cross the sea again, a woman who is healed when she secretly touches the cloak of Jesus is filled with "fear and trembling" when Jesus asks who has touched him (5:31, 33). Again Jesus contrasts faith and fear (5:34).

Today's Gospel is part of a series of Markan passages articulating the perspective that accepting the arrival of God's reign means the violent overthrow of the forces of evil in the world. God's reign comes not smoothly but through upheavals in our lives.

Reflecting on the Word

Fear of nature's power is understandable. Consider what the survivors of the Indian Ocean tsunami or of Hurricane Katrina went through, or the people who were the victims of the earthquake in China more recently. There is good reason to fear nature's destructive power. But we must look deeper, beyond the surface, at the event described in today's Gospel.

Some experienced fishermen were in that boat, yet they were terrified as it began to fill with water. At first, they let Jesus sleep, but finally, sensing that things were out of control, they wakened him, asking accusingly, "[D]o you not care that we are perishing?" (Mark 4:38). This statement is both an act of believing he could do something, and fear that he would not. Jesus responds to this ambivalence when he asks: "Why are you terrified? Do you not yet have faith?" (4:40).

Many of us have those moments when we turn to Jesus, half believing, half disbelieving that he will take care of us. Through the centuries, people have asked, "Don't you care that we are perishing?" Don't you care that we are being threatened by all kinds of storms that can overwhelm and sink us? Don't you care that our lives are hanging by a thread? This story resonates with those moments.

As he did then, Jesus stands before us and says: "Why are you terrified? Do you not yet have faith?" Don't you see that I am with you? Don't you know I can calm the winds and quiet the sea that threatens? Do you not trust that all will be well? Perhaps the most common exhortation in scripture is: "Be not afraid." It is spoken by the angel to Mary at Nazareth, to the shepherds in Bethlehem, to the women at the tomb, and many times in between. So, be not afraid; our God is with us.

CONSIDER/
DISCUSS:
- What are your greatest fears?
- Do you believe that Jesus is with you and that you will not be swept away by the storms that threaten?
- Can it be that the storms that threaten are the harbingers of old things passing away and new things coming, as Paul writes to the Corinthians?

Responding to the Word

Let us pray with confidence to the God revealed in the book of Job as one who is Lord of the sea, no matter what violent form it takes, physical or metaphorical. Let us turn with confidence to hear the words Jesus addresses to our fearful hearts: "Quiet. Be still. Know that I am God." Let us rest at peace in the arms of the Lord.

June 28, 2009

THIRTEENTH SUNDAY IN ORDINARY TIME

Today's Focus: A Touching Tale

Whether we are threatened with death by the chaos of a storm at sea or physical failures on land, Jesus calls out to us: "Do not be afraid; just have faith." But Jesus brings a more personal touch to this tale of two untouchable women.

FIRST READING
Wisdom 1: 13–15; 2:23–24

God did not make death,
　　nor does he rejoice in the destruction of the living.
For he fashioned all things
　　that they might have being;
and the creatures of the world are wholesome,
and there is not a destructive drug among them
　　nor any domain of the netherworld on earth,
　　for justice is undying.
For God formed man to be imperishable;
　　the image of his own nature he made him.
But by the envy of the devil, death entered the world,
　　and they who belong to his company experience it.

PSALM RESPONSE
Psalm 30:2a

I will praise you, Lord, for you have rescued me.

SECOND READING
2 Corinthians 8: 7, 9, 13–15

Brothers and sisters: As you excel in every respect, in faith, discourse, knowledge, all earnestness, and in the love we have for you, may you excel in this gracious act also.

For you know the gracious act of our Lord Jesus Christ, that though he was rich, for your sake he became poor, so that by his poverty you might become rich. Not that others should have relief while you are burdened, but that as a matter of equality your abundance at the present time should supply their needs, so that their abundance may also supply your needs, that there may be equality. As it is written:

Whoever had much did not have more,
and whoever had little did not have less.

In the shorter form of the reading, the passage in brackets is omitted.

GOSPEL
Mark 5:21–43 or 21–24, 35b–43

When Jesus had crossed again in the boat to the other side, a large crowd gathered around him, and he stayed close to the sea. One of the synagogue officials, named Jairus, came forward. Seeing him he fell at his feet and pleaded earnestly with him, saying, "My daughter is at the point of death. Please, come and lay your hands on her that she may get well and live." He went off with him, and a large crowd followed him and pressed upon him.

145

[There was a woman afflicted with hemorrhages for twelve years. She had suffered greatly at the hands of the many doctors and had spent all that she had. Yet she was not helped but only grew worse. She had heard about Jesus and came up behind him in the crowd and touched his cloak. She said, "If I but touch his clothes, I shall be cured." Immediately her flow of blood dried up. She felt in her body that she was healed of her affliction. Jesus, aware at once that power had gone out from him, turned around in the crowd and asked, "Who has touched my clothes?" But his disciples said to Jesus, "You see how the crowd is pressing upon you, and yet you ask, 'Who touched me?' " And he looked around to see who had done it. The woman, realizing what had happened to her, approached in fear and trembling. She fell down before Jesus and told him the whole truth. He said to her, "Daughter, your faith has saved you. Go in peace and be cured of your affliction."]

While he was still speaking, people from the synagogue official's house arrived and said, "Your daughter has died; why trouble the teacher any longer?" Disregarding the message that was reported, Jesus said to the synagogue official, "Do not be afraid; just have faith." He did not allow anyone to accompany him inside except Peter, James, and John, the brother of James. When they arrived at the house of the synagogue official, he caught sight of a commotion, people weeping and wailing loudly. So he went in and said to them, "Why this commotion and weeping? The child is not dead but asleep." And they ridiculed him. Then he put them all out. He took along the child's father and mother and those who were with him and entered the room where the child was. He took the child by the hand and said to her, "Talitha koum," which means, "Little girl, I say to you, arise!" The girl, a child of twelve, arose immediately and walked around. At that they were utterly astounded. He gave strict orders that no one should know this and said that she should be given something to eat.

Understanding the Word

According to the evangelist Mark, a fruitful follower of Christ must believe that the reign of God is coming powerfully through upheavals in our lives and in the world. In today's Gospel, Mark emphasizes again the degree of faith necessary to conquer our fear at such turbulence.

Mark painstakingly points out that all the tumult that caused the fear in last Sunday's Gospel took place around the Sea of Galilee (Mark 4:35; 5:1, 21). In the Old Testament, the sea often represents the chaotic elements of life. For Mark, faith is lived in the face of chaos.

In this Sunday's Gospel the stories of the healing of the woman with hemorrhages and the raising of Jairus' daughter are intertwined. The women in both stories are in desperate situations. The woman with the hemorrhages "had suffered greatly at the hands of many doctors and had spent all that she had. Yet she was not helped but only grew worse" (5:26). The daughter of Jairus who was "at the point of death" dies (5:23, 35). To both the woman and the girl's parents Jesus speaks of faith in the face of fear, faith that will open them to the reign of God in their lives: "Do not be afraid; just have faith" (5:36; cf. 5:33–34).

The faith that accepts the inbreaking reign of God comes not only in the face of upheavals but also in the teeth of the chaos that seems to have won the day.

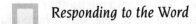

Reflecting on the Word

These two stories are quite touching, perhaps because they involve so much touching—forbidden touching, as a matter of fact. The father starts it off by falling at Jesus' feet and begging Jesus to help his dying daughter: "[C]ome lay your hands on her that she may get well and live" (Mark 5:23). Only touching her will do.

Then as Jesus is passing through the crowd, a woman suddenly appears on the scene, reaching out to Jesus and saying to herself: "If I but touch his clothes, I shall be cured" (5:28). Jesus knows immediately that he's been touched: "Who has touched my clothes?" he asks (5:30). And the disciples wryly observe that the crowd is . . . well, crowding him . . . so how can you ask "Who touched me?"

It is important to remember that because the woman was bleeding, a condition that made her "unclean" according to the law of Moses, her touch would have made Jesus unclean. However, her touching Jesus has the opposite effect: the bleeding stops and she is made clean once again.

When word comes that the little girl is dead, Jesus calls on the father to set aside fear and put on faith. Arriving at the house, Jesus goes in and takes the child by the hand and says, "Little girl, I say to you, arise!" (Mark 5:41). Sixteen times in Mark's Gospel Jesus touches or takes someone by the hand. She does arise and he tells them to bring her some food. Again, touching her would have made Jesus unclean, but instead his touch cleanses her of death's hold.

Two desperate people—a dying girl and a bleeding woman. Jesus touches them and they both touch him—the woman through her own faith, the little girl through the faith of her father. It seems that healing depends on a flow between healer and the one being healed. The great news is that God allows a proxy.

CONSIDER/
DISCUSS:
- Do you trust that your faith in the Lord might bring God's healing touch to others?
- Do you need to reach out to touch Jesus through prayer?
- Are there people whom Jesus wishes to touch through you?

Responding to the Word

Today we might pray for those who are in need of the healing touch of Jesus, and for those who care for them and suffer with them.

July 5, 2009

FOURTEENTH SUNDAY IN ORDINARY TIME

Today's Focus: The High Cost of Unbelief

Jesus' power worked in the face of chaos, sickness, and death. It could not work in the face of unbelief. For two weeks we have heard Jesus call for faith rather than fear. When faith was present, things happened. Today we get a snapshot of what happens when faith is not present.

FIRST READING
Ezekiel 2:2–5

As the LORD spoke to me, the spirit entered into me and set me on my feet, and I heard the one who was speaking say to me: Son of man, I am sending you to the Israelites, rebels who have rebelled against me; they and their ancestors have revolted against me to this very day. Hard of face and obstinate of heart are they to whom I am sending you. But you shall say to them: Thus says the LORD God! And whether they heed or resist — for they are a rebellious house — they shall know that a prophet has been among them.

PSALM RESPONSE
Psalm 123:2cd

Our eyes are fixed on the Lord, pleading for his mercy.

SECOND READING
2 Corinthians 12: 7–10

Brothers and sisters: That I, Paul, might not become too elated, because of the abundance of the revelations, a thorn in the flesh was given to me, an angel of Satan, to beat me, to keep me from being too elated. Three times I begged the Lord about this, that it might leave me, but he said to me, "My grace is sufficient for you, for power is made perfect in weakness." I will rather boast most gladly of my weaknesses, in order that the power of Christ may dwell with me. Therefore, I am content with weaknesses, insults, hardships, persecutions, and constraints, for the sake of Christ; for when I am weak, then I am strong.

GOSPEL
Mark 6:1–6

Jesus departed from there and came to his native place, accompanied by his disciples. When the sabbath came he began to teach in the synagogue, and many who heard him were astonished. They said, "Where did this man get all this? What kind of wisdom has been given him? What mighty deeds are wrought by his hands! Is he not the carpenter, the son of Mary, and the brother of James and Joses and Judas and Simon? And are not his sisters here with us?" And they took offense at him. Jesus said to them, "A prophet is not without honor except in his native place and among his own kin and in his own house." So he was not able to perform any mighty deed there, apart from curing a few sick people by laying his hands on them. He was amazed at their lack of faith.

As Mark's story progresses, Jesus returns home from the places where chaos rules. The startling aspect of today's Gospel is that while Jesus' power was manifested in the chaos, it is stifled here at home by lack of faith.

This Gospel reading picks up a Markan theme of Jesus' family serving as a foil to those who, by attending to Jesus' word, share his perspective and life. This theme is first encountered in Mark 3 when Jesus' family sets out to seize him upon hearing that he is attracting crowds so big that he cannot sit down to eat. Although they might have been seen as acting in Jesus' best interests, Mark gives their action a negative spin when he has the family say of Jesus, "He is out of his mind" (3:21). To emphasize the inappropriateness of this remark, Mark immediately has the scribes pronounce him "possessed by Beelzebul" (3:22). When his family does arrive to take him home, Jesus tells the crowd listening to him that those who do the will of God are his mother and brothers (3:31–34), and they have been doing so by listening to him (3:23–30).

In today's Gospel Jesus is back in his hometown, and he is again teaching (6:2). This time, however, no one in the city believes in him. This occasions Jesus' saying, "A prophet is not without honor except in his native place and among his own kin and in his own house" (6:4). Amazed at the lack of faith among his own and "unable to perform any mighty deeds there" (6:5), Jesus departs and goes elsewhere to teach (6:6).

Mark distinguishes between the faith of those in the places where chaos rules and the lack of faith of those closest to him. The former leads to the actualization of Jesus' power while the latter diminishes his ability to express it. Mark's purpose is to show that remaining close to the word of Jesus is what makes a Christian productive, that is, a means by which the reign of God is active. Such closeness establishes the true family of Jesus.

Reflecting on the Word

God describes the people to whom Ezekiel is being sent as "hard of face and obstinate of heart" (Ezekiel 2:4). They are a people who have rebelled and revolted against God, but still God persists in sending them a prophet: this time Ezekiel, last time Jeremiah, the time before that Isaiah, all the way back to Samuel and Nathan, Elijah and Elisha. Even today, God continues to send prophets to soften our faces and make yielding our own hearts.

Jesus found hardened faces and stubborn hearts when he went to his hometown. Impenetrable seems to be the best description. His words could not get through. He was proclaiming the kingdom of God, the presence of God among them, and they couldn't hear him. It all depended on what they saw and all they saw was the carpenter, questioning where he got such wisdom and how he did these mighty deeds. He was just the son of Mary! We know the family. Go figure.

And then we hear some of the saddest words in the Gospel: "So he was not able to perform any mighty deed there, apart from curing a few sick people by laying his hands on them" (Mark 6:5). Why? Their lack of faith.

So Jesus started a new family. It began with the people whom we have been hearing about—the disciples, for all their struggles to believe in him right up to the very end, but also people like the woman with the hemorrhage, Jairus and his daughter, the man lowered through the roof, the fellow who had an evil spirit. The list goes on and on, down to our own day.

By baptism, we became part of the family, the new family whose bond is not based on blood, but on faith. The ever-recurring question is: Is he able to work any signs among us, or is he amazed at our lack of faith?

CONSIDER/
DISCUSS:
- When has being close to someone blinded you to knowing who that person really was?
- Are there ways of thinking about Jesus that need to be discarded? Do you really see him with the eyes of faith?
- Does your pride, your need to be independent, serve as a barrier to drawing closer to God?

Responding to the Word

We pray that when we gather on Sundays we know ourselves as the family of Jesus, striving to hear the word of God and keep it. We pray that we might recognize in others the brothers and sisters of the Lord, the beloved children of God.

July 12, 2009

FIFTEENTH SUNDAY IN ORDINARY TIME

Today's Focus: "Travel Light!"

Today we find Jesus sending out the Twelve, those he had specially chosen to be with him and join him in his ministry. The directions he gives them are instructive for all who have been called to take part in the ongoing work of spreading the gospel—a work given to all of the baptized.

FIRST READING
Amos 7:12–15

Amaziah, priest of Bethel, said to Amos, "Off with you, visionary, flee to the land of Judah! There earn your bread by prophesying, but never again prophesy in Bethel; for it is the king's sanctuary and a royal temple." Amos answered Amaziah, "I was no prophet, nor have I belonged to a company of prophets; I was a shepherd and a dresser of sycamores. The LORD took me from following the flock, and said to me, Go, prophesy to my people Israel."

PSALM RESPONSE
Psalm 85:8

Lord, let us see your kindness, and grant us your salvation.

In the shorter form of the reading, the passage in brackets is omitted.

SECOND READING
Ephesians 1: 3–14 or 1:3–10

Blessed be the God and Father of our Lord Jesus Christ, who has blessed us in Christ with every spiritual blessing in the heavens, as he chose us in him, before the foundation of the world, to be holy and without blemish before him. In love he destined us for adoption to himself through Jesus Christ, in accord with the favor of his will, for the praise of the glory of his grace that he granted us in the beloved. In him we have redemption by his blood, the forgiveness of transgressions, in accord with the riches of his grace that he lavished upon us. In all wisdom and insight, he has made known to us the mystery of his will in accord with his favor that he set forth in him as a plan for the fullness of times, to sum up all things in Christ, in heaven and on earth.

[In him we were also chosen, destined in accord with the purpose of the One who accomplishes all things according to the intention of his will, so that we might exist for the praise of his glory, we who first hoped in Christ. In him you also, who have heard the word of truth, the gospel of your salvation, and have believed in him, were sealed with the promised holy Spirit, which is the first installment of our inheritance toward redemption as God's possession, to the praise of his glory.]

Jesus summoned the Twelve and began to send them out two by two and gave them authority over unclean spirits. He instructed them to take nothing for the journey but a walking stick — no food, no sack, no money in their belts. They were, however, to wear sandals but not a second tunic. He said to them, "Wherever you enter a house, stay there until you leave. Whatever place does not welcome you or listen to you, leave there and shake the dust off your feet in testimony against them." So they went off and preached repentance. The Twelve drove out many demons, and they anointed with oil many who were sick and cured them.

Understanding the Word

The message and mission of Jesus are too important to let rejection overcome them. This is the point that Mark's Gospel makes today. Jesus has been teaching in his hometown but has been rejected there (6:2–5). He responds with persistence, continuing his teaching in nearby villages (6:6b). In fact, Jesus responds to rejection by increasing the dispersion of his message and mission. He ratchets up his efforts by sending out the apostles to different locales to drive out unclean spirits, preach, and heal (6:7, 12–13). Rejection is met with renewed vigor.

In the process Jesus assures the apostles that they will be provided for when they focus on the mission. This is why he tells them not to take food, sack, money, or a second tunic, and to stay at the house they enter (6:9–10). Rejection is still to be expected from some (6:11). This will not, however, prevent acceptance by others of the apostles' message or the arrival of the reign of God in the healing of people's lives (6:12–13).

Rejection of the message of Mark's Jesus is never the last word and so proclaiming the message must continue despite all setbacks. Although the lack of faith in his own hometown caused Jesus not "to perform any mighty deed there, apart from curing a few sick people by laying his hands on them" (6:5), the apostles whom Jesus sends elsewhere "drove out many demons, and they anointed with oil many who were sick and cured them" (6:13). The tactile healings that are few in one place are followed by tactile healings that are many in another locale. With persistence in spreading the gospel message, rejection becomes a springboard for greater success.

Reflecting on the Word

Traveling by plane these days calls for careful preparation. One airline recently posted notice that if your bag weighs more than fifty pounds, there is an additional fee of fifty dollars. Add in the restrictions on carry-on baggage: no liquids more than three ounces, no bags beyond a certain size. It encourages you to travel light.

Jesus is issuing his own travel instructions to those he chose to work with him. First, he gives them "authority over unclean spirits" (Mark 6:7), a sharing in the authority the Father has given him for the work of spreading the gospel that the reign of evil is over and the reign of God is beginning.

Then, Jesus gets practical: Take nothing but a walking stick—to be used in climbing hills, driving off wild animals, or pushing away snakes found on the paths. No food, no sack to hold extra clothing—not even a second tunic—or to carry off anything from the towns you visit, and no money! Permission granted to wear sandals.

Finally, when you get to a place, do not look for the most comfortable lodging, take what comes first and be content there. The focus is clear: Stay on message—God's kingdom is at hand. Repent and believe. And show it in action: Deliver the sick and possessed from what burdens them. If people don't like the message? Move on.

Over two thousand years later, Jesus, risen Lord, continues to call ordinary folk. Back then it was some fishermen, a tax collector, a political activist; now it's workers from every way of life, every profession and job. People raising families, singles, the elderly, anyone willing to confess that God is at work in our world, that evil will not have the last word, and that all creation finds its deepest meaning in Christ.

CONSIDER/ DISCUSS:
- What instructions would Jesus give today?
- Do I take seriously the call to work for the coming of God's reign in the world, my world?
- Do I have the support Jesus intended when he sent them out two by two?

Responding to the Word

Let us pray that we will recognize where God wants us to do the work of spreading the news of God's kingdom.

July 19, 2009

SIXTEENTH SUNDAY IN ORDINARY TIME

Today's Focus: God's People ISO . . .

The apostles return from their first mission as preachers and healers and Jesus invites them to go away for some "R and R," but no sooner do they get there then a "vast crowd" shows up. Jesus' heart goes out to them and he responds to their needs.

FIRST READING
Jeremiah 23: 1–6

Woe to the shepherds who mislead and scatter the flock of my pasture, says the LORD. Therefore, thus says the LORD, the God of Israel, against the shepherds who shepherd my people: You have scattered my sheep and driven them away. You have not cared for them, but I will take care to punish your evil deeds. I myself will gather the remnant of my flock from all the lands to which I have driven them and bring them back to their meadow; there they shall increase and multiply. I will appoint shepherds for them who will shepherd them so that they need no longer fear and tremble; and none shall be missing, says the LORD.

Behold, the days are coming, says the LORD,
    when I will raise up a righteous shoot to David;
as king he shall reign and govern wisely,
    he shall do what is just and right in the land.
In his days Judah shall be saved,
    Israel shall dwell in security.
This is the name they give him:
    "The LORD, our justice."

PSALM RESPONSE
Psalm 23:1

The Lord is my shepherd; there is nothing I shall want.

SECOND READING
Ephesians 2: 13–18

Brothers and sisters: In Christ Jesus you who once were far off have become near by the blood of Christ.

For he is our peace, he who made both one and broke down the dividing wall of enmity, through his flesh, abolishing the law with its commandments and legal claims, that he might create in himself one new person in place of the two, thus establishing peace, and might reconcile both with God, in one body, through the cross, putting that enmity to death by it. He came and preached peace to you who were far off and peace to those who were near, for through him we both have access in one Spirit to the Father.

The apostles gathered together with Jesus and reported all they had done and taught. He said to them, "Come away by yourselves to a deserted place and rest a while." People were coming and going in great numbers, and they had no opportunity even to eat. So they went off in the boat by themselves to a deserted place. People saw them leaving and many came to know about it. They hastened there on foot from all the towns and arrived at the place before them.

When he disembarked and saw the vast crowd, his heart was moved with pity for them, for they were like sheep without a shepherd; and he began to teach them many things.

Understanding the Word

Last Sunday we learned that rejecting Mark's message of the coming of the reign of God is not the last word. Resolve to spread this message despite opposition leads to the belief in it that opens the way for its coming. This Sunday we discover that successful witness itself is not the last word in ushering in the reign of God.

We have seen before that Mark likes to make a point by surrounding one passage with two others that deal with the same topic. This has been called the "sandwich" or intercalation technique. In today's Gospel, this technique reveals the culminating step in the life of any follower of Christ, by which they do their part in becoming a means through which God acts definitively.

Today we hear the apostles report to Jesus "all they had done and taught" (Mark 6:30). This refers to their casting out demons, preaching, and curing people, that we heard last week (6:7–13). In between these two passages from last week and this week, which form the "bread" of this Markan sandwich, is an account involving Herod (6:14–29). When Herod hears about what Jesus and his disciples are doing, he equates it with the work of John the Baptist (6:16). Next we learn how Herod had John the Baptist killed (6:27–28). This account of Herod's actions, ending with the disciples of John the Baptist coming and taking his body, juxtaposed with the next verse that begins with the apostles returning to Jesus from their mission, links the sufferings of the Baptist with what the apostles can expect (6:29–30).

On the horizon of all effective striving for the reign of God is suffering, the final means through which the reign of God comes.

Most newspapers and even some magazines have personal ads with their ISO ("in search of . . .") pleas. Some can be quite poignant: "Young man in search of companionship . . ." "Young woman looking for someone to share thoughts and dinner and hiking . . ." People turn to a newspaper column to help resolve their loneliness and desire for intimacy, hoping to find someone who will care and make their lives more meaningful. It is not only individuals who are searching for something more. Sometimes it can be a community, a country, even most of the world.

Jesus has taken his apostles off to a quiet place so they can "rest a while" (Mark 6:31). But even "a deserted place" provides no getaway from the needs of the people who search them out. Jesus' response to them gives us an insight into what he was like. The Gospel tells us "his heart was moved with pity for them" (6:34). The word in Greek for "moved with pity" has its roots in the word for "womb" or "loins," the innermost part of a person, where life begins.

What evokes this response is their being "like sheep without a shepherd" (6:34). Sheep without a shepherd would be likely to wander off and get lost, vulnerable to being picked off by wolves, or just starve to death. The kings of Israel and Judah and the religious leaders were called to shepherd God's people. They were to govern, guide, and guard them. Often they did a poor job. Today we hear the Lord castigate these shepherds through the words of the prophet Jeremiah. God promises to appoint new shepherds.

The need for good shepherds continues in our day, for men and women who will care for the ones most vulnerable in our society. This is not just a matter for those in obvious positions of power, whether church or state, but for all those who have the capacity to reach out to any in physical need, to any searching for deeper meaning, to those looking for signs of the presence of God.

CONSIDER/ DISCUSS:
- What are people searching for in our day? Where do they look?
- What does it mean to be baptized into a people called to share in the work of Jesus, the Good Shepherd?
- How can my community show itself as a community dedicated to the work of the Good Shepherd?

Responding to the Word

We can pray that the Lord will send us shepherds who will shepherd the people "so that they need no longer fear and tremble; and none shall be missing" (Jeremiah 23:4). We can pray that God will send leaders of church and state, on all levels, who will govern wisely.

July 26, 2009

SEVENTEENTH SUNDAY IN ORDINARY TIME

Today's Focus: Jesus, Sign of God

We depart from the Gospel of Mark for the next five weeks to hear the great discourse of Jesus as the Bread of Life in the Gospel of John (chapter 6). During these weeks we will consider Jesus as the great sign of God, sent by the Father, to reveal the face of the living God.

FIRST READING
2 Kings 4: 42–44

A man came from Baal-shalishah bringing to Elisha, the man of God, twenty barley loaves made from the firstfruits, and fresh grain in the ear. Elisha said, "Give it to the people to eat." But his servant objected, "How can I set this before a hundred people?" Elisha insisted, "Give it to the people to eat. For thus says the LORD, 'They shall eat and there shall be some left over.'" And when they had eaten, there was some left over, as the LORD had said.

PSALM RESPONSE
Psalm 145:16

The hand of the Lord feeds us; he answers all our needs.

SECOND READING
Ephesians 4: 1–6

Brothers and sisters: I, a prisoner for the Lord, urge you to live in a manner worthy of the call you have received, with all humility and gentleness, with patience, bearing with one another through love, striving to preserve the unity of the spirit through the bond of peace: one body and one Spirit, as you were also called to the one hope of your call; one Lord, one faith, one baptism; one God and Father of all, who is over all and through all and in all.

<table>
<tr>
<td>GOSPEL
John 6:1–15</td>
<td>Jesus went across the Sea of Galilee. A large crowd followed him, because they saw the signs he was performing on the sick. Jesus went up on the mountain, and there he sat down with his disciples. The Jewish feast of Passover was near. When Jesus raised his eyes and saw that a large crowd was coming to him, he said to Philip, "Where can we buy enough food for them to eat?" He said this to test him, because he himself knew what he was going to do. Philip answered him, "Two hundred days' wages worth of food would not be enough for each of them to have a little." One of his disciples, Andrew, the brother of Simon Peter, said to him, "There is a boy here who has five barley loaves and two fish; but what good are these for so many?" Jesus said, "Have the people recline." Now there was a great deal of grass in that place. So the men reclined, about five thousand in number. Then Jesus took the loaves, gave thanks, and distributed them to those who were reclining, and also as much of the fish as they wanted. When they had had their fill, he said to his disciples, "Gather the fragments left over, so that nothing will be wasted." So they collected them, and filled twelve wicker baskets with fragments from the five barley loaves that had been more than they could eat. When the people saw the sign he had done, they said, "This is truly the Prophet, the one who is to come into the world." Since Jesus knew that they were going to come and carry him off to make him king, he withdrew again to the mountain alone.</td>
</tr>
</table>

Understanding the Word

Today let us focus on the reaction of Philip to Jesus' multiplying the five loaves and two fish to feed about five thousand (John 6:1–15). This reaction clarifies the evangelist John's perspective on how to derive enough from life to be open through prayer to the powerful working of God in our lives.

Philip is the disciple who always wants more. Thus, when Jesus asks where they can buy "enough" food to feed such a large crowd, Philip responds that even with two hundred days' wages they could not procure enough for a morsel for each (6:5, 7). Later, when some Greeks want to see Jesus, it is to Philip that they communicate this wish and Philip and Andrew convey this information to Jesus (12:20–22). This event follows right on the heels of a "great crowd" welcoming Jesus to Jerusalem, one so great that the Pharisees claim that "the whole world has gone after him" (12:12, 19). Philip is part of the process of attempting to increase the acclaim. Finally, at one point during his last discourse Jesus claims that to see him is to see and know the Father (14:7). Philip replies, "Master, show us the Father and that will be enough for us" (14:8). This is the disciple who is always looking for something else to confirm his faith.

Jesus' final response to Philip redirects the disciple's focus. The "more" that Philip is looking for is implicit in what he has already experienced in Jesus, and particularly in the works that Jesus has performed (14:10–11). If Philip wants more it will be present through him. Jesus assures him that greater works than Jesus has done will be done through the disciple who believes and asks for such works (14:12–13). In order to be the medium of the divine "moreness" Philip needs to believe in this excess on the basis of the power that he has already experienced Jesus exercising in his life.

158

Philip must look to this past (such as today's multiplication of the loaves and fishes) as the basis for his expectation of more works to be done *through* him rather than to the future for more signs to be done *for* him.

Reflecting on the Word

It's easy to misread a sign, sometimes to humorous effect. I was driving through a little town in Vermont when I saw a sign that I read as "Guilt Festival." I did a double take and then discovered it read "Quilt Festival." We can easily misread signs as we are moving along through life, sometimes with a more serious result. We watch someone do something and we interpret it one way, then later discover this "reading" was really off the mark, and that we had misjudged or rashly judged that person.

In today's Gospel, signs are being misread several times. The people following after Jesus were reading the sign of his healings as indicating that someone special was among them. After he feeds them, they interpret this action as a sign that the Prophet who was to come had arrived (which was correct), but then they want to make him king (which was not God's plan). The apostles read the sign of a hungry crowd as impossible to feed with limited resources.

But they had forgotten the example of Elisha the prophet, who fed a hundred people with only twenty barley loaves. Jesus did one better, feeding five thousand men, not to say how many women and children were there, with only five barley loaves and two fish, and having twelve baskets of leftovers. (An interesting note is that barley was the food of the poor.)

The Prophet foretold by Moses had indeed come into the world, but not to be king. What he came for will be revealed in the coming weeks. But as a start, we can reflect on how he came to be a sign of the generosity of the Father who sent him out of love for the world to feed the children of the world.

CONSIDER/ DISCUSS:
- If he knew what he was going to do, why did Jesus ask Philip, "Where can we buy enough food for them to eat?"
- Is the Lord asking you to do something that you feel is beyond your resources?
- What does Jesus teach us about turning to the Father when our resources are limited?

Responding to the Word

With so much hunger in our world, we pray that all who have more than enough will see "the large crowd" that has so little. We pray that we might read the sign of hunger as an invitation to be a sign of God's generous care for the poor.

August 2, 2009

EIGHTEENTH SUNDAY IN ORDINARY TIME

Today's Focus: Jesus, Bread for Life

A day has passed since Jesus fed the five thousand. The crowd has followed him to Capernaum, apparently looking for another free meal. Jesus invites them to recognize a deeper hunger that he can satisfy. The bread they ate yesterday no longer satisfies; the bread he will give will satisfy forever.

FIRST READING
Exodus 16:2–4, 12–15

The whole Israelite community grumbled against Moses and Aaron. The Israelites said to them, "Would that we had died at the Lord's hand in the land of Egypt, as we sat by our fleshpots and ate our fill of bread! But you had to lead us into this desert to make the whole community die of famine!"

Then the Lord said to Moses, "I will now rain down bread from heaven for you. Each day the people are to go out and gather their daily portion; thus will I test them, to see whether they follow my instructions or not.

"I have heard the grumbling of the Israelites. Tell them: In the evening twilight you shall eat flesh, and in the morning you shall have your fill of bread, so that you may know that I, the Lord, am your God."

In the evening quail came up and covered the camp. In the morning a dew lay all about the camp, and when the dew evaporated, there on the surface of the desert were fine flakes like hoarfrost on the ground. On seeing it, the Israelites asked one another, "What is this?" for they did not know what it was. But Moses told them, "This is the bread that the Lord has given you to eat."

PSALM RESPONSE
Psalm 78:24b

The Lord gave them bread from heaven.

SECOND READING
Ephesians 4: 17, 20–24

Brothers and sisters: I declare and testify in the Lord that you must no longer live as the Gentiles do, in the futility of their minds; that is not how you learned Christ, assuming that you have heard of him and were taught in him, as truth is in Jesus, that you should put away the old self of your former way of life, corrupted through deceitful desires, and be renewed in the spirit of your minds, and put on the new self, created in God's way in righteousness and holiness of truth.

GOSPEL
John 6:24–35

When the crowd saw that neither Jesus nor his disciples were there, they themselves got into boats and came to Capernaum looking for Jesus. And when they found him across the sea they said to him, "Rabbi, when did you get here?" Jesus answered them and said, "Amen, amen, I say to you, you are looking for me not because you saw signs but because you ate the loaves and were filled. Do not work for food that perishes but for the food that endures for eternal life, which the Son of Man will give you. For on him the Father, God, has set his seal." So they said to him, "What can we do to accomplish the works of God?" Jesus answered and said to them, "This is the work of God, that you believe in the one he sent." So they said to him, "What sign can you do, that we may see and believe in you? What can you do? Our ancestors ate manna in the desert, as it is written:

He gave them bread from heaven to eat."

So Jesus said to them, "Amen, amen I say to you, it was not Moses who gave the bread from heaven; my Father gives you the true bread from heaven. For the bread of God is that which comes down from heaven and gives life to the world."

So they said to him, "Sir, give us this bread always." Jesus said to them, "I am the bread of life; whoever comes to me will never hunger, and whoever believes in me will never thirst."

Understanding the Word

Today's reading from the Gospel of John shows how easily faith in Jesus can be based on the wrong thing. The crowd that eats its fill of the bread and fish that Jesus has miraculously provided for them is ready to believe in the one who can and will take care of their physical needs.

Thus, their first reaction to this event is to declare Jesus "the Prophet, the one who is to come into the world" and to seek to make him king (John 6:14–15). When Jesus escapes from them, they get into boats, cross the Sea of Galilee, and find him on the other side (6:22–25). Physical satisfaction is a powerful drive that can even be a means by which people interpret the value of their faith.

What follows is a dialogue in which Jesus seeks to help them seek something else and the people seek to make Jesus conform to their own wishes. Jesus tells them that they should be working for the food that lasts for eternal life rather than "the food that perishes" (6:26–27). The people seem to begin on a promising note by asking how they can do this work of God.

Following Jesus' response that they do so by believing in him, however, we begin to see that the people are intent on squeezing belief into the matrix of their own appetites. They ask Jesus what sign he can show them as a basis for their belief (6:30). Have they forgotten the previous day's multiplication of the loaves and fishes? No, this is a gambit to procure an endless supply for their hungers. They subtly suggest, by noting that their ancestors were given manna, that always providing satisfaction for their appetites would be an appropriate sign (6:31). Their response to Jesus' next comment makes clear their intentions: "Sir, give us this bread always" (6:34).

How often do people bargain with God for God's work to be directed to their convenience?

Reflecting on the Word

Do you remember Wonder® Bread? The ad campaign from decades ago trumpeted the claim that it "helped build strong bodies twelve ways." I can't remember exactly how it did this, but the claim stays with me. What stays with me is not that it tasted good or bad, but that it was rather bland. But when you are hungry . . .

The people in today's readings are hungry, both the grumbling crowd that Moses faced out in the desert, and the crowd that Jesus filled when he fed them up on the mountain, who tracked him down the next day, going by boat to the lakeside town of Capernaum. In both cases, the people wanted more food.

In both cases God acted to feed the people. For the Israelites in the desert, God provided manna (a word that literally means "what is it?"), which most likely was the juice secreted by certain desert insects after eating the desert bushes—a form of "bug juice," sweet, but short-lived. God provided this for Israel during their entire time in the desert. Not much variety, it would seem, but no one starved either.

When the crowd comes to Jesus looking for another course of barley bread, Jesus directs their attention to a deeper hunger that can be satisfied only by the "true bread from heaven" (John 6:32), himself: "I am the bread of life; whoever comes to me will never hunger" (6:35).

Paul calls on us to put on a new self, one "created in God's way in righteousness and holiness of truth" (Ephesians 4:24). This deep inner growth into a new self will demand more than "bug juice"; only bread from heaven that gives eternal life will do.

CONSIDER/ DISCUSS:
- Even the greatest meals soon fade from memory and give way to hunger. When was the last time you had a meal whose effects were long lasting?
- When you think of your "deepest hungers," what comes to mind?
- How has Jesus been "bread for life" for you?

Responding to the Word

Place yourself in the presence of the Lord and speak to God of your deepest hunger. How do you want the Lord to respond to this hunger? Is it possible that this hunger is leading you to a yet deeper hunger, the hunger for communion with Jesus Christ and with the Father?

August 9, 2009

NINETEENTH SUNDAY IN ORDINARY TIME

Today's Focus: Jesus, Food for the Journey

The dialogue between Jesus and the crowd he has fed continues, but with a change in tone. The impulse to make Jesus king and the desire for the bread that gives life to the world now gives way to dismissing Jesus because they know the man and his parents. The journey of faith Jesus is calling them to make is only possible with the help of the Father.

FIRST READING
1 Kings 19:4–8

Elijah went a day's journey into the desert, until he came to a broom tree and sat beneath it. He prayed for death, saying: "This is enough, O LORD! Take my life, for I am no better than my fathers." He lay down and fell asleep under the broom tree, but then an angel touched him and ordered him to get up and eat. Elijah looked and there at his head was a hearth cake and a jug of water. After he ate and drank, he lay down again, but the angel of the LORD came back a second time, touched him, and ordered, "Get up and eat, else the journey will be too long for you!" He got up, ate, and drank; then strengthened by that food, he walked forty days and forty nights to the mountain of God, Horeb.

PSALM RESPONSE
Psalm 34:9a

Taste and see the goodness of the Lord.

SECOND READING
Ephesians 4:30 — 5:2

Brothers and sisters: Do not grieve the Holy Spirit of God, with which you were sealed for the day of redemption. All bitterness, fury, anger, shouting, and reviling must be removed from you, along with all malice. And be kind to one another, compassionate, forgiving one another as God has forgiven you in Christ.

So be imitators of God, as beloved children, and live in love, as Christ loved us and handed himself over for us as a sacrificial offering to God for a fragrant aroma.

The Jews murmured about Jesus because he said, "I am the bread that came down from heaven," and they said, "Is this not Jesus, the son of Joseph? Do we not know his father and mother? Then how can he say, 'I have come down from heaven'?" Jesus answered and said to them, "Stop murmuring among yourselves. No one can come to me unless the Father who sent me draw him, and I will raise him on the last day. It is written in the prophets:

They shall all be taught by God.

Everyone who listens to my Father and learns from him comes to me. Not that anyone has seen the Father except the one who is from God; he has seen the Father. Amen, amen, I say to you, whoever believes has eternal life. I am the bread of life. Your ancestors ate the manna in the desert, but they died; this is the bread that comes down from heaven so that one may eat it and not die. I am the living bread that came down from heaven; whoever eats this bread will live forever; and the bread that I will give is my flesh for the life of the world."

Understanding the Word

Today we hear Jesus' response to those who were upset about his explanation that the multiplication of the bread and fish signifies that he himself is the heavenly bread that gives eternal life. In this response we find that the acceptance of Jesus' message is facilitated or hindered by how people have appropriated the Old Testament.

Jesus' initial response to those who were "murmuring" against his words is to say no one is able to come to Jesus unless the Father brings them to Jesus (John 6:43–44). How the Father does so is immediately explained when Jesus, citing a prophetic verse, says that the one who listens and learns from the Father comes to Jesus (6:45). Then Jesus himself points to the scripture of the wilderness generation eating manna in the desert, as the people who were murmuring against Jesus had also done (6:31, 49). He does so in order to illustrate his claim that he is the true bread from heaven that enables eternal life (6:50–51).

The people Jesus is talking to wanted bread simply to satisfy their appetites. They have not learned from the scriptures that the manna from heaven was to sustain them on their journey to the promised land and not just to satisfy their hunger. They have not learned from the Exodus account that the purpose of the manna was sustenance toward a greater goal and not the goal itself. In John 5:45–47, too, we read that the reason that the people do not believe in Jesus is because they have not believed in Moses.

Understanding the Old Testament leads to belief in Jesus; failure to understand it leads to unbelief. The New Testament and its witness stand or fall for these people on the basis of their appreciation and understanding of the Old Testament witness that undergirds it.

Reflecting on the Word

The poet Constantinos Cavafys offers a wonderful insight in his poem "Ithaca," whose title refers to the hometown Odysseus spends years journeying toward in *The Odyssey*. Ithaca stands for every destination for which we set out in our lives; every goal we try to achieve. Cavafys concludes that, while arriving there is your ultimate goal, Ithaca's greatest gift is the voyage she provokes you to take: "Without her you would never have set out on the road."

The God of the Bible is a God who invites people to journey. It begins with Abraham, then with Moses and the Israelites. Then there are the journeys the prophets take, like Elijah in today's reading, who is tired of being "on the road," but to whom God sends an angel of the Lord to feed so he can be on his way again to the mountain where he will meet God. God is a God who calls us to journey, and while we are on the journey God provides food: manna in the desert, a hearth cake on the way to the mountains.

Sometimes the journey is a physical one, but not always. The Jews in today's Gospel are invited to take a journey of faith: to see Jesus not as the son of Joseph but as one who came down from heaven. But they resist. They don't want to go far from their "home," their comfort zone. To take this journey, they have to listen to the Father and learn that Jesus is indeed the Son, the living bread come down from heaven. And heaven knows where that will lead. Who knows what they will be given to eat?

CONSIDER/ DISCUSS:
- If you think of your life as a journey God is taking with you, where have you been and where are you heading?
- What do you need to know to complete the journey?
- How has God fed you over the years? Do you see God feeding you now?

Responding to the Word

Like Elijah, we can get weary on the journey; like the crowd in the Gospel today, we can resist when God is doing something new in our lives. Ask God to help you be attuned to how God is speaking to you, how God is feeding you.

August 15, 2009

THE ASSUMPTION OF THE BLESSED VIRGIN MARY

Today's Focus: Mary, Mother of Hope

This venerable solemnity of Mary has its origins in the Eastern Church in the fifth century, where it was called her "Dormition" (that is, her "falling asleep"). Later, when it came into the West, it was named the Assumption. What we celebrate is the taking up of the Blessed Virgin Mary, Mother of God, body and soul, into heaven. It is a feast of hope that what has been done for her will also be done for all who hear the word of God and keep it.

FIRST READING
Revelation 11: 19a; 12:1–6a, 10ab

God's temple in heaven was opened, and the ark of his covenant could be seen in the temple.

A great sign appeared in the sky, a woman clothed with the sun, with the moon beneath her feet, and on her head a crown of twelve stars. She was with child and wailed aloud in pain as she labored to give birth. Then another sign appeared in the sky; it was a huge red dragon, with seven heads and ten horns, and on its heads were seven diadems. Its tail swept away a third of the stars in the sky and hurled them down to the earth. Then the dragon stood before the woman about to give birth, to devour her child when she gave birth. She gave birth to a son, a male child, destined to rule all the nations with an iron rod. Her child was caught up to God and his throne. The woman herself fled into the desert where she had a place prepared by God.

Then I heard a loud voice in heaven say: "Now have salvation and power come, and the kingdom of our God and the authority of his Anointed One."

PSALM RESPONSE
Psalm 45:10bc

The queen stands at your right hand, arrayed in gold.

SECOND READING
1 Corinthians 15: 20–27

Brothers and sisters: Christ has been raised from the dead, the first-fruits of those who have fallen asleep. For since death came through man, the resurrection of the dead came also through man. For just as in Adam all die, so too in Christ shall all be brought to life, but each one in proper order: Christ the firstfruits; then, at his coming, those who belong to Christ; then comes the end, when he hands over the kingdom to his God and Father, when he has destroyed every sovereignty and every authority and power. For he must reign until he has put all his enemies under his feet. The last enemy to be destroyed is death, for "he subjected everything under his feet."

GOSPEL
Luke 1:39–56

Mary set out and traveled to the hill country in haste to a town of Judah, where she entered the house of Zechariah and greeted Elizabeth. When Elizabeth heard Mary's greeting, the infant leaped in her womb, and Elizabeth, filled with the Holy Spirit, cried out in a loud voice and said, "Blessed are you among women, and blessed is the fruit of your womb. And how does this happen to me, that the mother of my Lord should come to me? For at the moment the sound of your greeting reached my ears, the infant in my womb leaped for joy. Blessed are you who believed that what was spoken to you by the Lord would be fulfilled."

And Mary said:

"My soul proclaims the greatness of the Lord;
  my spirit rejoices in God my Savior
  for he has looked upon his lowly servant.
From this day all generations will call me blessed:
  the Almighty has done great things for me,
  and holy is his Name.
He has mercy on those who fear him
  in every generation.
He has shown the strength of his arm,
  and has scattered the proud in their conceit.
He has cast down the mighty from their thrones,
  and has lifted up the lowly.
He has filled the hungry with good things,
  and the rich he has sent away empty.
He has come to the help of his servant Israel
  for he has remembered his promise of mercy,
  the promise he made to our fathers,
  to Abraham and his children for ever."

Mary remained with her about three months and then returned to her home.

Understanding the Word

The story of the assumption of Mary first appears in post-biblical literature. Nevertheless, the Church understands it to be congruent with the scriptures.

Mary is seen as a model for the church. The reading from the book of Revelation treats with vivid apocalyptic imagery the divine protection of the Messiah and the people of God from whom the Messiah was born. In typical apocalyptic fashion, the powerful hold of evil on the world is highlighted. Thus, the devil (Revelation 12:3, 9) is portrayed as a cosmic seven-headed dragon. Its power is signified by the diadem it wears on each of its heads, and its action of sweeping a third of the stars down to earth with its tail (12:3–4a). All of this malevolent power then becomes focused against the Messiah who is to be born from a woman, as the dragon prepares to devour it when it is born (12:4b). In this text, it appears that the woman represents the people of God and the child symbolizes the Messiah. It is easy to see, however, that the message of this passage could be applied to the Blessed Mother. The passage continues to speak of God's deliverance of the child and protection of the woman in order to show that no evil is powerful enough, no evil has a firm enough hold on life to stand in the way of God's salvation (12:5–6).

The threat of imminent death to God's special agent of salvation, the deliverance of this agent, and the protection of the woman are in a trajectory that leads the church to expect the deliverance of the woman as well. God's protection of the child is described with the words, "Her child was caught up to God and his throne" (12:5). It is this type of scriptural imagery that nourishes the development of the doctrine that the Blessed Mother was assumed bodily into the heavens.

Reflecting on the Word

I find that the feast of the Assumption has begun to take on more meaning for me as I get older. From its early days the tradition has been handed down that Mary, the mother of the Lord, was taken up into heaven at the completion of her life. Some may see this as one of those feasts that sets her apart from us. But I think it is a feast that upholds the promise in which we all share: that in Christ we shall have eternal life.

The second reading from St. Paul's First Letter to the Corinthians offers a reflection on the hope that we have because of the resurrection of Christ. Paul speaks of Christ as "the firstfruits of those who have fallen asleep" (1 Corinthians 15:20). Just as Christ was raised from the dead, so too shall all be who are baptized into Christ. Paul says this will occur in proper order: Christ the firstfruits, then, at his coming, those who belong to Christ.

When I said this feast has more meaning the older I get, this has to do with all those who have passed on ahead of me: grandparents and parents, other members of my family, members of my religious community, friends, parishioners, and so many good people who have passed through my life for a short time, never to be seen again. I cannot believe that all this goodness has ceased to be forever.

Our faith tells us we are destined for the resurrection of the flesh and life eternal. This has already happened for Jesus and his mother. In this we find a promise rooted in the God who is the source of all life; in this we have a continued basis for hope and a motive to live now in light of what is to come.

CONSIDER/ DISCUSS:
- Does the feast of the Assumption make Mary seem more distant from you or, paradoxically, closer to you?
- How do you relate this feast to Mary as Mother of Hope?

Responding to the Word

We pray today for all those who have passed on and rest in the Lord. We pray that we might not lose sight of the promise of this feast for ourselves and that we will live faithful to God and as keepers and doers of the word of God that has been entrusted to us.

August 16, 2009

TWENTIETH SUNDAY IN ORDINARY TIME

Today's Focus: Eating Wisely or Feasting Like Fools

The Bread of Life discourse in John 6 builds to this proclamation of Jesus as bread broken and blood poured out for us. Today we are at the heart of this discourse in which Jesus says that his body must be eaten and his blood must be drunk. Creation itself, in the form of food and drink, provides the signs of his self-giving.

FIRST
READING
Proverbs 9:1–6

Wisdom has built her house,
    she has set up her seven columns;
she has dressed her meat, mixed her wine,
    yes, she has spread her table.
She has sent out her maidens; she calls
    from the heights out over the city:
"Let whoever is simple turn in here;
    to the one who lacks understanding, she says,
Come, eat of my food,
    and drink of the wine I have mixed!
Forsake foolishness that you may live;
    advance in the way of understanding."

PSALM
RESPONSE
Psalm 34:9a

Taste and see the goodness of the Lord.

SECOND
READING
Ephesians 5:
15–20

Brothers and sisters: Watch carefully how you live, not as foolish persons but as wise, making the most of the opportunity, because the days are evil. Therefore, do not continue in ignorance, but try to understand what is the will of the Lord. And do not get drunk on wine, in which lies debauchery, but be filled with the Spirit, addressing one another in psalms and hymns and spiritual songs, singing and playing to the Lord in your hearts, giving thanks always and for everything in the name of our Lord Jesus Christ to God the Father.

169

GOSPEL
John 6:51–58

Jesus said to the crowds: "I am the living bread that came down from heaven; whoever eats this bread will live forever; and the bread that I will give is my flesh for the life of the world."

The Jews quarreled among themselves, saying, "How can this man give us his flesh to eat?" Jesus said to them, "Amen, amen, I say to you, unless you eat the flesh of the Son of Man and drink his blood, you do not have life within you. Whoever eats my flesh and drinks my blood has eternal life, and I will raise him on the last day. For my flesh is true food, and my blood is true drink. Whoever eats my flesh and drinks my blood remains in me and I in him. Just as the living Father sent me and I have life because of the Father, so also the one who feeds on me will have life because of me. This is the bread that came down from heaven. Unlike your ancestors who ate and still died, whoever eats this bread will live forever."

Understanding the Word

The reading from the Old Testament today is part of the culmination of the first nine chapters of the book of Proverbs. This summation describes life as a journey in which conflicting voices beckon to us.

In order to appreciate today's reading it is necessary to understand its original primary audience. Proverbs is a compilation of the wisdom of Israel that had been formulated to function as a guide to young males who are coming of age. This is why so much of the counsel is addressed to "my son." Two major problems that these young men face are newly developed physical strength and raging hormones, and so at the very beginning of the book the author inveighs against gang violence for robbery and the lure of the prostitute (Proverbs 1:10–14; 2:16–19; 5:1–23; 6:20–35; 7:6–27).

In our reading today Wisdom has a house and calls to people to eat and drink of her nourishment and to "forsake foolishness" (9:1, 3, 5–6). The banquet that Wisdom prepares leads to understanding and life (9:4, 6). These activities of Wisdom are presented as alternatives to the activities by which the prostitute lures men. Thus, in 2:16–19 the wanton lures with "smooth words" (2:16; 6:24; 7:5, 21); her lips "drip with honey" and her words are "smoother than oil" (5:3). So, too, the prostitute offers the man a drink of love (6:18). Finally, whereas going to Wisdom leads to life (9:6), going to the prostitute leads to death (2:18–19; 5:5, 11; 7:22–23, 26–27).

We live at a time when so many hunger for the basics, when millions are threatened with famine and even the lack of such a necessity as water. It takes no large degree of empathy to feel great compassion in the face of those images of gaunt-faced adults and children with swollen bellies. This common human experience of the importance of eating and drinking has also served as an image for the necessary nourishment needed for eternal life, for our ongoing life in God.

From the beginning in Eden, God was concerned with what Adam and Eve ate—and what they should not eat. "You can eat from all the trees except this one," God told them. Nourishment came in two forms: the food of creation and the food of God's word, calling for obedience. In the journey through the desert God fed the people with manna for their bodies, then offered the Torah for their spirits.

Today we have a poetic image of God in the first reading as Lady Wisdom—or Woman Wisdom, as might be preferred—pictured as gracious figure who has prepared her meat and given attention to her wine so that the simple might be nourished, food for the spirit that offers understanding in the place of foolishness for one reason: "that you may live" (Proverbs 9:6). Forsaking foolishness and living wisely is again echoed in the letter to the Ephesians.

Jesus' words today are the most challenging of all. In place of the manna and the Torah, he calls on the crowds to eat his flesh and drink his blood, offering himself as food that will bring eternal life. While we can certainly hear in this a reference to the Eucharist, it is first of all a call to accept Jesus as the Wisdom of God, as the Revelation of God who feeds us for eternal life.

CONSIDER/ DISCUSS:
- Do you see a connection between Jesus calling us to eat his flesh and drink his blood and the figure of Wisdom setting a table and calling us to forsake foolishness and grow in understanding?
- How does the eating and drinking of the Eucharist call for a life given for others, poured out for others?
- How is the Spirit leading you away from foolishness to a life of wisdom and understanding?

Responding to the Word

The purpose of Proverbs 9:1–6 is to present the value of wisdom as a counterforce to those voices in society that take young men away from a full life. Each generation must identify the harmful voices to which various segments of the community are exposed and present Wisdom as the better option.

TWENTY-FIRST SUNDAY IN ORDINARY TIME

Today's Focus: Following the Leader

Joshua of the Hebrew scriptures and Joshua (Jesus) of the Christian scriptures are set before us today. Each is laying down a challenge to the people, calling them to choose life with the God of the covenant. Both make it clear where their allegiance lies. Where does our allegiance lie?

FIRST READING
Joshua 24:1–2a, 15–17, 18b

Joshua gathered together all the tribes of Israel at Shechem, summoning their elders, their leaders, their judges, and their officers. When they stood in ranks before God, Joshua addressed all the people:

"If it does not please you to serve the LORD, decide today whom you will serve, the gods your fathers served beyond the River or the gods of the Amorites in whose country you are now dwelling. As for me and my household, we will serve the LORD."

But the people answered, "Far be it from us to forsake the LORD for the service of other gods. For it was the LORD, our God, who brought us and our fathers up out of the land of Egypt, out of a state of slavery. He performed those great miracles before our very eyes and protected us along our entire journey and among the peoples through whom we passed. Therefore we also will serve the LORD, for he is our God."

PSALM RESPONSE
Psalm 34:9a

Taste and see the goodness of the Lord.

In the shorter form of the reading, the passage in brackets is omitted

SECOND READING
Ephesians 5: 21–32 or 5:2a, 25–32

Brothers and sisters: [Be subordinate to one another out of reverence for Christ. Wives should be subordinate to their husbands as to the Lord. For the husband is head of his wife just as Christ is head of the church, he himself the savior of the body. As the church is subordinate to Christ, so wives should be subordinate to their husbands in everything.] Husbands, love your wives, even as Christ loved the church and handed himself over for her to sanctify her, cleansing her by the bath of water with the word, that he might present to himself the church in splendor, without spot or wrinkle or any such thing, that she might be holy and without blemish. So also husbands should love their wives as their own bodies. He who loves his wife loves himself. For no one hates his own flesh but rather nourishes and cherishes it, even as Christ does the church, because we are members of his body.

> For this reason a man shall leave his father and his mother
>   and be joined to his wife,
>   and the two shall become one flesh.

This is a great mystery, but I speak in reference to Christ and the church.

GOSPEL
John 6:60–69

Many of Jesus' disciples who were listening said, "This saying is hard; who can accept it?" Since Jesus knew that his disciples were murmuring about this, he said to them, "Does this shock you? What if you were to see the Son of Man ascending to where he was before? It is the spirit that gives life, while the flesh is of no avail. The words I have spoken to you are Spirit and life. But there are some of you who do not believe." Jesus knew from the beginning the ones who would not believe and the one who would betray him. And he said, "For this reason I have told you that no one can come to me unless it is granted him by my Father."

As a result of this, many of his disciples returned to their former way of life and no longer accompanied him. Jesus then said to the Twelve, "Do you also want to leave?" Simon Peter answered him, "Master, to whom shall we go? You have the words of eternal life. We have come to believe and are convinced that you are the Holy One of God."

Understanding the Word

Today's reading from John's Gospel is the conclusion of the lengthy section in chapter 6 on Jesus as the bread of life. This reading illustrates Jesus' forthright clarity in proclaiming the word of God and calling people to accept this word no matter what the cost.

Earlier in John 6 we heard about people complaining about what Jesus is saying (John 6:41–42, 52). But today's passage marks a watershed. Now it is no longer the larger crowd who complain, but Jesus' own disciples have problems with his "hard sayings"; they cannot see how Jesus' words can be accepted (6:60). Jesus' response is to confront the issue head-on. He asks them if they take offense at his words, and then he startles them with even more difficult words: that he will ascend to God from whom he came (6:61–62).

Why burden his disciples with another difficult saying when they are already having problems believing? Is Jesus not concerned that he might lose disciples if he doesn't move them more gradually to the understanding necessary to accept his words? For Jesus, two ideas seem to be at work. First, people have already had preparation from God. If they have learned from God, they will come to Jesus (6:44–45, 65). Second, there is a need for unambiguous witness in a society in which clear witness is threatened with death (5:18). Without such witness, one might keep disciples but there would be no chance for mature belief.

The result of Jesus' question to the disciples who cannot accept his words is predictable: many leave him (6:66). But then Jesus calls the Twelve who were silent to make a decision based on what they have heard (6:67). His unambiguous witness must be met with unambiguous declarations of faith. Candor enables people to receive and accept the rich implications of faith.

Joshua/Jesus means "God saves." The first Joshua was the servant of Moses who ended up leading the Israelites into the Promised Land. God chose him as Moses' successor and he received the Spirit of God when Moses laid his hands on him. In today's first reading Joshua calls the people to renew their fidelity to the covenant with God. The people are united in their choice.

A choice is also made in today's Gospel. (It may be helpful to read all of chapter 6 from the Gospel of Saint John in order to appreciate what is happening here, what is being rejected or accepted.) Jesus' words that we have heard over the last few weeks now receive a mixed reaction from the disciples present. Some say, "This saying is hard. Who can accept it?" (John 6:60). We are told that many of those who had been following him "returned to their former way of life and no longer accompanied him" (6:66).

But for Peter and the rest of the Twelve, there is trust in Jesus and what he has been saying. Peter speaks for them all when he quickly responds to Jesus' question about whether they too are going to walk away: "Master, to whom shall we go? You have the words of eternal life" (6:68). This is one time I doubt that Jesus was upset at Peter's impetuousness. In contrast to the story of Joshua, the people around Jesus are divided in their choice.

The choice needs to be made again and again over the course of a lifetime. Have you made your choice to follow our leader, Jesus, who has the words of eternal life?

CONSIDER/ DISCUSS:
- Who has been a leader for you in life? Whom have you followed?
- When Jesus says, "No one can come to me unless it is granted him by my Father" (6:65), does this mean that the Father might not want some to come to him?
- Are you convinced that Jesus "has the words of eternal life," that he is "the Holy One of God" (6:68, 69)?

Responding to the Word

To be able to follow Jesus is a gift of the Father. We pray today that all will recognize the gift that is offered to all: faith in the one whom the Father sent. We pray that we will follow Jesus wherever he wishes to lead us.

August 30, 2009

TWENTY-SECOND SUNDAY IN ORDINARY TIME

Today's Focus: "Wash Your Hands!"

The Pharisees were out to trap Jesus into being careless about the law of Moses. In this way, they hoped to discredit him. The discussion today concerns the laws of cleanliness with regard to food and how it was prepared. But Jesus serves up for them a dish different from the one they had planned.

FIRST READING
Deuteronomy 4: 1–2, 6–8

Moses said to the people: "Now, Israel, hear the statutes and decrees which I am teaching you to observe, that you may live, and may enter in and take possession of the land which the LORD, the God of your fathers, is giving you. In your observance of the commandments of the LORD, your God, which I enjoin upon you, you shall not add to what I command you nor subtract from it. Observe them carefully, for thus will you give evidence of your wisdom and intelligence to the nations, who will hear of all these statutes and say, 'This great nation is truly a wise and intelligent people.' For what great nation is there that has gods so close to it as the LORD, our God, is to us whenever we call upon him? Or what great nation has statutes and decrees that are as just as this whole law which I am setting before you today?"

PSALM RESPONSE
Psalm 15:1a

The one who does justice will live in the presence of the Lord.

SECOND READING
James 1:17–18, 21b–22, 27

Dearest brothers and sisters: All good giving and every perfect gift is from above, coming down from the Father of lights, with whom there is no alteration or shadow caused by change. He willed to give us birth by the word of truth that we may be a kind of firstfruits of his creatures.

Humbly welcome the word that has been planted in you and is able to save your souls.

Be doers of the word and not hearers only, deluding yourselves.

Religion that is pure and undefiled before God and the Father is this: to care for orphans and widows in their affliction and to keep oneself unstained by the world.

175

GOSPEL
Mark 7:1–8,
14–15, 21–23

When the Pharisees with some scribes who had come from Jerusalem gathered around Jesus, they observed that some of his disciples ate their meals with unclean, that is, unwashed, hands. — For the Pharisees and, in fact, all Jews, do not eat without carefully washing their hands, keeping the tradition of the elders. And on coming from the marketplace they do not eat without purifying themselves. And there are many other things that they have traditionally observed, the purification of cups and jugs and kettles and beds. — So the Pharisees and scribes questioned him, "Why do your disciples not follow the tradition of the elders but instead eat a meal with unclean hands?" He responded, "Well did Isaiah prophesy about you hypocrites, as it is written:

This people honors me with their lips,
  but their hearts are far from me;
in vain do they worship me,
  teaching as doctrines human precepts.

You disregard God's commandment but cling to human tradition." He summoned the crowd again and said to them, "Hear me, all of you, and understand. Nothing that enters one from outside can defile that person; but the things that come out from within are what defile.

"From within people, from their hearts, come evil thoughts, unchastity, theft, murder, adultery, greed, malice, deceit, licentiousness, envy, blasphemy, arrogance, folly. All these evils come from within and they defile."

Understanding the Word

Our reading today from the Gospel of Mark presents Jesus' effort to keep his disciples properly focused in the face of an attempt by Pharisees and scribes to redirect the way the disciples express their religious commitment.

The religious leaders complain that the disciples are eating with unwashed hands. In the Old Testament such washings were necessary for priests in preparation for sacrificial offerings (Exodus 30:18–21). Apparently during Mark's time the matter of extending this practice to everyday meals was also being discussed.

The real underlying question addressed in this passage apparently concerns where and how we address our limited psychic energy. In other words, how can our life be permeated with religious conviction? Notice how time-consuming the religious leaders' concern over purification must be. Mark writes that it is not only to hands, but also to "many other things" that their concern over purification extends: "the purification of cups and jugs and kettles and beds" (Mark 7:5).

According to Jesus, it is a much better use of one's time to concentrate on purifying the thoughts that are within us and that lead to immoral activities. Corresponding to the many things that the religious leaders seek to purify are the many types of thoughts—and the activities that spring from them—that Jesus calls to his disciples' attention: "evil thoughts, unchastity, theft, murder, adultery, greed, malice, deceit, licentiousness, envy, blasphemy, arrogance, folly" (7:21–22). Moral cleanliness is from within and not from without.

176

Jesus advises his disciples that holiness is not a matter of extending temple rituals into all the various spheres of one's life, but rather a matter of allowing only those thoughts that we have purified to be the ones to which we give assent. To monitor and refine thoughts and feelings are sacred activities.

Reflecting on the Word

I remember a book from years ago called *All I Really Need to Know I Learned in Kindergarten* by Robert Fulghum. At the outset, the author listed numerous sayings from his childhood that articulated attitudes, values, and practices for living a satisfying life. Such things as taking another's hand while crossing the street and always saying thank you come to mind. From my own list I remember "Wash your hands." I was convinced that my parents obsessed over germs.

Listening to our Gospel today, you could get the impression that the Pharisees also obsessed over germs with all the fuss over cleaning hands, cups, jugs, kettles, and even beds! But the real tension here is between keeping or ignoring the "traditions of the elders." So when the religious laymen of Jesus' day—the Pharisees (the word itself means "the separate ones")—complained, they were perceived as taking the traditions of the law very seriously, whereas Jesus' disciples came across as clueless about the niceties of the law of Moses.

Nevertheless, Jesus gets right to the point. Calling the Pharisees and scribes hypocrites, he goes on to name the real problem—not pots and pans or unclean hands, but escaping into externals rather than practicing what is at the heart of their religion: true love of God and neighbor. Jesus knew that God is not as caught up in the dirt on one's hands as with the corruption of one's spirit. So-called "religious" people could be careful about the cleanliness of their cutlery but totally oblivious to the neglect of the needy, even their own parents—all in the name of God.

Not what goes in, but what comes out is what renders a person unworthy before God. So conduct an inventory of what's being held in storage within.

CONSIDER/ DISCUSS:
- Can you think of an experience of treating something as God's law when it was only a human tradition?
- What makes for true religion?
- James calls us to "welcome the word that has been planted in you and is able to save your souls" (James 1:21). Did you hear such a word in today's readings?

Responding to the Word

It is not always easy to know what is most important. We ask the Father of lights to enlighten us by sending the Holy Spirit, so that we can be "doers of the word and not hearers only" (James 1:22).

September 6, 2009

TWENTY-THIRD SUNDAY IN ORDINARY TIME

Today's Focus: Making Contact

A man who is deaf and has a speech impediment is at the heart of today's Gospel. He is brought to Jesus, who leads him to a quiet place and heals him. Being able to hear and speak is crucial to being in communion with others. Jesus continues to touch ears and tongues so that we might hear his voice and sing his praise.

FIRST READING
Isaiah 35:4–7a

Thus says the LORD:
    Say to those whose hearts are frightened:
        Be strong, fear not!
    Here is your God,
        he comes with vindication;
    with divine recompense
        he comes to save you.
    Then will the eyes of the blind be opened,
        the ears of the deaf be cleared;
    then will the lame leap like a stag,
        then the tongue of the mute will sing.
    Streams will burst forth in the desert,
        and rivers in the steppe.
    The burning sands will become pools,
        and the thirsty ground, springs of water.

PSALM RESPONSE
Psalm 146:1b

Praise the Lord, my soul!

SECOND READING
James 2:1–5

My brothers and sisters, show no partiality as you adhere to the faith in our glorious Lord Jesus Christ. For if a man with gold rings and fine clothes comes into your assembly, and a poor person in shabby clothes also comes in, and you pay attention to the one wearing the fine clothes and say, "Sit here, please," while you say to the poor one, "Stand there," or "Sit at my feet," have you not made distinctions among yourselves and become judges with evil designs?

Listen, my beloved brothers and sisters. Did not God choose those who are poor in the world to be rich in faith and heirs of the kingdom that he promised to those who love him?

Again Jesus left the district of Tyre and went by way of Sidon to the Sea of Galilee, into the district of the Decapolis. And people brought to him a deaf man who had a speech impediment and begged him to lay his hand on him. He took him off by himself away from the crowd. He put his finger into the man's ears and, spitting, touched his tongue; then he looked up to heaven and groaned, and said to him, *"Ephphatha!"* — that is, "Be opened!" — And immediately the man's ears were opened, his speech impediment was removed, and he spoke plainly. He ordered them not to tell anyone. But the more he ordered them not to, the more they proclaimed it. They were exceedingly astonished and they said, "He has done all things well. He makes the deaf hear and the mute speak."

Understanding the Word

Now Mark's Jesus has left for Gentile lands as our story takes place east of the Jordan River (Mark 7:31–37). Already he has journeyed to other Gentile territory (7:24–30). In both places Jesus performs a miracle. Both miracles occur right after a discussion between Jewish religious leaders and Jesus concerning what true purity is all about.

The context of this discussion colors the meaning of the passage for today. Life should not be spent constructing a sanctuary around oneself, but rather going out to those beyond our comfort zone, with holiness guiding our thoughts and feelings. Holiness is outward-flowing and inclusive rather than inward-tending and exclusive.

In the prior discussion Pharisees and scribes had advocated extensive purifications. This was a means of sanctifying life by extending temple practices into daily life. In today's passage Jesus moves out to the unclean Gentile areas, and there he heals a man unable to hear and speak. The contrast between this healing and the earlier concern of the religious leaders for purification is striking and instructive. The leaders do not eat without washing their hands (7:2–3); Jesus puts saliva on his hands and with it touches the tongue of a man with a speech impediment (7:33).

The result is that the man can now speak *orthos*, a word that can mean "plainly" but that also commonly means "rightly." This new-found type of speech contrasts with the religious leaders who were not speaking rightly but only honoring Jesus with their lips (7:6–7). The man is not only mute but deaf as well. Jesus responds to this condition by putting his hands in the man's ears (7:33). By going out and being concerned to touch people where they hurt (here the tongue and ears), Jesus brought people to a correct perspective. This healing is similar to a later healing, also involving Jesus' saliva and touch, of the blind man in Bethsaida (8:22–26). This latter miracle is commonly looked upon as symbolic of the spiritual enlightenment that the disciples need to achieve.

Rather than being concerned with keeping oneself pure (washing of hands), Jesus heals the man in a tactile way. So this passage shows that moral cleanliness comes not only by monitoring and refining one's thoughts and feelings (7:1–23), but also by trying to touch others in healing ways where they are hurting.

I remember being at the shrine of Saint Anne de Beaupré outside Quebec City one summer many years ago. Another Redemptorist priest and I were preaching the novena before the feast of Saint Anne at the end of July. Busloads of people would come up. One bus brought a number of people disabled in different ways. I remember one young woman coming to confession who had a severe speech impediment, and to assure her I was understanding her, I would repeat after her what I heard her saying. She was so determined to have me understand and was trying with such vigor that I remember her teeth cutting her tongue, and yet she paid no attention to the pain it must have caused. All she cared about was having me understand what she was saying. I was never more aware how much it means to be understood by another.

We know that the miracles of Jesus were signs of the inbreaking of the kingdom of God. Jesus came to remove all obstacles that prevent the kingdom from coming and that block us from being in communion with each other. Being unable to hear or speak clearly could certainly remove a person from being present to or for others. I say this as one who has begun to lose his hearing. Yet these miracles, like the healing of the man in today's Gospel, speak to us of a deeper healing that happens when Jesus enters our lives.

Jesus came to restore all men and women to communion with God and with each other. He came to take away fear from hearts that are frightened, as the prophet Isaiah proclaims. This fear can prevent us from hearing God's word drawing us near and from witnessing to others about the living God and what God wishes for us: fullness of life.

CONSIDER/ DISCUSS:
- Have you known times when fear has prevented you from saying what needed to be said or from hearing what God was telling you?
- Is there someone you know who needs the healing touch of Jesus?
- How does Jesus continue to use ordinary things in creation, such as the spit he used in this story, to bring his healing touch to our world?

◻ *Responding to the Word*

We need to bring to Jesus in our prayer those who cannot hear what God is saying to them or respond to what God is calling them to be—and this always includes the possibility of ourselves. Sometimes God speaks to us through the scriptures, at other times through the events of our lives and the happenings in our world. Lord, help us to hear, and help us to speak clearly a word of thanksgiving and praise.

September 13, 2009

TWENTY-FOURTH SUNDAY IN ORDINARY TIME

Today's Focus: The Labor of Learning

Jesus teaches his disciples today the most important lesson they have to learn: who he is. Notice how Jesus goes from asking a question with which they would be comfortable to one with which they might feel less at ease, finally speaking a lesson that could only bring great distress.

FIRST READING
Isaiah 50:5–9a

The Lord GOD opens my ear that I may hear;
    and I have not rebelled,
    have not turned back.
I gave my back to those who beat me,
    my cheeks to those who plucked my beard;
my face I did not shield
    from buffets and spitting.
The Lord GOD is my my help,
    therefore I am not disgraced;
I have set my face like flint,
    knowing that I shall not be put to shame.
He is near who upholds my right;
    if anyone wishes to oppose me,
    let us appear together.
Who disputes my right?
    Let that man confront me.
See, the Lord GOD is my help;
    who will prove me wrong?

PSALM RESPONSE
Psalm 116:9

I will walk before the Lord, in the land of the living.

SECOND READING
James 2:14–18

What good is it, my brothers and sisters, if someone says he has faith but does not have works? Can that faith save him? If a brother or sister has nothing to wear and has no food for the day, and one of you says to them, "Go in peace, keep warm, and eat well," but you do not give them the necessities of the body, what good is it? So also faith of itself, if it does not have works, is dead.

Indeed someone might say, "You have faith and I have works." Demonstrate your faith to me without works, and I will demonstrate my faith to you from my works.

Jesus and his disciples set out for the villages of Caesarea Philippi. Along the way he asked his disciples, "Who do people say that I am?" They said in reply, "John the Baptist, others Elijah, still others one of the prophets." And he asked them, "But who do you say that I am?" Peter said to him in reply, "You are the Christ." Then he warned them not to tell anyone about him.

He began to teach them that the Son of Man must suffer greatly and be rejected by the elders, the chief priests, and the scribes, and be killed, and rise after three days. He spoke this openly. Then Peter took him aside and began to rebuke him. At this he turned around and, looking at his disciples, rebuked Peter and said, "Get behind me, Satan. You are thinking not as God does, but as human beings do."

He summoned the crowd with his disciples and said to them, "Whoever wishes to come after me must deny himself, take up his cross, and follow me. For whoever wishes to save his life will lose it, but whoever loses his life for my sake and that of the gospel will save it."

Understanding the Word

In Mark 8:27–10:45 Jesus turns his attention to preparing his disciples for his passion and death and for the necessity of accepting suffering in their own lives. Like the religious leaders, the disciples substitute their own perspectives on what constitutes a religious life for God's perspective. Thus, Jesus contrasts the views of both Peter and the religious leaders with that of God (7:8; 8:33b) and criticizes both of them in harsh terms (7:6–13; 8:33).

Peter rebukes Jesus for saying that Jesus will suffer, be killed, and rise again (8:31–32). The disciples express no hesitancy about making the sacrifices necessary to guide their thoughts and feelings or about trying to heal those who are suffering (7:17–37). But to witness to a suffering messiah and not to be ashamed of such a message seems too much for them.

Is it easier to witness to what God does for us ("Grant that in your glory we may sit one at your right hand and the other at your left" [10:37]) than to what God suffers because of us ("the Son of Man came . . . to give his life as a ransom for many" [10:45])? The former speaks indirectly about the richness of our lives because of God, but the latter about our poverty because of our need for conversion. In Mark's Gospel Jesus has attempted, by enjoining silence on those he healed, to get people to concentrate on their need for reform rather than on a temporal life made full. For Jesus the wise long-term perspective focuses on eternal life (8:38). What it takes for such life is much reform, not profit or gain in the world (8:36).

Mark says that the witness to Jesus' suffering on our behalf and then to his resurrection links us to the pattern of continuing reform leading to eternal life. This witness is important enough to die for because it leads to the fullness of life (8:35).

Going to the school of Jesus was not always easy for the disciples. Beginning with this event, Jesus begins to educate them about what it means to be his disciple. He starts with the basics: who he is. Like a good teacher, he engages them in a discussion, asking two questions, going from the easier one to the more demanding one: Who do others say I am? Who do you say I am?

The first question gets a quick answer, but the second one gets only Peter's response. By saying "You are the Christ" (Mark 8:29), Peter was naming Jesus as the long-awaited Anointed One, the one who would come to restore Israel's political kingdom and overthrow the Romans. But this was not to be. Jesus counters Peter by speaking of himself as the Son of Man who must suffer, be rejected, and be killed, and then rise after three days.

Peter is aghast at this and places himself in front of Jesus so that Jesus has to tell him to get behind him. Peter is blocking his way, like an obstacle, a stumbling block, an adversary (Satan) preventing Jesus from going in the direction he is heading. Peter had learned about a Messiah of power and prestige and Jesus was talking about a Man of pain and punishment. Peter wanted a political Messiah, not a suffering one. Peter saw the disciples taking part in the pomp and pageantry of a new age, and Jesus was speaking of denying oneself and picking up a cross.

But to graduate from the school of Jesus means moving out of your comfort zone into a distressful district: a place where you take up the cross of self-denial and self-sacrifice. Of course, it all depends on how you answer his question: Who do you say that I am?

CONSIDER/ DISCUSS:
- How would you answer today if Jesus asked, "Who do you say that I am?"
- Peter the rock becomes Peter the block by trying to impose his own agenda on Jesus. Is there an agenda belonging to me, my family, my parish community, my country, that runs counter to the agenda of Jesus?
- Does God want us to suffer?

Responding to the Word

We pray that we come to know who Jesus is and how he is calling us to enter into his ministry to bring life to our world. We pray that we might better understand what we need to die to, so that God's reign might become more present in our world.

September 20, 2009

TWENTY-FIFTH SUNDAY IN ORDINARY TIME

Today's Focus: Kingdom Etiquette

Once more we find Jesus teaching his disciples about the destiny of the Son of Man, who is to be handed over, killed, and then raised up. But this time no one questions or objects. Instead they end up bickering about who is the greatest. Jesus' response is to instruct them in kingdom etiquette.

FIRST READING
Wisdom 2:12, 17–20

The wicked say:
    Let us beset the just one, because he is obnoxious to us;
        he sets himself against our doings,
    reproaches us for transgressions of the law
        and charges us with violations of our training.
    Let us see whether his words be true;
        let us find out what will happen to him.
    For if the just one be the son of God, God will defend him
        and deliver him from the hand of his foes.
    With revilement and torture let us put the just one to the test
        that we may have proof of his gentleness
        and try his patience.
    Let us condemn him to a shameful death;
        for according to his own words, God will take care of him.

PSALM RESPONSE
Psalm 54:6b

The Lord upholds my life.

SECOND READING
James 3:16 — 4:3

Beloved: Where jealousy and selfish ambition exist, there is disorder and every foul practice. But the wisdom from above is first of all pure, then peaceable, gentle, compliant, full of mercy and good fruits, without inconstancy or insincerity. And the fruit of righteousness is sown in peace for those who cultivate peace.

Where do the wars and where do the conflicts among you come from? Is it not from your passions that make war within your members? You covet but do not possess. You kill and envy but you cannot obtain; you fight and wage war. You do not possess because you do not ask. You ask but do not receive, because you ask wrongly, to spend it on your passions.

184

GOSPEL
Mark 9:30–37

Jesus and his disciples left from there and began a journey through Galilee, but he did not wish anyone to know about it. He was teaching his disciples and telling them, "The Son of Man is to be handed over to men and they will kill him, and three days after his death the Son of Man will rise." But they did not understand the saying, and they were afraid to question him.

They came to Capernaum and, once inside the house, he began to ask them, "What were you arguing about on the way?" But they remained silent. They had been discussing among themselves on the way who was the greatest. Then he sat down, called the Twelve, and said to them, "If anyone wishes to be first, he shall be the last of all and the servant of all." Taking a child, he placed it in their midst, and putting his arms around it, he said to them, "Whoever receives one child such as this in my name, receives me; and whoever receives me, receives not me but the One who sent me."

 ## Understanding the Word

Have the disciples learned from Jesus' criticism of Peter's response to the first prediction of his passion? This is the topic addressed in today's passage from the Gospel of Mark, when we hear Jesus' second prediction of his passion and the beginning of his disciples' response to it.

This time the disciples are more cautious in their reply to Jesus, no doubt the recent censure of Peter still on their minds. The first thing we hear following this second prediction is that the disciples did not understand it "and they were afraid to question him" (9:32). It soon becomes clear, however, from what the disciples discuss among themselves shortly afterwards, how far they have come in seeing the significance of Jesus' passion. They are wondering which of them is the greatest (9:34).

Jesus uses this preoccupation of theirs to turn them back to the meaning of his passion. He says that the first will be the last and that the last is the one who serves everyone (9:35). This statement links up to the third Passion prediction in which Jesus will talk about giving his life as a ransom for many in terms of service (10:45). So Jesus' suffering, to which the disciples are called to witness and follow, is a service to all.

Have they got it now? No. As we will hear next week, they respond that they saw, and attempted to stop, a man who was performing miracles in Jesus' name "because he does not follow us" (9:38). It is their privileged status in relation to Jesus that they are concerned to uphold rather than being servant to everyone.

The desire for distinction is so strong that it needs to be incessantly weeded out by a deliberate focus on the extent of Jesus' suffering service as a model for our lives as disciples.

Reflecting on the Word

The Letter of James asks where wars and conflict come from, and then answers with another question, "Is it not from your passions that make war within your members?" (James 4:1). We find a clear example of this in today's Gospel. After Jesus has spoken again about what was going to happen to him, the disciples say nothing, even though they do not understand what he is saying. Instead they go back to bickering among themselves about who is the greatest.

The passion to be great, to achieve, to be "on top," is profoundly human. We get a sense of importance by being over others, and we can get quite passionate when we feel that someone is in any way diminishing us or "dissing" us. But this is not the way of Jesus.

Greatness lies not in being first, on top, at the head of the class, accumulating the adulation and admiration of the crowd. Greatness is to be found in a willingness to be last and the servant of all. "You go first," is the motto of the kingdom. And it is not just a matter of good manners. The willingness to be the last and the least comes from the example of Jesus himself.

The wisdom he taught results in an inner world that makes us "peaceable, gentle, compliant, full of mercy and good fruits, without inconstancy or insincerity" (James 3:17). Kingdom etiquette will bring the peace for which we long.

CONSIDER/ DISCUSS:
- What criteria do you use to determine "greatness"?
- Who would Jesus place in our midst today in calling us to care for the least and the most vulnerable?
- What is your passion? Do your passions bring you peace or conflict?

Responding to the Word

We pray that we receive the wisdom of God that moves our inner being from living in conflict to being at peace. We ask God to help us to live out the etiquette of the kingdom, and to be willing to change our definition of "greatness" as the world often defines it to what Jesus proposes to his disciples today, a life of service in which we receive both Jesus and the Father who sent him.

September 27, 2009

TWENTY-SIXTH SUNDAY IN ORDINARY TIME

Today's Focus: God's Work Has Priority

In the first reading and the Gospel, we see God's power working through "outsiders." But Moses' deputy, Joshua, complains when two men start prophesying, men who were not among the seventy who were with Moses when the Lord bestowed the spirit. Similarly John tells Jesus how "we" tried to prevent someone from driving out demons in Jesus' name. Both Jesus and Moses have similar reactions: Good for God!

FIRST READING
Numbers 11: 25–29

The LORD came down in the cloud and spoke to Moses. Taking some of the spirit that was on Moses, the LORD bestowed it on the seventy elders; and as the spirit came to rest on them, they prophesied.

Now two men, one named Eldad and the other Medad, were not in the gathering but had been left in the camp. They too had been on the list, but had not gone out to the tent; yet the spirit came to rest on them also, and they prophesied in the camp. So, when a young man quickly told Moses, "Eldad and Medad are prophesying in the camp," Joshua, son of Nun, who from his youth had been Moses' aide, said, "Moses, my lord, stop them." But Moses answered him, "Are you jealous for my sake? Would that all the people of the LORD were prophets! Would that the LORD might bestow his spirit on them all!"

PSALM RESPONSE
Psalm 19:9a

The precepts of the Lord give joy to the heart.

SECOND READING
James 5:1–6

Come now, you rich, weep and wail over your impending miseries. Your wealth has rotted away, your clothes have become moth-eaten, your gold and silver have corroded, and that corrosion will be a testimony against you; it will devour your flesh like a fire. You have stored up treasure for the last days. Behold, the wages you withheld from the workers who harvested your fields are crying aloud; and the cries of the harvesters have reached the ears of the Lord of hosts. You have lived on earth in luxury and pleasure; you have fattened your hearts for the day of slaughter. You have condemned; you have murdered the righteous one; he offers you no resistance.

At that time, John said to Jesus, "Teacher, we saw someone driving out demons in your name, and we tried to prevent him because he does not follow us." Jesus replied, "Do not prevent him. There is no one who performs a mighty deed in my name who can at the same time speak ill of me. For whoever is not against us is for us. Anyone who gives you a cup of water to drink because you belong to Christ, amen, I say to you, will surely not lose his reward.

"Whoever causes one of these little ones who believe in me to sin, it would be better for him if a great millstone were put around his neck and he were thrown into the sea. If your hand causes you to sin, cut it off. It is better for you to enter into life maimed than with two hands to go into Gehenna, into the unquenchable fire. And if your foot causes you to sin, cut it off. It is better for you to enter into life crippled than with two feet to be thrown into Gehenna. And if your eye causes you to sin, pluck it out. Better for you to enter into the kingdom of God with one eye than with two eyes to be thrown into Gehenna, where 'their worm does not die, and the fire is not quenched.'"

Understanding the Word

How can service be the driving force in one's life? Mark provides three perspectives on an answer to this question. Mark's Jesus initially defines excellence in terms of service. The first of all will be the last of all, and the last of all will be the servant of all (9:36). Second, Mark presents Jesus as showing the value of everyone who is served as a means of encouraging service to them. One finds Jesus and the Father precisely in the one who needs help. So assisting the needy is welcoming God (9:37).

The third way that the Markan Jesus encourages service is by promoting inclusivity rather than exclusivity. Thus, when John says to Jesus that the disciples forbade a man who was casting out demons to do so "because he was not following us," Jesus offers them a one hundred eighty–degree change of perspective (9:38–41). He says, "Do not prevent him. There is no one who performs a mighty deed in my name who can at the same time speak ill of me" (9:39). This saying is piercingly ironic. In fact, by exorcising demons in Jesus' name the man was not only unlikely to speak ill of Jesus but was also undoubtedly causing many others to speak favorably of Jesus. So the question is, where is the love of the disciples directed: to themselves or to Jesus? If their love is for Jesus, then they will foster the inclusivity that promotes the service of others where Jesus is met. Nurturing more people's gifts for ministry will lead to more people being served.

Finally, Jesus bolsters the disciples' desire to serve by intertwining their future with the future of the people they serve. Impairing the faith of anyone is impairing one's own faith and so risking the loss of eternal life (9:42–48).

Distinction through service, the great value of those who are served, inclusivity, and interconnected destinies are the means through which Jesus energizes a life of service.

Reflecting on the Word

Focus on God's agenda, not your own. This message could be the link between the reading from the book of Numbers and the Gospel. When Joshua gets upset at the two men who are suddenly prophesying and wants Moses to stop them, Moses asks "Are you jealous for my sake? Would that all the people were prophets!" (Numbers 11:29). And Jesus responds to his disciple John, also upset that someone outside their group was casting out demons in Jesus' name, that "whoever is not against us is for us" (Mark 9:40).

Both Jesus and Moses recognized that God's spirit blows where it will: it sometimes ends up in the strangest places, working through very unexpected people. At the same time, no one can presume that the Spirit will always be working through a particular group or the proper channels. We must be careful of trying to box in or corral the spirit of God.

Being on the inside is no guarantee. Thus, we get Jesus' hard words about cutting off a hand or a leg or plucking out an eye rather than letting it cause us to sin and be cast into hell. Most say this is hyperbole, Middle Eastern exaggeration. I think Jesus is calling his disciples to look honestly at their lives and face whatever it is that leads them away from God. "Deal with it," he says. We must always watch what we hold, the path we choose to walk, and the vision that guides us.

Those on the inside can lose sight of, lose touch with, go off the path that takes us to the kingdom. And they can take others with them. What matters is that God's work be done. God will see to it; don't get in the way.

CONSIDER/ DISCUSS:
- Have you ever been surprised at God's choice of working partners?
- Who are the "little ones"?
- What is your first reaction to Jesus' words about cutting off a hand or leg or plucking out an eye rather than letting anything lead you to sin? Was he just exaggerating for effect?

Responding to the Word

We ask for the discernment to recognize when God is working in unexpected ways through unexpected people who do unexpected things . . . and for the wisdom to distinguish the wise from the wacky, much less the wicked. And we pray both that we never let ourselves fall from grace or lead another away from God.

October 4, 2009

TWENTY-SEVENTH SUNDAY IN ORDINARY TIME

Today's Focus: Family Values

We hear Jesus teaching about marriage and children in today's Gospel. While it may not sound very radical to us, Jesus was being counter-cultural both in speaking about God's plan for marriage and in enacting God's love for children. His teaching continues to challenge our own culture.

FIRST READING
Genesis 2: 18–24

The LORD God said: "It is not good for the man to be alone. I will make a suitable partner for him." So the LORD God formed out of the ground various wild animals and various birds of the air, and he brought them to the man to see what he would call them; whatever the man called each of them would be its name. The man gave names to all the cattle, all the birds of the air, and all wild animals; but none proved to be the suitable partner for the man.

So the LORD God cast a deep sleep on the man, and while he was asleep, he took out one of his ribs and closed up its place with flesh. The LORD God then built up into a woman the rib that he had taken from the man. When he brought her to the man, the man said:

"This one, at last, is bone of my bones
and flesh of my flesh;
this one shall be called 'woman,'
for out of 'her man' this one has been taken."

That is why a man leaves his father and mother and clings to his wife, and the two of them become one flesh.

PSALM RESPONSE
Psalm 128:5

May the Lord bless us all the days of our lives.

SECOND READING
Hebrews 2:9–11

Brothers and sisters: He "for a little while" was made "lower than the angels," that by the grace of God he might taste death for everyone.

For it was fitting that he, for whom and through whom all things exist, in bringing many children to glory, should make the leader to their salvation perfect through suffering. He who consecrates and those who are being consecrated all have one origin. Therefore, he is not ashamed to call them "brothers."

In the shorter form of the reading, the passage in brackets is omitted.

GOSPEL
Mark 10:2–16
or 10:2–12

The Pharisees approached Jesus and asked, "Is it lawful for a husband to divorce his wife?" They were testing him. He said to them in reply, "What did Moses command you?" They replied, "Moses permitted a husband to write a bill of divorce and dismiss her." But Jesus told them, "Because of the hardness of your hearts he wrote you this commandment. But from the beginning of creation,

> God made them male and female.
> For this reason a man shall leave his father and mother
>   and be joined to his wife,
>   and the two shall become one flesh.

So they are no longer two but one flesh. Therefore what God has joined together, no human being must separate." In the house the disciples again questioned Jesus about this. He said to them, "Whoever divorces his wife and marries another commits adultery against her; and if she divorces her husband and marries another, she commits adultery."

[And people were bringing children to him that he might touch them, but the disciples rebuked them. When Jesus saw this he became indignant and said to them, "Let the children come to me; do not prevent them, for the kingdom of God belongs to such as these. Amen, I say to you, whoever does not accept the kingdom of God like a child will not enter it." Then he embraced them and blessed them, placing his hands on them.]

Understanding the Word

Today's Gospel reading of Mark 10:1–16 is usually divided into two parts: 10:1–12, which is a prohibition of divorce, and 10:13–16, in which Jesus affirms and welcomes children.

The passages for today emphasize the point that service should lead to closeness rather than to separation. Thus, Jesus responds to the Pharisees' question about whether a man may divorce his wife by forbidding it on the grounds that God has joined them and made them one (10:7–12). Jesus responds to the disciples' attempt to prevent people from bringing children to him by affirming, blessing, and embracing children (10:13–16).

One might think that the disciples would have already learned at least the lesson of welcoming children because Jesus had just put his arms around another child and told them that to receive a child is to receive him and to receive him is to receive the Father (9:36–37). But the thought of their own importance as members of the group traveling with Jesus had been uppermost on their minds at that time. That is why in 9:38 John tells Jesus that they had tried to stop one who was not one of them from exorcising in Jesus' name. John's words that the healer "was not following us" are instructive. The verb "to follow" is used in Mark's Gospel to indicate discipleship of Jesus. John broadens the use of the term to indicate that people follow the disciples as well, giving them a special status.

Now the disciples continue their habit of seeking to distinguish themselves by excluding others. This time they do so by acting as gatekeepers for who may and who may not approach Jesus (10:13). The desire to draw boundaries to set ourselves apart is so powerful that we must constantly guard against it.

Reflecting on the Word

A famous actress once commented on her own record of multiple marriages that she certainly believed in the institution. Statistics show that more than fifty percent of marriages today end in divorce. A sociologist has called marriage in our day a "porous institution" that no longer holds people securely. But Jesus offers another vision.

Jesus takes a rather strict position on marriage in today's Gospel. There were two schools of thought on marriage at that time. One allowed for divorce on almost any grounds: all a husband had to do was to sign a writ of divorce and his wife would have to leave his home. The other line of reasoning held that only for the most serious reason—adultery—was divorce allowed. Jesus himself goes back to the first book of the Torah. God's plan is that marriage is to be lasting; man and woman are to grow in unity.

We may not realize how much a woman could be victimized under the more liberal teaching. Jesus is coming down on the side of the woman here, that she, too, had rights and wasn't merely under the control of her husband. But his teaching also addresses the possibility of a woman divorcing her husband and recognizes that the husband also has rights. Marriage is described as a holy relationship, designed by God.

In a similar fashion, children were also seen in that culture as having little value, possibly a defense mechanism against the prevalence of infant and child mortality. No matter; in Jesus' eyes these little ones belong to the kingdom of God. Furthermore, we can learn from them to accept the kingdom with arms as open as a child's when receiving an unexpected gift.

CONSIDER/
DISCUSS:
- Was Moses a realist and Jesus an idealist? Would Jesus change his mind if he were teaching about marriage today?
- Do you think about marriage as a religious commitment?
- Have you learned anything from children that influences your own spirituality?

Responding to the Word

We need to pray for all couples as they prepare for marriage, as they struggle to become "one flesh" over the course of their love together. We must pray for the children of our time, for those who suffer abuse and neglect. We must cherish the children entrusted to us to become children of the kingdom of God.

October 11, 2009

TWENTY-EIGHTH SUNDAY IN ORDINARY TIME

Today's Focus: More Now or More Later

Last week we heard Jesus' teaching on marriage and children; today his teaching is about money. A man's enthusiasm quickly turns to reticence in the Gospel. The open hand generously stretched out becomes the closed hand lowered in disappointment. Was too much asked or too little really offered?

FIRST READING
Wisdom 7:7–11

I prayed, and prudence was given me;
  I pleaded, and the spirit of wisdom came to me.
I preferred her to scepter and throne,
  and deemed riches nothing in comparison with her,
    nor did I liken any priceless gem to her;
because all gold, in view of her, is a little sand,
  and before her, silver is to be accounted mire.
Beyond health and comeliness I loved her,
  and I chose to have her rather than the light,
    because the splendor of her never yields to sleep.
Yet all good things together came to me in her company,
  and countless riches at her hands.

PSALM RESPONSE
Psalm 90:14

Fill us with your love, O Lord, and we will sing for joy!

SECOND READING
Hebrews 4:12–13

Brothers and sisters: Indeed the word of God is living and effective, sharper than any two-edged sword, penetrating even between soul and spirit, joints and marrow, and able to discern reflections and thoughts of the heart. No creature is concealed from him, but everything is naked and exposed to the eyes of him to whom we must render an account.

In the shorter form of the reading, the passage in brackets is omitted.

GOSPEL
Mark 10:17–30 or 10:17–27

As Jesus was setting out on a journey, a man ran up, knelt down before him, and asked him, "Good teacher, what must I do to inherit eternal life?" Jesus answered him, "Why do you call me good? No one is good but God alone. You know the commandments:

You shall not kill;
you shall not commit adultery;
you shall not steal;
you shall not bear false witness;
you shall not defraud;
honor your father and your mother."

He replied and said to him, "Teacher, all of these I have observed from my youth." Jesus, looking at him, loved him and said to him, "You are lacking in one thing. Go, sell what you have, and give to the poor and you will have treasure in heaven; then come, follow me." At that statement his face fell, and he went away sad, for he had many possessions.

Jesus looked around and said to his disciples, "How hard it is for those who have wealth to enter the kingdom of God!" The disciples were amazed at his words. So Jesus again said to them in reply, "Children, how hard it is to enter the kingdom of God! It is easier for a camel to pass through the eye of a needle than for one who is rich to enter the kingdom of God." They were exceedingly astonished and said among themselves, "Then who can be saved?" Jesus looked at them and said, "For human beings it is impossible, but not for God. All things are possible for God." [Peter began to say to him, "We have given up everything and followed you." Jesus said, "Amen, I say to you, there is no one who has given up house or brothers or sisters or mother or father or children or lands for my sake and for the sake of the gospel who will not receive a hundred times more now in this present age: houses and brothers and sisters and mothers and children and lands, with persecutions, and eternal life in the age to come."]

Understanding the Word

At the end of last week's Gospel reading Jesus said that "whoever does not accept the kingdom of God like a child will not enter it" (Mark 10:15). Today's reading is the passage that follows in Mark's Gospel (10:17–30). Its purpose is to show how one receives the kingdom like a child.

The Gospel we hear today is about the man who runs up and asks Jesus what to do to inherit eternal life. After ascertaining that the man has kept all the commandments from his youth, Jesus tells him that he lacks one thing: giving up his possessions so as to follow Jesus. The man goes away sorrowful. Jesus uses this experience to tell his disciples, whom he now addresses as "children," how difficult it is "to enter the kingdom of God" and about how such entrance is possible (10:27–30).

It is the idea of entering the kingdom and the references to children that explicitly connect this reading to the notion of entering the kingdom of God by receiving it like a child (10:15, 25). In essence, Jesus is saying that what the man lacked was his realization of his dependence on God in order to enter the kingdom. He failed to recognize his need. The man had come to Jesus asking what he needed to "do to inherit eternal life" (10:17). He had done almost all that needed to be done. He had followed all the commandments as Jesus said he should do (10:19–20).

What was still missing was a return to a childlike acceptance of a greater power to sustain and save us. Counting up our achievements, even religious ones, is easier than recognizing our need. And yet, it is in the very recognition of our need and in our persisting in ministry in the face of this recognition that God sustains us in this life and leads us into the next (10:29–30).

Reflecting on the Word

The responsorial psalm has a thoughtful verse today: "Teach us to number our days aright, / that we may gain wisdom of heart" (Psalm 90:12). A man approached Jesus asking how he could inherit eternal life. An inheritance can come to us by chance, as a windfall, or by right because of something we are or have done. The man was willing to work for this inheritance of eternal life: "What must I do?" he asked. And he must have been sincere because we are told Jesus looked at him and loved him.

At first, when Jesus told him what he had to do, the man came back with a quick "Already taken care of." But when Jesus moved up to the next category of higher demand, "sell what you have and give to the poor," the man walked away sad, "for he had many possessions," we are told (Mark 10:21, 22).

"It's hard if you have a lot of stuff," Jesus later tells Simon. It weighs you down. You just can't get through the gate. Like trying to get through a subway turnstile with a lot of baggage. Only God can make it possible. But the promise is that God will make it profitable to take the narrow way, not in terms of things, but in terms of family and a place to call home even now.

Gaining wisdom of heart means acquiring what Solomon speaks of in the first reading. Riches are nothing compared to the gifts of the Spirit of wisdom: "all good things together came to me in her company, / and countless riches at her hands" (Wisdom 7:11).

CONSIDER/ DISCUSS:
- What do we consider "gain" in our lives? What are our priorities as a country? As a parish community?
- Are there any particular things that make it hard for me to move toward the kingdom of God?
- Do I believe that while I may feel that certain things are simply not possible, "all things are possible for God" (Mark 17:27)?

Responding to the Word

It is good to pray for the wisdom that is God's gift and enables us to evaluate things properly in the light of eternal life. We can pray that God will do what we may consider impossible, allowing us to move away from those attitudes and habits that prevent us from drawing more closely to Jesus, who continues to lead us to the kingdom.

October 18, 2009

TWENTY-NINTH SUNDAY IN ORDINARY TIME

Today's Focus: What's on Your Agenda?

The second half of Mark's Gospel reveals not only who Jesus is (the Son of Man) and why he came (to be handed over, to suffer, die, and then be raised), but also how difficult it was for the apostles to accept this. Today's focus on the request of James and John and the reaction of the rest of the disciples reveals their agenda, one quite different from that of Jesus.

FIRST READING
Isaiah 53:10–11

The LORD was pleased
    to crush him in infirmity.

If he gives his life as an offering for sin,
    he shall see his descendants in a long life,
    and the will of the LORD shall be accomplished through him.

Because of his affliction
    he shall see the light in fullness of days;
through his suffering, my servant shall justify many,
    and their guilt he shall bear.

PSALM RESPONSE
Psalm 33:22

Lord, let your mercy be on us, as we place our trust in you.

SECOND READING
Hebrews 4:14–16

Brothers and sisters: Since we have a great high priest who has passed through the heavens, Jesus, the Son of God, let us hold fast to our confession. For we do not have a high priest who is unable to sympathize with our weaknesses, but one who has similarly been tested in every way, yet without sin. So let us confidently approach the throne of grace to receive mercy and to find grace for timely help.

GOSPEL
Mark 10:35–45
or 10:42–45

[James and John, the sons of Zebedee, came to Jesus and said to him, "Teacher, we want you to do for us whatever we ask of you." He replied, "What do you wish me to do for you?" They answered him, "Grant that in your glory we may sit one at your right and the other at your left." Jesus said to them, "You do not know what you are asking. Can you drink the cup that I drink or be baptized with the baptism with which I am baptized?" They said to him, "We can." Jesus said to them, "The cup that I drink, you will drink, and with the baptism with which I am baptized, you will be baptized; but to sit at my right or at my left is not mine to give but is for those for whom it has been prepared." When the ten heard this, they became indignant at James and John.] Jesus summoned [them] the Twelve and said to them, "You know that those who are recognized as rulers over the Gentiles lord it over them, and their great ones make their authority over them felt. But it shall not be so among you. Rather, whoever wishes to be great among you will be your servant; whoever wishes to be first among you will be the slave of all. For the Son of Man did not come to be served but to serve and to give his life as a ransom for many."

Understanding the Word

There is a powerful voice within us that can drown out the voice that guides us aright. The Gospel passage for today is the last one in a section in which Jesus tries to improve the disciples' understanding about the need for his passion and for their participation in this suffering through their own service of others (Mark 8:27 — 10:45).

This section contains three statements about Jesus' coming passion (8:31; 9:31; 10:33–34). The last of them is the most detailed and specific about how Jesus will suffer, and it comes right before today's Gospel reading. This section also contains a number of instructions for the disciples regarding how to serve others (8:34–38; 9:29, 35–37, 38–41, 42–50; 10:13–16, 23–31).

Today James and John ask Jesus if they can sit at his right and left hand when he comes into his glory. This request causes anger at the brothers among the other disciples. It also becomes an occasion for Jesus to teach about real leadership, which consists not in lording it over others but rather in serving them (10:35–45).

Recall that James and John were two of the three disciples who had recently witnessed the transfiguration of Jesus on a high mountain (9:2–8). Their experience on the mountain has given them a taste for glory. For them glory is associated with authority. Status is still a goal that captivates the human heart.

But at the Transfiguration the divine voice had told the three disciples to listen to Jesus (9:7). What James and John have done is to ask Jesus to listen to them: "Teacher, we want you to do for us whatever we ask of you" (10:35). How difficult it is to hear a voice beyond, especially over the clamor for prestige that we hear within us.

One day after church a woman went up to my friend who had just preached and said, "Father, do you want to make God laugh?' My friend smiled and said, "Sure. Tell me how." She smiled and said, "Tell God your plans."

I think most of us have our "plans" now and then about how we want the future to be. Today we overhear James and John's plans. They want to sit next to Jesus when he comes into glory. And their plans are at the top of their wish list. Notice how they approach Jesus: "Teacher, we want you to do for us whatever we ask of you" (Mark 10:35). They have their eye on the road to glory. When the others hear of this, they get angry at James and John, fearing that these two brothers have gotten an edge on them.

First Jesus tells the two that they will indeed share in his suffering, but positions of honor are up to the Father, but then he realizes it's back to basics for the whole bunch of them. Once again Jesus has to call them to the gospel meaning of life. God's agenda is about serving the least, those most vulnerable, those most looked down upon. It's not about amassing power and prestige, or getting the places of honor and privilege. If that's your agenda, know it's not God's!

CONSIDER/ DISCUSS:
- What are the three top items on your agenda? What guides how you plan your future?
- What place does God's agenda have in your life?
- Do you think of Jesus as one who came "to serve and to give his life as a ransom for many" (Mark 10:45)? What does that mean for the community that follows him?

■ *Responding to the Word*

We pray that we can honestly look at what guides and governs our lives, our plans and future hopes, and that we can ask for the grace to align them with God's plan. Then God will not simply smile but laugh in delight. "Thy kingdom come, thy will be done on earth as it is in heaven."

October 25, 2009

THIRTIETH SUNDAY IN ORDINARY TIME

Today's Focus: Seeing the Way to God

The blind beggar Bartimaeus sits by the wayside as Jesus passes. He is stationary, stuck there, when suddenly he is moved to cry out, "Jesus, son of David, have pity of me" (Mark 10:47). When Jesus answers, his life is changed forever. It can be risky to ask Jesus to change things.

FIRST READING
Jeremiah 31: 7–9

Thus says the LORD:
Shout with joy for Jacob,
    exult at the head of the nations;
    proclaim your praise and say:
The LORD has delivered his people,
    the remnant of Israel.
Behold, I will bring them back
    from the land of the north;
I will gather them from the ends of the world,
    with the blind and the lame in their midst,
the mothers and those with child;
    they shall return as an immense throng.
They departed in tears,
    but I will console them and guide them;
I will lead them to brooks of water,
    on a level road, so that none shall stumble.
For I am a father to Israel,
    Ephraim is my first-born.

PSALM RESPONSE
Psalm 126:3

The Lord has done great things for us; we are filled with joy.

SECOND READING
Hebrews 5:1–6

Brothers and sisters: Every high priest is taken from among men and made their representative before God, to offer gifts and sacrifices for sins. He is able to deal patiently with the ignorant and erring, for he himself is beset by weakness and so, for this reason, must make sin offerings for himself as well as for the people. No one takes this honor upon himself but only when called by God, just as Aaron was. In the same way, it was not Christ who glorified himself in becoming high priest, but rather the one who said to him:

You are my son:
    this day I have begotten you;
just as he says in another place:
You are a priest forever
    according to the order of Melchizedek.

GOSPEL

Mark 10:46–52

As Jesus was leaving Jericho with his disciples and a sizable crowd, Bartimaeus, a blind man, the son of Timaeus, sat by the roadside begging. On hearing that it was Jesus of Nazareth, he began to cry out and say, "Jesus, son of David, have pity on me." And many rebuked him, telling him to be silent. But he kept calling out all the more, "Son of David, have pity on me." Jesus stopped and said, "Call him." So they called the blind man, saying to him, "Take courage; get up, Jesus is calling you." He threw aside his cloak, sprang up, and came to Jesus. Jesus said to him in reply, "What do you want me to do for you?" The blind man replied to him, "Master, I want to see." Jesus told him, "Go your way; your faith has saved you." Immediately he received his sight and followed him on the way.

Understanding the Word

Mark 10:46–52 is the last passage before Jesus enters Jerusalem. It is a transition passage between Jesus' instruction of the disciples in 8:27 — 10:45 and his final days in Jerusalem beginning in Mark 11. It is also one of the "brackets" for the instruction of the disciples. Right before and right after Jesus teaches his disciples about suffering and service, we find stories of Jesus healing blind men (8:22–26; 10:46–53). These miracles serve to show how Jesus is attempting by his words to bring spiritual sight to the disciples.

The healings of the blind men are also revealing in how they differ from each other. In the first one a blind man is brought to Jesus, and the people who bring him make the request for Jesus to heal him (8:22). Jesus takes the man aside and first spits and then touches the man. The result is that the man sees dimly (8:23–24). So Jesus touches the man again, and this results in the man being able to see clearly (8:25). This healing comes before all of Jesus' teaching on how to be of service. The progression of the healing suggests how difficult it is to accept the teaching of Jesus and how people have to grow into it.

The healing of the blind man in today's Gospel is different from the other healing in several important ways. First, it is the man himself who approaches Jesus and not other people who bring him up. In fact, this second blind man struggles against many who want him to keep quiet and stop calling for Jesus (10:46–48). Second, Jesus heals him quickly and not progressively (10:52). This healing appears to signify how the disciples may acquire the spiritual perspective that Jesus has been inculcating in them about service. It is by asking, as the second blind man does three times, for Jesus to give them sight. This prayer is the childlike realization that the kingdom is a gift that is received.

A great English actress told an interviewer about a time when she was in Washington, D.C. performing in a play. She had not had time to see the city, but on her last day there she had a few hours, so she went down to the National Gallery, where there was a Picasso exhibit. She only had about forty-five minutes, and decided that instead of rushing through the exhibit she would spend the time on just one painting. She noted, "After about forty minutes, I began to see it."

Mark's Gospel often reminds us how difficult it was for people to see who Jesus really was. For the people he was a miracle worker and healer. For his family and neighbors he was just the carpenter's son. For the religious leaders and the Pharisees he was a troublemaker who broke the law of Moses. For his disciples he was the Messiah but not one who would suffer.

When Bartimaeus hears Jesus coming he begins to shout out, and when Jesus asks what he wants him to do, the blind man answers, "Master, I want to see" (Mark 10:51). Jesus recognizes his faith: "Go your way; your faith has saved you" (10:52). Bartimaeus saw Jesus in faith before he saw him with his eyes. The final line confirms this when Mark says "he followed him on the way" (10:52). To follow Jesus on the way means to be a disciple.

CONSIDER/
DISCUSS:

- How do you see Jesus? Who is he for you these days?
- Is there a "way" you are being asked to walk with Jesus?
- How much of your life is lived seeing through the eyes of faith?

■ *Responding to the Word*

Our daily prayer can be, "Lord, I want to see." We can ask to see Jesus as he truly is, the crucified and risen Lord who came to call disciples to serve others. We can pray to see the way we are being called to follow the Lord.

November 1, 2009

THE SOLEMNITY OF ALL SAINTS

Today's Focus: A Cloud of Witnesses

As early as the fourth century the saints were remembered during the celebration of the Eucharist. At first it was the martyrs, then the confessors—holy men and women not martyred but who lived a life that imitated Christ. Today we remember all those throughout history who have allowed the face of God to be seen in them.

FIRST READING
Revelation 7: 2–4, 9–14

I, John, saw another angel come up from the East, holding the seal of the living God. He cried out in a loud voice to the four angels who were given power to damage the land and the sea, "Do not damage the land or the sea or the trees until we put the seal on the foreheads of the servants of our God." I heard the number of those who had been marked with the seal, one hundred and forty-four thousand marked from every tribe of the Israelites.

After this I had a vision of a great multitude, which no one could count, from every nation, race, people, and tongue. They stood before the throne and before the Lamb, wearing white robes and holding palm branches in their hands. They cried out in a loud voice:

"Salvation comes from our God,
  who is seated on the throne,
and from the Lamb."

All the angels stood around the throne and around the elders and the four living creatures. They prostrated themselves before the throne, worshiped God, and exclaimed:

"Amen. Blessing and glory, wisdom and thanksgiving,
  honor, power, and might
  be to our God forever and ever. Amen."

Then one of the elders spoke up and said to me, "Who are these wearing white robes, and where did they come from?" I said to him, "My lord, you are the one who knows." He said to me, "These are the ones who have survived the time of great distress; they have washed their robes and made them white in the blood of the Lamb."

PSALM RESPONSE
Psalm 24:6

Lord, this is the people that longs to see your face.

SECOND READING
1 John 3:1–3

Beloved: See what love the Father has bestowed on us that we may be called the children of God. Yet so we are. The reason the world does not know us is that it did not know him. Beloved, we are God's children now; what we shall be has not yet been revealed. We do know that when it is revealed we shall be like him, for we shall see him as he is. Everyone who has this hope based on him makes himself pure, as he is pure.

GOSPEL
Matthew 5: 1–12a

When Jesus saw the crowds, he went up the mountain, and after he had sat down, his disciples came to him. He began to teach them, saying:

"Blessed are the poor in spirit,
for theirs is the kingdom of heaven.
Blessed are they who mourn,
for they will be comforted.
Blessed are the meek,
for they will inherit the land.
Blessed are they who hunger and thirst for righteousness,
for they will be satisfied.
Blessed are the merciful,
for they will be shown mercy.
Blessed are the clean of heart,
for they will see God.
Blessed are the peacemakers,
for they will be called children of God.
Blessed are they who are persecuted for the sake of righteousness,
for theirs is the kingdom of heaven.
Blessed are you when they insult you and persecute you and utter every kind of evil against you falsely because of me. Rejoice and be glad, for your reward will be great in heaven."

 Understanding the Word

The Beatitudes in the Gospel of Matthew have both captivated people's fascination and left them wondering exactly what they mean. For example, what is it to be "poor in spirit" or righteous or meek, and why are those who mourn blessed (5:3–6)?

Matthew gives guidelines on what these Beatitudes mean in a section of his Gospel (5:21–48) called the "Antitheses," so called because in it Jesus first quotes what the law says about an issue and then gives his own views on it, beginning with the words, "But I say to you."

The first Beatitude calls the "poor in spirit" blessed (5:3). For Matthew this Beatitude may be viewed in the context of the larger Sermon on the Mount of which it is a part. It has often been said that this sermon presents an impossible ideal that the Christian should strive to achieve. Impossible or not, the Sermon on the Mount certainly contains some of the loftiest ethical exhortations found in the scriptures. Blessed are those who attempt to live by them, and in the process see their own poverty of spirit in light of the ideal.

The second Beatitude, which blesses those who mourn, may be viewed in connection with the two Beatitudes on righteousness. Mourning implies suffering, and the only suffering explicitly treated in the Beatitudes is that of those who suffer "for righteousness' sake" (5:10). How to live righteously is defined by living according to Jesus' words in the Antitheses, which express a righteousness exceeding that found in the scribes and Pharisees (5:20).

Matthew provides guidance for living the other Beatitudes as well. "Blessed are the meek" is explained by the section in the Antitheses that addresses not being angry with another (5:21–26). "Blessed are the peacemakers" is explained by Jesus' instruction not to use speech that could lead to friction and to make efforts at reconciliation (5:21–26). Clarification for "blessed are the pure in heart" comes in the passage on not even looking at a woman lustfully (5:27–30). Finally, the Beatitude "Blessed are the merciful" is illuminated in 5:38–48, in which Jesus talks about how to respond to those who have harmed you.

Reflecting on the Beatitudes in the light of these corresponding passages opens up rich perspectives for ethical living.

Reflecting on the Word

Try this. Draw three circles, each within the other—make them large, not tiny; then put a dot in the middle of the innermost circle. Write on the border of innermost circle the names of those who have handed on the faith to you, who taught you what it means to live your faith. These are the people we have known during our life.

Along the outermost circle record the names of the biblical people who have had an impact on your life—the women and men of the Old and New Testaments, of course, but also the authors of any books of the Bible that have had an impact on you. Finally, around the edge of the middle circle, write the names of anyone in the intervening two thousand years who has influenced you as a believer— saints with a capital "S" and a small "s." This is your own personal "cloud of witnesses" spoken of in the letter to the Hebrews (12:1), who have surrounded you during your life, praying for you and urging you on to live more fully in Christ.

The circles are actually much larger in reality, but these are the ones who have taught us to be poor in spirit, to mourn injustices in the world, to be meek and merciful, pure of heart and peacemakers. They have embodied what it means to hunger and thirst for justice and to be willing to undergo suffering for the sake of our faith. How impoverished our lives would be without them. Today is a day to say thank you to God for all these men and women and for sending us Jesus, our "leader and perfecter of faith" (12:2), who continues to draw us into the life shared by the Father, Son, and Holy Spirit.

CONSIDER/ DISCUSS:
- What does it mean to be a saint?
- Do you think of yourself as a saint?
- Do you think of yourself and those around you as destined for the kingdom of heaven, to be like God because you shall see God as God is?

Responding to the Word

We pray today thanking God for all the saints—men and women who grew into sanctity—who struggled as we do, who at times were overcome by the power of sin and evil in their own lives, but eventually came to be witnesses to Jesus and profess him Lord and Savior. We pray to the Lord to continue to send the Holy Spirit to sanctify, that is, to make saints of us.

November 8, 2009

THIRTY-SECOND SUNDAY IN ORDINARY TIME

Today's Focus: When Less Is More

Of all the people in biblical times, among the most vulnerable were women. Considered little more than property, a woman went from the house of her father to the house of her husband. If her husband died, she was dependent on her sons; if there were no sons, she was in a very precarious position. We meet two courageous widows today, whose small gifts were great indeed.

FIRST READING
1 Kings 17: 10–16

In those days, Elijah the prophet went to Zarephath. As he arrived at the entrance of the city, a widow was gathering sticks there; he called out to her, "Please bring me a small cupful of water to drink." She left to get it, and he called out after her, "Please bring along a bit of bread." She answered, "As the LORD, your God, lives, I have nothing baked; there is only a handful of flour in my jar and a little oil in my jug. Just now I was collecting a couple of sticks, to go in and prepare something for myself and my son; when we have eaten it, we shall die." Elijah said to her, "Do not be afraid. Go and do as you propose. But first make me a little cake and bring it to me. Then you can prepare something for yourself and your son. For the LORD, the God of Israel, says, 'The jar of flour shall not go empty, nor the jug of oil run dry, until the day when the LORD sends rain upon the earth.' " She left and did as Elijah had said. She was able to eat for a year, and he and her son as well; the jar of flour did not go empty, nor the jug of oil run dry, as the LORD had foretold through Elijah.

PSALM RESPONSE
Psalm 146:1b

Praise the Lord, my soul!

SECOND READING
Hebrews 9: 24–28

Christ did not enter into a sanctuary made by hands, a copy of the true one, but heaven itself, that he might now appear before God on our behalf. Not that he might offer himself repeatedly, as the high priest enters each year into the sanctuary with blood that is not his own; if that were so, he would have had to suffer repeatedly from the foundation of the world. But now once for all he has appeared at the end of the ages to take away sin by his sacrifice. Just as it is appointed that human beings die once, and after this the judgment, so also Christ, offered once to take away the sins of many, will appear a second time, not to take away sin but to bring salvation to those who eagerly await him.

GOSPEL
Mark 12:38–44
or 41–44

[In the course of his teaching Jesus said to the crowds, "Beware of the scribes, who like to go around in long robes and accept greetings in the marketplaces, seats of honor in synagogues, and places of honor at banquets. They devour the houses of widows and, as a pretext, recite lengthy prayers. They will receive a severe condemnation."]

He sat down opposite the treasury and observed how the crowd put money into the treasury. Many rich people put in large sums. A poor widow also came and put in two small coins worth a few cents. Calling his disciples to himself, he said to them, "Amen, I say to you, this poor widow put in more than all the other contributors to the treasury. For they have all contributed from their surplus wealth, but she, from her poverty, has contributed all she had, her whole livelihood."

Understanding the Word

In 12:38–44 Mark contrasts the behavior of the scribes with the behavior of a poor widow in order to show the attitude toward God and others that opens one to the coming of the kingdom of God. The scribes have been at the forefront of the attack on Jesus during his final days in the temple (Mark 11:18, 27; 12:12, 13). Throughout this attack the scribes have manifested a concern for how they are viewed by others. They are jealous of the admiration of the multitude for Jesus because of his teaching (11:18). They are also afraid of answering Jesus in a certain way because of what the people would say about their answer (11:32). They also exhibit concern over the reaction of the crowd if they attempt to arrest Jesus (12:12).

The Gospel for today puts the capstone on this tendency of the scribes toward self-promotion and acclaim. Jesus tells the disciples of five ways in which the scribes parade themselves: they "like to go around in long robes and accept greetings in the market places, seats of honor in synagogues, and the places of honor at banquets . . . and . . . recite lengthy prayers" (12:38–40). On the other hand, the poor widow does not worry about how undistinguished she looks as she is seen putting in the equivalent of a penny while "many rich people" can be seen putting in "large sums" (12:41–42).

The widow is often viewed in the Old Testament in terms of her vulnerability. By giving "all she had, her whole livelihood," this widow has shown that she accepts the kingdom of God as a child would, as a gift from God, as the Markan Jesus said one needs to do in order to enter it (10:15). The kingdom does not come about through acquiring the good opinions of others but through the complete self-giving that acknowledges God's parent-like care.

When Elijah asked the widow of Zarephath not only for water, but for something to eat as well, he must have suspected the gravity of his request. The land was beset by famine. The widow confirms this, saying she has nothing baked; moreover, she was just about to use the last handful of flour to make something for herself and her son, adding "when we have eaten it, we shall die" (1 Kings 17:12). Dire straits, indeed!

Elijah calls on her to put faith in place of fear, to trust in the Lord, the God of Israel, who says, "The jar shall not go empty, nor the jug of oil run dry" until God sends rain upon the earth (17:14). She takes the prophet at his word—or rather, God's word—and she and her young son eat for a year on the little flour that was there.

The widow whom Jesus was watching drops two coins into the temple coffers, worth about one sixty-fourth of a day's salary, a pittance compared with the money given by the wealthy around her. But Jesus speaks admiringly of her for giving, from her poverty, all that she had. Unlike the scribes, those religious leaders who were careful to display themselves before others as pious while "devouring the houses of widows" (Mark 12:40), this woman is giving her very life to God in her seemingly small offering, a model for all disciples of Jesus who gave all for us.

CONSIDER/
DISCUSS:
- What does it mean to be a "religious person"?
- What kind of generosity is Jesus asking of his disciples today? What does it look like?
- How can religious institutions betray their calling?

Responding to the Word

We pray that we might hear the voice of God speaking through others, calling us to be generous. Think of those whom we have ceased to "see." Rather than judging them as lazy, pathetic, or getting what they deserve, consider how Christ might approach them.

November 15, 2009

THIRTY-THIRD SUNDAY IN ORDINARY TIME

Today's Focus: And All Shall Be Well

Some sections in the Bible are called "apocalyptic literature," that is, writings that reveal or disclose truths not apparent to others living at the time. The book of Daniel and the thirteenth chapter of Mark's Gospel were written at a time of persecution and contain a message that is meant to encourage people to hold onto their faith: God will not abandon us.

FIRST READING
Daniel 12:1–3

In those days, I, Daniel,
    heard this word of the Lord:
"At that time there shall arise
    Michael, the great prince,
    guardian of your people;
it shall be a time unsurpassed in distress
    since nations began until that time.
At that time your people shall escape,
    everyone who is found written in the book.

Many of those who sleep in the dust of the earth shall awake;
    some shall live forever,
    others shall be an everlasting horror and disgrace.

But the wise shall shine brightly
    like the splendor of the firmament,
and those who lead the many to justice
    shall be like the stars forever."

PSALM RESPONSE
Psalm 16:1

You are my inheritance, O Lord!

SECOND READING
Hebrews 10: 11–14, 18

Brothers and sisters: Every priest stands daily at his ministry, offering frequently those same sacrifices that can never take away sins. But this one offered one sacrifice for sins, and took his seat forever at the right hand of God; now he waits until his enemies are made his footstool. For by one offering he has made perfect forever those who are being consecrated.

Where there is forgiveness of these, there is no longer offering for sin.

Jesus said to his disciples:

"In those days after that tribulation
the sun will be darkened,
   and the moon will not give its light,
and the stars will be falling from the sky,
   and the powers in the heavens will be shaken.

"And then they will see 'the Son of Man coming in the clouds' with great power and glory, and then he will send out the angels and gather his elect from the four winds, from the end of the earth to the end of the sky.

"Learn a lesson from the fig tree. When its branch becomes tender and sprouts leaves, you know that summer is near. In the same way, when you see these things happening, know that he is near, at the gates. Amen, I say to you, this generation will not pass away until all these things have taken place. Heaven and earth will pass away, but my words will not pass away.

"But of that day or hour, no one knows, neither the angels in heaven, nor the Son, but only the Father."

Understanding the Word

Mark 13:24–32 comes toward the end of the longer discourse that Jesus gives about the final days (13:5–32) before his second coming, when there would be a new age of fulfillment for the just. Mark uses this discourse to energize the service of others that Jesus has been stressing in his Gospel as necessary for his disciples.

Today's Gospel begins by describing the final coming of Jesus in spectacular terms: the moon's light going out, stars falling, " 'the Son of man coming in the clouds' with great power and glory," and angels being sent throughout the earth to gather the elect (13:24–27). Psychological studies have shown that vivid imagery has a great capacity to capture people's attention.

The passage then holds the attention of its audience by assuring them that these world-changing events would occur before the present generation passes away (13:28–31). This seems to imply that some in Jesus' own generation would experience these events. Opening the experience of world transformation up to future generations, however, we hear Jesus' caveat: "But of that day or that hour, no one knows, neither the angels in heaven, nor the Son, but only the Father" (13:32).

Now that our attention is riveted by the action of God on the horizon, Mark goes on to tell us, in the verses beyond today's Gospel reading, how to be prepared for it. Followers of Jesus are to watch, like the doorkeeper looking for the master's return no matter what hour of the day or night (13:33–36). To stress how all Christians are to live in such attentive expectation of God's transformation, Jesus concludes, "What I say to you I say to all: Watch" (13:37). One watches by being there for others in need. This is shown when shortly Jesus will say to Peter, James, and John in Gethsemane, "My soul is very sorrowful, even to death; remain here and watch" (14:34).

Reflecting on the Word

Several years ago, the biblical scholar Luke T. Johnson wrote that over the last half-century Catholics have lost their clear sense of how things will come to an end. We recite the Creed weekly at Sunday Mass, professing that "[h]e will come again in glory to judge the living and the dead," and that "[w]e look for the resurrection of the dead, and the life of the world to come," yet if many Catholics were asked how they are preparing for the "four last things" (death, judgment, heaven, and hell), they would look at you quite blankly.

By contrast, today's readings come from a time when "what happens next" was very much on people's minds. The book of Daniel with its vision of the archangel Michael, guardian of the Jewish people, arising and awakening those who sleep in the dust was written to comfort and give hope to a people suffering under a cruel king who persecuted and killed Jewish believers. The chapter in Mark's Gospel that we hear today, part of a longer discourse in which Jesus' words speak of a day when the Son of Man will come in the clouds with great power and glory and gather his elect, was written to give hope to the early church persecuted by the Roman emperor Nero.

We do not know exactly how things will end, but we do know that God will be there, that Christ will come again, and that we are not meant to end in the dust bin of history. As the psalm refrain reminds us today: "You are my inheritance, O Lord!" (Psalm 16:1).

CONSIDER/ DISCUSS:
- How do you think of the "four last things": death, judgment, heaven, and hell?
- Do you look to the future with hope?

Responding to the Word

We pray that we will remain watchful, living in hope, no matter how dark it sometimes appears to be. The promise of God to be with us all our days, the assurance of Christ to be with us until the end of time, the gift of the Holy Spirit as the ongoing presence of God in our midst, guiding and praying with and for us, bring assurance that we are not abandoned. You are my inheritance, loving God.

November 22, 2009

THE SOLEMNITY OF OUR LORD JESUS CHRIST THE KING

Today's Focus: Pledging Allegiance to Our King

At Mass we pray "Thy kingdom come, thy will be done on earth as it is in heaven." In celebrating the feast of Christ the King, we acknowledge Jesus as the One in whom creation comes to completion, through whom salvation comes to our world, and for whom we act in the world. Thy kingdom come in us, through us, for us and all creation.

FIRST READING
Daniel 7:13–14

As the visions during the night continued, I saw
  one like a Son of man coming,
    on the clouds of heaven;
when he reached the Ancient One
  and was presented before him,
the one like a Son of man received dominion, glory, and kingship;
  all peoples, nations, and languages serve him.
His dominion is an everlasting dominion
  that shall not be taken away,
    his kingship shall not be destroyed.

PSALM RESPONSE
Psalm 93:1a

The Lord is king; he is robed in majesty.

SECOND READING
Revelation 1: 5–8

Jesus Christ is the faithful witness, the firstborn of the dead and ruler of the kings of the earth. To him who loves us and has freed us from our sins by his blood, who has made us into a kingdom, priests for his God and Father, to him be glory and power forever and ever. Amen.

Behold, he is coming amid the clouds,
  and every eye will see him,
    even those who pierced him.
All the peoples of the earth will lament him.
  Yes. Amen.

"I am the Alpha and the Omega," says the Lord God, "the one who is and who was and who is to come, the almighty."

GOSPEL
John 18:33b–37

Pilate said to Jesus, "Are you the King of the Jews?" Jesus answered, "Do you say this on your own or have others told you about me?" Pilate answered, "I am not a Jew, am I? Your own nation and the chief priests handed you over to me. What have you done?" Jesus answered, "My kingdom does not belong to this world. If my kingdom did belong to this world, my attendants would be fighting to keep me from being handed over to the Jews. But as it is, my kingdom is not here." So Pilate said to him, "Then you are a king?" Jesus answered, "You say I am a king. For this I was born and for this I came into the world, to testify to the truth. Everyone who belongs to the truth listens to my voice."

Understanding the Word

Sometimes situations are so bad that the very idea of a godly reign is easier to envision as taking place in the afterlife. This is the case in the Gospel of John and its idea of Christ the King. When one thinks of kingship in the New Testament one often thinks of God the Father as the king. This is so because the concept of "the kingdom of God" is so important in the synoptic Gospels. In John's Gospel, however, Jesus is presented as a king (John 18:34, 36). Moreover, this Gospel prefers to address not how the kingdom of God is being ushered into the world by Jesus, as do the synoptic Gospels, but how Jesus the King empowers people to enter into the kingdom beyond this world.

For John most people in the world failed to accept either Jesus or the message that Jesus brings: "He was in the world, / and the world came to be through him, / but the world did not know him. / He came to what was his own, / but his own people did not accept him" (1:10–11). There are some, however, who do accept Jesus (1:12). What Jesus does for these people is not to bring the kingdom into the hostile world, but rather to make them effective witnesses in the world (17:20–23), to preserve them in the world (17:11, 12, 15), and to intercede with the Father to take them to Jesus' kingdom with the Father (17:24).

In John's Gospel today Jesus the king brings truth (18:37). Acceptance of this truth welcomes God into one's life. The effect of this welcome is that God is active in us for protection, witness, and movement to the realm of the glory that Jesus had with the Father "before the foundation of the world" (17:24). Jesus' kingship, then, is something toward which we move, and our acceptance of Jesus and his message removes the self-imposed obstacles to entering this realm.

Reflecting on the Word

Political power meets spiritual power in today's conversation between Jesus and Pilate. "Are you the King of the Jews?" Pilate asks Jesus (John 18:33). Pilate is concerned about whether Jesus is a threat to Roman rule, just as the Jewish leaders see Jesus as a threat to their authority. Jesus is thus either guilty of fomenting insurrection as a militant messiah or of speaking blasphemy by presenting himself as one who inaugurates the reign of God.

Jesus, however, speaks not about himself as a king but about a kingdom that "does not belong to this world." This kingdom may not be of this world but it is in this world. God's kingdom is present in Jesus as one who comes to bear witness to the truth. And what is this truth? That "God so loved the world that he gave his only Son, so that everyone who believes in him might not perish but might have eternal life" (John 3:16).

Jesus is the Word become flesh who made his dwelling among us, so that we might see his glory, "the glory of the Father's only Son, / full of grace and truth" (John 1:14). The hour of glory was the hour of the cross, the hour not of political power, but God's power shining through human weakness, bringing light into the darkness, revealing self-sacrificing love so that we might have life.

Political power tends to be an upward climb into dominance and authority that must be protected at all costs. It frequently leads to isolation and abuse, to clinging to power as its own end. Spiritual power is having the strength to trust God and surrender so that God can reign, not by conquest or political alliances, but through human weakness and surrender to God.

**CONSIDER/
DISCUSS:**
- Does the image of Jesus as king help you to understand who he is for us?
- What is the difference between political power and spiritual power? Are they always in conflict?
- What does it mean to "belong to the truth" to which Jesus testifies?

Responding to the Word

We pray that we might be part of God's people who continue to proclaim Jesus as the One to whom we give our allegiance, and that we show this in the world by working to bring about God's kingdom where mercy and justice, peace and love rule.

Dennis Sylva is Director of Lifelong Faith Formation at St. Jerome Parish in Oconomowoc, Wisconsin and an adjunct professor of biblical studies at Stritch University in Milwaukee, Wisconsin. Dr. Sylva has authored books and articles on the Old and New Testaments that have appeared in American, British, French, and German publications. He is currently working on commentaries on the book of Wisdom and the Pentateuch, and developing a series of books about discipleship in the Gospel of John. Recent publications include articles on 2 Peter and about the portrayal of Isaac in Genesis. Dr. Sylva specializes in addressing the human concerns that undergird biblical texts, and the ways that the biblical authors portray God's response to these concerns so as to help people live to their full potential. He is a member of the Society of Biblical Literature, the Catholic Biblical Association of America, and the Rhetoric of Religious Antiquity group.

James A. Wallace, CSsR, is professor of homiletics at the Washington Theological Union, Washington, D.C. He is the author of *Preaching to the Hungers of the Heart* (Liturgical Press, 2002) and co-author of three books of homilies, *Lift Up Your Hearts: Homilies for the A, B, and C Cycles* (Paulist Press 2004, 2005, and 2006). He has served as president of the Academy of Homiletics, the Catholic Association of Teachers of Homiletics, and the Religious Speech Communication Association. His articles have appeared in various journals, and he has lectured on preaching in this country, Europe, and Asia.